THE PLOT TO HACK AMERICA

2ND EDITION

Also by Malcolm Nance

Defeating ISIS
The Terrorist Recognition Handbook
The Terrorists of Iraq
An End to Al-Qaeda

THE PLOT TO HACK AMERICA

2ND EDITION

How Putin's Cyberspies and WikiLeaks
Tried to Steal the 2016 Election

MALCOLM NANCE

SKYHORSE PUBLISHING

Skyhorse Publishing books may be purchased in bulk at special discounts for sales promotion, corporate gifts, fund-raising, or educational purposes. Special editions can also be created to specifications. For details, contact the Special Sales Department, Skyhorse Publishing, 307 West 36th Street, 11th Floor, New York, NY 10018 or info@skyhorsepublishing.com.

Skyhorse® and Skyhorse Publishing® are registered trademarks of Skyhorse Publishing, Inc.®, a Delaware corporation.

Visit our website at www.skyhorsepublishing.com.

10 9 8 7 6 5 4 3

Library of Congress Cataloging-in-Publication Data is available on file.

Cover design by Brian Peterson
Cover photo: AP Images

ISBN: 978-1-5107-3468-5
Ebook ISBN: 978-1-5107-2333-7

Dedicated to Captain Humayun Khan, US Army

CONTENTS

Foreword. ix
Preface. xi

1 Watergate 2.0 1
2 Suspicions of Something More Sinister 17
3 The Spymaster-in-Chief. 24
4 Trump's Agents, Putin's Assets. 37
5 Operation LUCKY-7: The Kremlin Plan
   to Elect a President. 65
6 Battles of the CYBER BEARS. 83
7 WikiLeaks: Russia's Intelligence Laundromat 110
8 When CYBER BEARS Attack 122
9 Cyberwar to Defend Democracy 145

Appendix 155
Endnotes 181

FOREWORD

THE 2016 PRESIDENTIAL ELECTION WAS ALREADY surreal—a former reality TV host fueled by white backlash had completed a hostile takeover of the Republican Party—before the bears emerged.

By the summer, as the campaign intensified, a WordPress page operated by someone claiming the mantle Guccifer2.0 was dumping embarrassing emails and memoranda stolen from the Democratic National Committee. When the anti-secrecy organization Wikileaks did the same thing, Guccifer2.0 claimed credit as the source; Wikileaks has kept its sourcing obscure. But the leaks showed the Democrats' political apparatus to be petty, vindictive, and determined to anoint Hillary Clinton as the Democratic nominee despite grassroots enthusiasm for challenger Bernie Sanders. Chairwoman Debbie Wasserman Schultz resigned.

Then something unexpected happened.

Cybersecurity researchers analyzing the committee network breach noticed that the particulars of the attack showed distinct patterns for gaining access—familiar patterns. Their tools were prohibitively expensive for random hackers, particularly their use of previously unknown software flaws. Instead, the researchers concluded, the hack was the work of two well-known groups tied to Russian intelligence. They are known by the weird names Fancy Bear and Cozy Bear.

Intelligence professionals weren't actually mad at the Russians for digitally breaking into the DNC. "That's a valid intelligence target," one cybersecurity analyst and Defense Intelligence Agency veteran told me. But usually they hoard stolen data, not spill it out onto the Internet. Suddenly, it looked like the bears had changed their game.

Attributing culpability for cyberattacks is difficult. Competent spy agencies labor to make it nigh-impossible. But it didn't take long before Obama administration and congressional leaders started expressing with unusual certainty—off the record, of course—that Russia was behind the assault. A theory emerged. The Russians were putting a digital thumb on the scale of the US election to help the aforementioned reality TV host—who just happened to be running on the most pro-Russia platform in GOP history.

As of this writing, the election is undecided. And there are knowledgeable cybersecurity researchers skeptical of Russian involvement. So here comes Malcolm Nance, an intelligence, counterterrorism, and national-security lifer, to sort out what's known, what's suspected, and what it all means. If you've read books like *The Terrorists of Iraq* and *Defeating ISIS*, you know Malcolm's expertise. If you've seen his 2007 congressional testimony using his firsthand experience with waterboarding to call it torture—back when that was controversial—you know Malcolm's integrity. And if you've spent any time with his fellow Navy senior chiefs, you know Malcolm's bluntness.

It's worth scrutinizing this bizarre episode in American politics and security. It's unlikely to be a one-off event. After all, bears tend to go where they want—unless something stops them.

Spencer Ackerman
US national security editor, *The Guardian*
September 2016

PREFACE

BEGINNING IN MARCH AND APRIL 2016, an unknown person or persons hacked into the computer servers of the Democratic National Committee. Over time it became clear that the hackers were targeting very specific information in the DNC files—the opposition research the Democrats had dug up on their Republican opponent Donald J. Trump. Once they had the information they wanted, the cyber-spies rooted around in the computers for several months thereafter, stealing other files such as personal emails, digital voice mails, and sensitive personal information on donors. This included the donors' bank account, credit card, and social security numbers. The DNC discovered the intrusion while performing a security check, and shut their network down. However, the damage was done.

For an old spy and codebreaker like myself, nothing in the world happens by coincidence. Intelligence officers are a peculiar lot. Whether they are active or retired, their brains are wired for a completely different way of seeing the world around them. Some come from the Human Intelligence world, where they learn to read, manipulate, and distrust everyone in order to "social engineer" intelligence from people who do not want to give them anything. Others are forged in the signals intelligence world, where all data is just a massive electronic puzzle to be constantly analyzed, turned over, and fused together into an exploitable product, or into a final code to be decrypted or broken. Some, like myself, come from both worlds, and are at turns analytical and skeptical of seemingly obvious information. This hybrid mindview doesn't approach the world as streams of linear data; it attempts to analyze information like a constantly flowing game of three-dimensional chess. All the moves are technically the same as in regular chess, but the traditional allowances of forward and backwards one square, or a lateral or L-shaped pattern, are too limiting for those trained to sniff out hostile intent; we require additional ways of processing information to be satisfied. Up vertically, down every angle of the compass rose and then across every median, line of longitude, latitude, and every other angle of measure are just about right . . . then we add layers of frequency analysis figuring out the timing, spacing, depth and distance between each item we call data points. When an event has been then identified on the continuum of intelligence, we compare it with everything that has ever occurred in history to see if it resembles other patterns played by another spy who employed that process. We then process the context and precedence of each observed activity against common sense to determine if an event chain is coincidence, or if it bears the marks of hostile intent. Ian Fleming, the old British Secret Intelligence Service officer who created the fictional character of James Bond, characterized the amazing events in his books with an observation in his 1959 book *Goldfinger*: "Once is happenstance. Twice is coincidence. Three times is enemy action."

Times have changed since Mr. Fleming's Dictum. In light of current trends in the intelligence business, I like to characterize this phenomenon as Nance's Law of Intelligence Kismet: "Coincidence takes a lot of planning."

Reading about the DNC hack was not initially alarming; hackers had also penetrated the Obama and McCain campaigns in 2008. The DNC hack was newsworthy but not really noteworthy until it was paired with two additional events. At the time of the hacks I was writing a massive tome on hackers associated with ISIS and al-Qaeda, so

I was attuned to any information about electronic data theft. Then on June 1, 2016 one of my military hacker friends pointed out that an entity who called himself Guccifer 2.0 had opened a WordPress page and was dumping information stolen from the DNC hack.

Guccifer 2.0 claimed he had all the hacked material from the DNC and would be releasing it through his webpage. The name Guccifer struck a nerve, as the real Guccifer, a prolific Romanian hacker, had just been extradited to the United States. Guccifer 2.0 was a copy-cat, and a lazy one at that. My hyper-suspicious intelligence mind started kicking into gear and the game of multidimensional chess was on.

Two weeks later Steve Biddle, the national security writer for the snarky web magazine *Gawker* posted the entire Donald J. Trump opposition file from the DNC's servers. Immediately both Fleming's Dictum and Nance's Law struck at the same time. There was no way that the single most damaging (and dull) file from the DNC hack would be "accidently" released weeks before the Republican National Committee convention. It was straight from the Karl Rove political playbook: Release damning information early, hold bad information until appropriate. More startling was that word was spreading across the global cyber security community that the DNC hack and Guccifer 2.0 had Russian fingerprints all over it.

I started my career in Naval Intelligence when I entered as a Russian language interpreter sent to DLI, the Defense Language Institute. For years before my Navy enlistment I had studied the Soviet Union and the KGB's history of political intrigue in preparation for a career in intelligence. Little did I know that two years of studying Russian on my own and four months of waiting at the Presidio of Monterey for my language school slot would result in my taking a completely different language. I was assigned to study Arabic, then I spent decades watching the Russian client states of Libya, Syria, and Iraq, as well as their ties to European terrorist groups Red Army Faction, Action Direct, the Irish Republican Army, and the Combatant Communist Cells. No matter what my target was, the KGB cast a shadow across every spectrum of my operations. Whenever we conducted a mission involving Syria, we watched for Russian cruisers and destroyers heading to Tartus, or the IL-38 "May" surveillance aircraft that dogged us and kept a weather eye on the Soviet naval units in the Gulf of Sollum anchorage off the Egyptian and Libyan border. Russian "Illegals"— covert intelligence officers—would try to attach themselves to us like leeches in seedy strip clubs in Naples or when puking on the streets of the Marseilles red light district. We went to monthly counterintelligence briefings that explained how the KGB recruited assets, and how they manipulated even the lowest-level young soldier, sailor, or marine through heterosexual and homosexual "honeytraps."

The formerly classified briefings of Yuri Bezmenov, now posted up on Youtube.com, are where we learned of the targeting and recruitment techniques of the KGB. Until the fall of the Soviet Union the watchword was "Beware of the Bears. The Bears are everywhere."

After the fall of the Soviet Union the KGB became known as the FSB. In the last ten years Russian intelligence melded all of its offensive techniques to create a new kind of war: Hybrid Warfare—a melange of hostile cyber, political, and psychological operations in support of their national objectives, whether during peacetime or in open war. It is now standard operating procedure.

A few months after the hacks, at the start of the Democratic Party Convention in Philadelphia, the WikiLeaks organization, led by the information transparency activist Julian Assange, leaked the stolen documents with the intent to "damage" Hillary Clinton. The information leak had the intended effect, as airing the DNC's dirty tricks conducted against the Sanders campaign created a rift between diehard Bernie Sanders supporters, and led to the resignation of Representative Debbie Wasserman-Schultz as chair of the DNC.

Once the emails were released the source of the hacking became the number one question asked by global security and intelligence experts. The story was literally a Whodunnit? How did information from just one political party get released to the benefit of the unpredictable Republican nominee, Donald Trump? Civilian security specialists joined the US and NATO allies as they commenced a massive cyber-sleuthing operation. The United States Cyber Command, headquartered at the National Security Agency (NSA) on Fort George G. Meade in Maryland, as well as the FBI and their cyber subcontractors, detected the leak source: The FSB and its sister the GRU—Russia's national and military intelligence bureaus. The metadata—information inside the emails showing the pathway from the DNC computers to WikiLeaks—led straight back to a suspected Russian intelligence organization, a conglomeration of cyber spying groups codenamed CYBER BEARS.

All of the old lessons of identifying Russian mantraps started to come back to me as the stolen DNC data was revealed. It had a pattern that was familiar and that virtually every other intelligence officer could recognize. The pattern showed that someone was playing 3-dimensional chess with our democracy.

Russia has perfected political warfare by using cyber assets to personally attack and neutralize political opponents. They call it *Kompromat*. They hack into computers or phones to gather intelligence, expose this intelligence (or false data they manufacture out of whole cloth) through the media to create scandal, and thereby knock an opponent or nation out of the game. Russia has attacked Estonia, the Ukraine, and Western nations using just these cyberwarfare methods. At some point Russia apparently decided to apply these tactics against the United States and so American democracy itself was hacked.

The president received a briefing days before WikiLeaks released the data to the public. The Russian spy agency had been ordered to make a bold move, hack the American elections, and engage in political warfare to elect Donald Trump President. Whether he knew it or not, Trump was the perfect candidate for a political asset. Former KGB officer Yuri Bezmenov said the KGB targeted "Ego-centric people who lack moral principles—who are either too greedy or who suffer from exaggerated self-importance. These are the people the KGB wants and finds easiest to recruit."

This activity could only have been directed from the highest level of the Russian Federation, from Vladimir Putin himself.

In *The Plot to Hack America*, I have attempted to explain the story of the first massive Russian cyberwarfare operation against the United States electorate, and how Vladimir Putin attempted to engineer Donald J. Trump's improbable election as president of the United States. Here you will find a fairly detailed breakdown of the entire CYBER BEARS organ of the Russian Federation: the FSB, the GRU, Russian military intelligence, and criminal cyberwarfare subcontractors. It will become clear that they are using every weapon in the Kremlin's propaganda arsenal. It will catalog the entirety of all of their known cyber and media activities related to the 2016 US political campaign. Within its chapters are revelations about how television media, global communications, and cyber operations were used to exploit and attack the US electoral system. There is strong evidence their work with WikiLeaks met clearly scripted dates and actively responded to events in order to destroy Hillary Clinton and the Democratic Party and to elect Donald Trump as president.

The Plot to Hack America will also try to explain how the CYBER BEARS group was detected; how CYBER BEARS hacks personal and intelligence data from its enemies and then uses that intelligence to choose political allies and "useful idiots" to do their bidding in the target nation; and why they may or may not be disseminating Black propaganda, forged emails, false statements, and computer viruses, that are released into the WikiLeaks data dumps. CYBER BEARS teams also often masquerade as American voters and post Pro-Trump positions and materials on Twitter, Facebook and other sites to support the election of Donald Trump.

The Plot to Hack America details how Russian intelligence, the FSB's "Active Measures" units, created and structured a strategic political warfare campaign, and how it influences the internet via distribution of international media through Russia Today (RT) television, which pushes political propaganda daily. The Russian television media arm of the Kremlin, Russia Today (RT) television is engaged in a strategic propaganda campaign to further Russia's political goals and has been used to co-opt the extreme wings of the American political parties including tacit and open support for neo-Nazis, anti-government extremist libertarians, conspiracy theorists, and the marginalized left such as the Green Party. RT gives these organizations an international mouthpiece in an attempt to validate them in mainstream media to the detriment of American stability.

This is a real-life spy thriller, happening in real time. It is my hope that *The Plot to Hack America* will inform the American electorate of how Russia executed a full-scale political and cyberwar on America, starting with Watergate 2.0, to elect Donald Trump president of the United States.

THE PLOT TO HACK AMERICA

2ND EDITION

1

WATERGATE 2.0

THE CENTRAL ORGANIZATIONAL HUB FOR THE Democratic Party is situated in a sand-colored modern building on Canal Street in Southeast Washington, DC, just a few blocks away from the Capitol. In late April 2016, the information technology division of the Democratic National Committee found problems in their system that indicated unauthorized access.

Upon discovery they called in CrowdStrike, an IT security company, to assess the damage. The hope was that it would be minor. Nuisance hackers attack with regularity, protesting various personal and political ideas and quack theories that usually involve the DNC and the Bilderbergs, the faking of the 9/11 attacks, or attempts to deny service in misguided attempts assist the opposition Republicans.

After CrowdStrike technicians implanted analytical software into the structure of the DNC's servers, they soon discovered that two unknown entities had made an unauthorized penetration of the committee's computers. The technicians immediately recognized that this was not a nuisance attack; it was a professional hit using professional tools and software. The CrowdStrike team started a series of analytical tests to discover the methods of entry and to outline the pathways that the hackers took into the server system. The tests would allow the cyber sleuths to determine where the hackers went, what they did while inside, and what data they may have taken. Another team checked the DNC's server logs to see what the hackers had manipulated out of parameter. All of the parameters of the hack would take weeks to lay out in an official report, but it was almost immediately clear that this was not the work of amateur hackers.

Once inside, the two unauthorized users had started rooting around. One entity had implanted itself and had been monitoring the emails and chats of the Democratic staff for months, stealing files, emails, and voice messages—almost everything. The second entity, seemingly operating independently, had targeted two very specific files.

The treasure in political espionage is to know precisely what your enemy knows about you. Every intelligence agency seeks to find the details of the inner management of their opposition, but finding the file summary of what they actually know, what they don't know and—equally important—*what they know that they don't know*, is intelligence gold. For the political season of 2016, the most highly prized information in the DNC's servers would be the opposition files held by the Democratic Party about the seventeen Republican Party candidates.

The CrowdStrike damage control team determined that the penetration operation conducted by the unknown hackers had left the servers of the Democratic Party severely compromised. They had copied or taken materials of all kinds, and had infiltrated virtually everything of value to a political opponent: personal file folders, official chat threads, digital voicemails, and the email content of virtually everyone's mailbox. The hackers also obtained the DNC's donor lists, and it is likely that the donors' credit card information was associated with these lists. One of the more fascinating aspects about this attack is that it was bold and brazen; many cyber security experts are a little surprised at how the hackers didn't cover their tracks deeply, as if they wanted to be discovered. There was just enough cover to be deniable, but as one expert observed, it was a "big cyber F-you." It was an electronic equivalent of a looting where the perpetrators throw everything around on the floor just to let you know they were there.

CrowdStrike quickly determined that the penetration into the servers started in the summer of 2015. Hand in hand with the successful penetration the next year, it would appear that the older attempt was an exploratory operation to determine the security settings on the server's network. This probe would lay the groundwork for the determined and focused 2016 attack. However one factor was unshakable; the timeline of the 2016 hacks on the computers of the Democratic National Committee clearly indicated that the collection and dissemination was timed to benefit only the opposition Republican Party. Worse, if the hack was truly malicious, even relatively innocent information such as personal discussions, preferences, and the rivalries or relationships among coworkers could be twisted and injected into the national conversation in the months leading up to the election. This was not lost on the chairperson of the DNC, Debbie Wasserman Schultz. She knew that scandal or not, the Republicans would use the hacked information to attack.

The Republican Party has shown an uncanny proclivity for taking an innocuous subject and by dint of repetition, inference, and outright false accusation making a seemingly innocent remark turn into years of acrimonious investigations. When Democratic staffers removed the letter "W" from a couple of Old Executive Office building computer keyboards, the Republicans turned it into a national campaign about how the White house itself was horribly vandalized by hordes of Democrats. When the staff at the White House travel office was routinely replaced upon the arrival of the freshly sworn-in President Bill Clinton, the scandal machine turned it into a witch hunt of national proportions that led to congressional investigations over abuse of power and personally targeted the first lady. It's been joked that had George Washington confessed to cutting down the cherry tree in the modern era, he would have been investigated for destruction of government property and abuse of authority, and promptly impeached.

However, this hack was unprecedented. The exposure of all of the internal discussions on the processes, procedures, strategy, beliefs, and thoughts of every staffer at the DNC from Debbie Wasserman Schultz down to the concerned citizen who calls and leaves a voice mail, was staggering. Any innocent comment could be turned into a political flamethrower. All discussions could be framed as conspiracies. The question at hand for the DNC became not who conducted the hack, but what would they do with the information.

Watergate 1.0

In 1972, President Richard Nixon, through his proxies in the White House called "The Plumbers" and in coordination with the Committee to Reelect the President (aka CREEP), sent five men into the offices of the Democratic National Committee in the offices at the luxurious Watergate Hotel in Washington, DC. The burglars had orders to install wiretaps, break into safes, and copy files to find out exactly what opposition research the Democrats had on Nixon in the months before the election. Although he won the presidential election, by August of 1973, the political scandal of covering up the crime led to Nixon being the first president to resign in disgrace.

The 2016 DNC hack conducted forty-four years later—almost to the day—was the exact same operation. However, this time there would be no security guard to detect the intrusion, and the burglars would not be caught wearing latex gloves and planting microphones. They would copy the information in a matter of seconds, their digital fingerprints would emerge long after the break-in, and discovery would occur well after the damage had been done to Hillary Clinton's presidential campaign.

There were a myriad of suspects on the political stage from Trump supporters to Black Hat members of Anonymous, the shadowy hacker collective that sought to expose hidden secrets though public sun lighting. Though the DNC is a political machine that manages the Democratic Party and the campaigns of its members to office, it also operates as the framework to express the political aspirations of a huge proportion of the American electorate.

When President Barack Obama won reelection to the presidency in 2012, he won more than 65 million votes representing 51.1 percent of American voters. The management team for that electoral success was the DNC. They not only represent the candidates, but once the candidates are selected the DNC is the principle agency for the grooming, funding, and support to meet the goals of the party. Now, all of their internal secrets were stolen.

The general understanding at the time was that the DNC could contain the damage resulting from the hack, and the DNC claimed that nothing had been pilfered.[1]

The general inner workings were relatively tame so long as they were not in the public domain. In June 2016, DNC Chairwoman Debbie Wasserman Schultz stated that,

> The security of our system is critical to our operation and to the confidence of the campaigns and state parties we work with. . . . When we discovered the intrusion, we treated this like the serious incident it is and reached out to CrowdStrike immediately. Our team moved as quickly as possible to kick out the intruders and secure our network.[2]

After the April hack had been discovered, the analytical study of what was stolen was compiled. Crowdstrike and DNC officials figured out very quickly that the attack was broad and that the hackers had access for as long as ninety or more days where they entered and exited the servers and reviewed and took what they pleased. However, there was an early indicator of the intent of the intrusion.

If an advocate of the Republican Party, a citizen hacktivist, or a malicious "Black Hat" hacker anarchist had perpetrated the intrusion, it would have been a much sloppier operation. Additionally, the perpetrators would likely have taken or destroyed the dossiers of every Republican Party candidate in a cyber version of a bonfire. Hacktivists love the anarchy of letting systems administrators know that they have been violated. On the other hand, "White Hat" hackers, internet security specialists who often win contracts by illegally entering systems, usually leave notes so they can be contacted and help fix security flaws. They generally let the administrators know by leaving "I told you that you were vulnerable" messages in high-value files. All of this would have been old hat for the DNC computer administrators and CrowdStrike protection analysts, but the target of this second hacking was peculiar. It ignored everything and everyone except one set of files: The opposition research folders on New York City billionaire Donald J. Trump. This 2016 intrusion could arguably be called Watergate 2.0, but unlike the original Watergate, this time the materials would be used in a political process to damaging effect.

Trump's Revenge: Erasing Obama's Presidency

The White House Correspondents' Dinner is an annual spring event hosted by the White House Correspondents' Association. Sometimes referred to as "nerd prom," the dinner brings journalists, politicians, and celebrities to the same room and is often criticized for fostering a cozy relationship between the media and the very people they are supposed to cover. The president usually delivers a humorous monologue that is then followed by a performance by a comedian. Donald Trump was a guest of the *Washington Post* at the 2011 White House Correspondents' Dinner.

It was just a month before the dinner that Trump had become a leading voice in the so-called birther movement, raising the preposterous charge that President Barack Obama was not born in Hawaii as he claimed, but rather in Kenya. Trump publically and repeatedly called on President Obama to release his birth certificate. The *New York Times* wrote, "The more Mr. Trump questioned the legitimacy of Mr. Obama's presidency, the better he performed in the early polls of the 2012 Republican field, springing from fifth place to a virtual tie for first."[3] Trump's notoriety as a blustering TV showman using blunt, racially tinged conspiracy theories was making him a rising star in conservative circles. These insults were not lost on the President, so Obama dedicated a notable portion of his nineteen-minute speech to making jabs at the New York businessman:

> Donald Trump is here tonight. Now I know that he's taken some flak lately, but no one is happier—no one is prouder—to put this birth certificate matter to rest than The Donald. And that's because he can finally get back to focusing on the issues that matter: Like, did we fake the moon landing? What really happened in Roswell? And where are Biggie and Tupac? But all kidding aside, obviously we all know about your credentials and breadth of experience. For example—no seriously, just recently, in an episode of *Celebrity Apprentice*, at the steakhouse, the men's cooking team did not impress the judges from Omaha Steaks. And there was a lot of blame to go around, but you, Mr. Trump, recognized that the real problem was a lack of leadership, and so ultimately you didn't blame Lil Jon or Meat Loaf, you fired Gary Busey. And these are the kinds of decisions that would keep me up at night. Well handled, sir. Well handled. Say what you will about Mr. Trump, he certainly would bring some change to the White House.[4]

After Obama's remarks, comedian Seth Meyers didn't let Trump off the hook. Many journalists noted Trump did not seem amused throughout the performance, particularly at Obama's and Meyers's insults. Roxanne Roberts, who sat next to Trump at the dinner, wrote in the *Washington Post* that Trump "didn't crack a smile" at Meyers's jabs. Meyers joked, "Donald Trump has been saying he will run for president as a Republican—which is surprising, since I just assumed he was running as a joke." He continued poking fun at Trump, as Roberts noted, "lobbing jokes like grenades."[5] Roberts wrote, "In retrospect, Trump broke the classic rule of political humor that says that the only response to a joke about you is to laugh harder than anyone else in the room.

Whatever he was thinking, Trump looked unhappy and gave pundits a reason to pounce."[6] Trump only fueled the fire when he didn't attend any after parties, and instead headed directly to his jet from the dinner.

The following day, Trump told *Fox News* that he "really understood what I was getting into" saying, "I didn't know that I'd be virtually the sole focus. I guess when you're leading in the polls that sort of thing tends to happen. But I was certainly in a certain way having a good time listening."[7]

If he was listening, what he heard did not appear to please him the slightest. He attacked Meyers directly. "Seth Meyers has no talent," Trump said in an interview with Michael Barbaro of the *New York Times* the day after the dinner. "He fell totally flat. In fact, I thought Seth's delivery was so bad that he hurt himself."[8] He told Barbaro the evening was "like a roast of Donald Trump." Still, Barbaro described him as "clearly reveling in the attention, if not the content."[9]

In retrospect, the events of the 2011 White House Correspondents' Dinner may have at least partially motivated Trump to run in 2016. The *New York Times'* Maggie Haberman and Alexander Burns wrote, "That evening of public abasement, rather than sending Mr. Trump away, accelerated his ferocious efforts to gain stature within the political world. And it captured the degree to which Mr. Trump's campaign is driven by a deep yearning sometimes obscured by his bluster and bragging: a desire to be taken seriously."[10]

Clearly stung by the dinner jokes, it would be natural to see how Trump might relish revenge. Harnessing the power of the conservative poll numbers running for president in 2016 would give him the power of dismantling Obama's legacy himself.

Trump Enters Politics

When Donald Trump announced his presidential run on June 16, 2015, he entered an unusually large field of eleven major Republican candidates seeking the White House. By the end of July, that field would expand to an unprecedented seventeen major Republican candidates, a hodgepodge that included nine current or former governors, senators, a retired neurosurgeon, and the former CEO of Hewlett Packard.[11] [12]

Polls early on in the contest showed Trump with an immediate edge over most of the candidates, with a June 26–28, 2015 CNN/ORC national poll showing him polling at 12 percent among Republicans, second after former Florida governor Jeb Bush at 19 percent.[13] By July 22–25, 2015, a CNN/ORC poll showed the New York businessman topping the polls at 19 percent, with Bush trailing at 15 percent.[14] Always outlandish, his brash style and ability to "tell it like it is" attracted crowds of admirers. He was an instant success among the conservative fringe and had the ability to bring that fringe into the mainstream.

The hallmark of his campaign was using hyperbole and personal insults with just a touch of Orwellian double speak. For example, he would make contradictory statements, on one hand praising veterans but insulting John McCain for being shot down and spending years as a prisoner of war in Vietnam. On July 18, 2015 Trump threw out an off-hand remark about McCain. "He's not a war hero," Trump said. "He was a war hero because he was captured. I like people who weren't captured."[15] When pressured he would claim he never said any such thing and allow the next outrageous statement to wash over the last one.

Despite his high poll numbers, most of the media and electorate did not initially take his campaign seriously. The *Huffington Post* went as far as to announce in July 2015 it would run all Trump-related stories in the Entertainment section. "Our reason is simple: Trump's campaign is a sideshow," the announcement read. "We won't take the bait. If you are interested in what The Donald has to say, you'll find it next to our stories on the Kardashians and *The Bachelorette*."[16]

Even the renowned statistician Nate Silver—founder of the polling analysis website *FiveThirtyEight*, who had a near-perfect track record of correctly predicting the winners of the presidential contests in each of the fifty states during the 2008 and 2012 elections—couldn't fathom Trump's rise.[17] In November of 2015, with the Republican field narrowed down to twelve candidates, Trump topped the polls. Silver put Trump's chances of winning the Republican nomination below 20 percent. Silver wrote, "For my money, that adds up to Trump's chances being higher than 0 but (considerably) less than 20 percent."[18]

As Christmas approached it looked increasingly probable that Trump would not lose his lead. It was at this time that Trump received a peculiar endorsement. Out of the blue, Vladimir Putin, president of the Russian Federation, made a series of comments about the US election that seemed to endorse Trump. Putin said of Trump in a press conference "He is a bright and talented person without any doubt. He is the absolute leader of the presidential race. . ."[19] Putin's endorsement was a surprise to most but not to those who had been noticing the penchant Trump had towards the Russian autocrat and his glowing admiration of other dictators such as Kim Il-Sung and Muammar Gaddafi.

Trump continued to top each poll as rivals began to fall. Former Florida Gov. Jeb Bush—once considered to be a shoo-in for the GOP nomination—continued to slip before dropping out after his February loss in the South Carolina primary. In the months leading up to Trump's nomination, former neurosurgeon Ben Carson, Texas Senator Ted Cruz, Florida Senator Marco Rubio, and former Hewlett-Packard CEO Carly Fiorina each at different times found themselves in second place to Trump, but none could catch up to his lead, according to various CNN/ORC polls.[20]

By spring the race to become the Republican presidential nominee had narrowed down to three candidates. On May 3, Trump became the presumptive GOP nominee when Senator Ted Cruz dropped out of the race after losing the Indiana primary. Ohio Governor John Kasich suspended his campaign the next day.[21] The field was vanquished and against all expectations, Donald Trump officially became the party's nominee at the Republican National Convention in June.[22]

Between August 2015 and March 2016, the Republicans held a total of twelve presidential primary debates. The Democrats held nine.[23] Trump certainly made splashes in the first Republican primary debate in August 2015, receiving both cheers and boos from the crowd at the Quicken Loans arena in Cleveland, Ohio.

When a moderator asked the ten Republican candidates on stage if anyone was unwilling to pledge their support to the eventual nominee, Trump was the only candidate to raise his hand. Receiving boos from the audience, Trump said, "I can totally make the pledge if I'm the nominee. I will pledge I will not run as an independent. I am discussing it with everybody. But I'm talking about a lot of leverage. We want to win and we will win. But I want to win as the Republican. I want to run as the Republican nominee."[24]

Trump also gained a reputation for his bluntness and constant criticism of political correctness. "I think the big problem this country has—is being politically correct," he said during the Fox debate, receiving cheers from the crowd and highlighting a theme he would exploit throughout his campaign. "And I don't frankly have time for total political correctness. And to be honest with you, this country doesn't have time either."[25]

Trump electrified a segment of the conservative electorate. He fired them up at unprecedented levels and relished the electricity in the air when the rallies had unusually high number of protesters and descended into violent altercations. Trump was repeatedly criticized for encouraging violence. Kevin Cirilli wrote for Bloomberg:

> Trump frequently chides protesters who seek to disrupt his rallies by shouting for authorities to "get 'em out" before sometimes adding "run home to mommy." In fact, even before the candidate begins speaking, a tongue-in-cheek audio-recording plays before each rally instructing attendees to "not hurt the protester," but to instead chant "Trump, Trump, Trump" and point to those seeking to disrupt the proceedings so as to notify authorities of their location.[26]

The violence wasn't limited to those in the crowd. His campaign staff mimicked the aggressive stance of the candidate. Trump's campaign manager Corey Lewandowski was accused of forcibly grabbing conservative *Breitbart News* reporter Michelle Fields hard enough to leave a bruise at a campaign rally in Florida. Lewandowski was charged with misdemeanor battery, charges that were ultimately dropped. But it was Trump's response to the incident that worried some. *Vox* explains:

> In fact, Trump supported Lewandowski since the accusations first surfaced. First he denied it ever happened. Then he denied the video footage existed. Then he said the video footage showed nothing. And then argued that Fields prompted the whole thing by first grabbing Trump while holding a pen (which Trump says Secret Service could have easily mistaken for a tiny bomb).[27]

The entire demeanor of the campaign was called into question. Trump chief strategist Paul Manafort addressed these concerns at an April closed-door meeting of the Republican National Committee. Ashley Parker writes in the *New York Times*:

> There, in a slide show, Mr. Manafort assured members that Mr. Trump was 'evolving' and simply playing a part with his incendiary style of campaigning, which has helped drive him to the front of the race but has caused party leaders to worry that Republicans will be punished in November.[28]

Trump himself has claimed that even his wife, Melania, and daughter, Ivanka, have called on him to act more presidential. Two days after Manafort addressed the RNC, Trump addressed the calls himself at a campaign rally in Connecticut, saying he wasn't about to start "toning it down." Parker writes:

I started thinking, and I said I can, you know being presidential is easy, much easier than what I have to do," Mr. Trump said, before quickly adding that, as a colorful entertainer-turned-politician, he might risk boring his audiences if he pivots too much toward general-election propriety.[29]

Worse than his mouth was his fingers when connected to an Android smartphone with access to Twitter. In 140 characters he managed to derail his candidacy with insulting, racy, or inappropriate comments including those retweeting neo-Nazi and white supremacist comments. The former host of *The Apprentice* often takes to Twitter to blast those who speak critically of him. The *New York Times* even kept a running list of the "People, Places and Things Donald Trump Has Insulted on Twitter."[30]

The Democratic Simmer

Compared to the unusually large number of candidates competing for the GOP nomination, a number that remained in the double digits through the Iowa caucuses, the Democratic side pitted two main candidates against one another from early on: former Secretary of State, US Senator, and First Lady Hillary Clinton and Vermont Senator Bernie Sanders.

Initial CNN/ORC polls showed Clinton with a big lead over Sanders, with a poll conducted June 26–28, 2015 showing Clinton polling at 58 percent to Sanders's 15 percent. Other would-be candidates Jim Webb, Lincoln Chafee, and former Maryland Governor Martin O'Malley never polled higher than 3 percent, according to an analysis of CNN/ORC polls.[31] O'Malley suspended his campaign after the February 1, 2016, Iowa caucus.

For a self-proclaimed democratic socialist from Vermont, Sanders had a decent showing in the 2016 race for nomination. A March 17–20 poll showed Sanders reaching a high of 44 percent support to Clinton's 51 percent.[32] Distrustful of Clinton and the Democratic Party machine, Sanders's followers were ardent and deeply believed that the power structure of the Democratic Party could be overturned in a new liberal progressive era. Accusations of vote rigging, favoritism, and delegate manipulation permeated the campaign. By the time Clinton secured the nomination, a great deal of mistrust between the Clinton and Sanders supporters had set in. Clinton supporters saw Sanders's campaigners as youthful, naïve, and ready to believe anything they read on the internet. Sanders's supporters saw the Clinton machine in terms that Trump and the Republicans could appreciate: for more than twenty-five years the Republicans had fostered an image of Clinton as a corrupt, dishonest, and manipulative liar who was ambitious at all costs, despite decades of investigations by Republican Congresses that had revealed no evidence of corruption or complicity in criminality.

The Benghazi Gambit and Email Questions

Sanders took a first shot at Clinton with his criticism of her emails related to the Benghazi scandal. In November 2015, after rejecting the scope of the Republican-led controversy, Sanders suddenly about faced, contending that any emails related to the subject were fair game.

A terrorist attack on the US mission compound in Benghazi, Libya on September 11, 2012, went from being a regrettable incident leading to the deaths of four Americans to a full-blown Republican-manufactured conspiracy theory positing that President Obama and Hillary Clinton allowed Ambassador J. Christopher Stevens and his staff to die by issuing a "stand-down order." Republicans attacked Clinton relentlessly for her handling of the Benghazi attacks as secretary of state. Critics charged the administration didn't listen to intelligence warnings ahead of the attack and subsequently covered up their actions. Nine separate congressional bodies investigated, and as *Vox* reported, "Each has identified problems with the way the incident was handled, but none have uncovered real evidence of an administration cover-up or failure to properly respond to the attacks."[33] In October 2015, Clinton testified before the House Select Committee on Benghazi for more than eleven hours. David Herszenhorn of the *New York Times* wrote, "The hearing was widely perceived to have backfired on Republicans, as she answered their questions and coolly deflected their attacks."[34]The Committee released its final report as the primary campaigns were wrapping up in June 2016. The *Times* reported "no new evidence of culpability or wrongdoing by Hillary Clinton."[35] Still, hours after the release of the report, Trump tweeted, "Benghazi is just another Hillary Clinton failure. It just never seems to work the way it's supposed to with Clinton."[36]

In the end nothing helped the Sanders campaign. Clinton had won more than three million more votes, and by June, however, Clinton had won enough delegates to secure the nomination, also beating Sanders in the superdelegate count.[37] On July 12, with less than two weeks until the Democratic National Convention, Sanders endorsed Hillary Clinton. In a post published the day of his endorsement, Sanders wrote he could not "in good conscience" allow Donald Trump to be elected president. "Today, I endorsed Hillary Clinton to be our next President. I know that some of you will be disappointed with that decision," he wrote. "But I believe that, at this moment, our country, our values, and our common vision for a transformed America, are best served by the defeat of Donald Trump and the election of Hillary Clinton."[38]

A hallmark of the 2016 campaign was the effort to damage Hillary Clinton with information related to a private email server located in her home while she was secretary of state, which first surfaced in March 2015. Republicans, as well as some in the Bernie Sanders campaign, desperately wanted Clinton to be found criminally liable for the usage of private emails for official business. Despite Sanders saying he was "sick and tired" of hearing about the emails, his campaign manager

Jeff Weaver bluntly told Fox news that it would be hard for Clinton to keep running for election if she were "under indictment."[39]

This level of talk got Sanders's supporters as frothed up as Trump supporters and the wait was on for the FBI investigation to conclude and rule against her so Sanders could walk away with the nomination. The email controversy was now the core of the Republican strategy; they theorized that if Clinton was indicted then her campaign and political career would be over and that Trump could easily insult Sanders to victory.

However, this was not to be. The FBI did conclude its investigation and determined that Secretary Clinton did not intentionally commit any crimes. There would be no indictment. The FBI determined that 110 of the 30,000 emails Clinton originally turned over contained information that was classified at the time she received them, but most had classification markers removed. Clinton had not deliberately misled anyone nor had she lied to the FBI. FBI Director James Comey called her actions "extremely careless," although the agency recommended no charges be filed against the former secretary of state.[40]

Seemingly nothing could derail the Clinton nomination. The Democratic Convention in Philadelphia was fast approaching and the last chance for Clinton's detractors to take down her campaign by the use of the emails had seemingly evaporated.

2

SUSPICIONS OF SOMETHING MORE SINISTER

The Trump Opposition Files

Late in the primaries, just two months before Donald Trump and Hillary Clinton would go to their respective conventions, the depth of the seriousness of the DNC hack was starting to sink in. It became apparent that the first successful hacks had stolen quite a bit from the DNC computers. The hackers took all manner of electronic information, particularly emails related to the internal conversations of the individual staff members, deliberations of the senior leadership, and internal correspondence. Additionally, Excel spreadsheets with donor information, contact lists, and even the voicemails of angry constituents were copied. However, the true treasure from this intrusion was a single file folder of the opposition research on the likely Republican opponent in the US presidential elections, Donald J. Trump.

The Trump Opposition Research dossier was put together by DNC staffer Alexandra Chalupa. On June 15, the website Gawker published the entirety of Chalupa's opposition files on Trump.[1] It was a collection of what dirt could be dredged up and used in tough political seas that were sure to come. To the DNC and the Clinton campaign, the dossier of data was rather mundane information from online sources collating the publically available information the DNC and Clinton campaign would use to characterize Trump. To a general hacker it would be of little interest except for amusement purposes. If the folder contained routine information, sophisticated narrative management could counter whatever the Clinton camp prepared. If the folder contained something explosive, leaking it early could defuse any interest, or it could be argued that the information was false based on the insecurity of the servers. For the Trump campaign, knowing in advance what the DNC and Team Clinton knew would prove invaluable to defending and counterattacking Hillary. And it is not unprecedented. One paranoid American president, so concerned with what secrets the DNC had on him, performed the same operation that appears to have occurred here.

There were early indications that a foreign nation had been targeting the opposition files before the news broke. In a May 3, 2013, email written on her DNC email account to Luis Miranda, the DNC communications director, Chalupa wrote in that she had spoken to Ukrainian journalists about her research on Trump. She also noted that when she started researching information on Paul Manafort, Trump's new campaign manager, and his ties to the Ukraine, Yahoo security started sending her numerous messages warning her that her email had become the target of "state-sponsored actors." Yahoo implemented a security protocol in December 2015 that would warn its users if any foreign government activity was seen impacting their accounts.[2] The Yahoo CIO issued a blog post stating, "We're committed to protecting the security and safety of our users, and we strive to detect and prevent unauthorized access to user accounts by third parties."[3] The main component of this early warning system is a pop-up banner that reads *Important Action Required. We strongly suspect that your account has been the target of state-sponsored actors. Learn how to better protect yourself.*

Chalupa noted at the end of her email to Miranda that "Since I started digging into [Trump campaign chairman Paul] Manafort, these messages have been a daily occurrence on my Yahoo account despite changing my password often." It was well known that Paul Manafort is the lawyer who led what is known as the "Torturer's Lobby."[4] In his portfolio was a rogue's gallery of dictators, strongmen, and autocrats, including the Ukraine's deposed pro-Moscow dictator Viktor Yanukovych.

Transmitting the Punch?

One of the most surprising events after the announcement of the DNC hack occurred a few weeks later in conservative media. During Fox News' May 9, 2016, show *The Megan File*, contributor Andrew Napolitano made an amazing statement to host Megan Kelly about the hacks. Napolitano claimed to have confidential information about what was going on at the highest levels of decision-making at the Kremlin, SVR (Russia's foreign intelligence service), and Putin's inner circle, saying "there's a debate going on in the Kremlin between the Foreign Ministry and the Intelligence Services about whether they should release the twenty thousand of Mrs. Clinton's emails that they have hacked into and received and stored. All of this is happening at once."[5]

Taken in the context of what we now know, it begs the question, how did Napolitano come upon this incredibly specific information? Was it information passed onto him from US intelligence, a Russian source, wishful thinking on his part, or just outright fabricated? Only the most senior ranking members of the Russian foreign ministry and intelligence apparatus know this, as it describes discussions at the inner sanctum of Russian intelligence, including Putin himself.

If the alleged source was American, then perhaps the director of the FBI, and only on an absolute need-to-know basis, together with the president, the national director of intelligence, the director of the CIA, and the director of NSA would be privy to this information. Access to such a source would be among the crown jewels of any intelligence community. If the story had any basis in fact and sourced from America there would have been a national security mole hunt by the FBI on par with the hunt to capture the Russian spies Aldrich Ames or Robert Hanssen.

It appears that the source of the story emanated from a mythical figure, a journalist named Sorcha Faal. Sorcha Faal is widely believed to be a pseudonym for David Booth. Booth hosts a wild-eyed conspiracy theory website called Whatdoesitmean.com.[6] Usually websites like this and the more popular and crazier Infowars.com are easily dismissed as tinfoil hat crowds who see government conspiracy everywhere. Yet in this case "Sorcha Faal" appears to be so well wired into the Kremlin that "her" work at this website was often copied by mainstream Russian information propaganda like Russia Insider's *Svobodnaya Pressa* ("Free Press"). This site pushes wild conspiracy theories such as the proposition that the US trains and directs ISIS, and writes op-eds about the dangers of European multiculturalism. It is a core component of the Russian propaganda system, and such news organs as *Ren TV* (a large, private, pro-Putin Russian television channel) and *Sputnik News* (a multinational propaganda organ of the Russian government) often cite its links as sources.

Did the Russians, after hacking the DNC, feed this story back to the West through Whatdoesitmean.com? Whatever the source, it would appear that Judge Napolitano and Fox News brought it right into the mainstream. It would not be out of the ordinary for the Russian information war strategists to insert false media stories during a global influence effort; they have a century of practice as the Soviet Union. Using Fox News, Andrew Napolitano may have unwittingly transmitted a secret Trump campaign punch; the thought came from conservative media, but it may have been created for propagation by Russia itself.

Foreign Shenanigans

This was not the first time that foreign players had tried influencing US elections. This time around appeared initially no different than prior nuisance hackings. However the calm on the surface was just hiding deep ripples in the US intelligence community. By summer of 2015 the National Security Agency knew that the FSB and other agencies were probing around the seams of the elections. Though they would never publicly admit it, the NSA, home to US Cyber Command, would have been the principal agency to tip off the FBI if there were any indicators of a cyber intrusion operation underway at the DNC. Apparently they passed on some kind of warning—also known as a tipper. The Bureau did give the DNC a hint but did not provide information as to the direction or severity of the threat because doing so would have identified the source, which could have only been tracked to its origin by the NSA.

On May 18, 2016, the director of national intelligence (DNI), James Clapper, briefed Congress about cyber-attacks and activities that may affect the 2016 presidential campaigns. Clapper said of the 2008 campaign that foreign intelligence agencies "met with campaign contacts and staff, used human-source networks for policy insights, exploited technology to get otherwise sensitive data, engaged in perception management to influence policy. . . . This exceeded traditional lobbying and public diplomacy."[7] He did not state which foreign agencies. Clapper stated that the US intelligence community has observed espionage activity in the past two presidential elections, and that interest by foreign spies was much higher than in past election cycles. According to Ellen Nakashima, who wrote several stories on hacking for the *Washington Post*, the public affairs director for the DNI, David P. Hale, stated "we're aware that campaigns and related organizations and individuals are targeted by actors with a variety of motivations—from philosophical differences to espionage—and capabilities—from defacements to intrusions."[8]

During the 2008 election season, Chinese government hackers penetrated the computers of the Obama and McCain campaigns and made off with numerous policy documents related to China.[9] Director of national security at the time, Dennis Blair said, "based on everything I know, this was a case of political cyberespionage by the Chinese government against the two American political parties."[10]

However, the nature of those hackings resembled traditional intelligence collection operations. Past operations include Chinese army hackers stealing a letter drafted by Senator John McCain supporting Taiwan. Chinese government officials contacted McCain's office to lodge a complaint not realizing that the stolen letter had never left his office computer. Such inadvertent collection versus exploitation foreshadowing is rare in a truly coordinated information war, and this Chinese attempt at propaganda was sloppy and almost amateurish.

President Obama made reference to the hacks by the Chinese on May 29, 2009. "Hackers gained access to emails and a range of campaign files, from policy position papers to travel plans."[11] He then laid out a new cyber security policy designed to deter attacks such as these. For all of the security measures and new legislation, the DNC of 2016 was still open to exploitation.

By the last week of August 2016, it would become patently clear that someone had stolen every facet of the Democratic Party system, taken what they pleased, and launched an organized campaign to discredit it in the media. Simply put, the Democratic machine was hit by a terrorist attack without bombs. The effect of the hacker's campaign was to influence a strategic outcome that could only help one American political party and indirectly help a foreign actor's strategic policy against the West. A hack of this magnitude could only be perpetrated by a determined foe that wanted to foment division in the Democratic Party, a foe with the advanced cyber technology to see to it that Donald J. Trump would take advantage of the chaos caused at a critical moment in the process, almost exactly one hundred days from the election.

That foe had been waiting patiently for the right opportunity to damage America. And his opportunity would come to him, on a golden platter, at the Miss Universe Pageant of 2013 in Moscow.

3

THE
SPYMASTER-IN-CHIEF

ACCORDING TO THE OFFICIAL KREMLIN BIOGRAPHY, Putin was interested in intelligence at an early age. When Putin attended a public KGB event as a teenager, he asked the amused officers how to achieve his goal of becoming an intelligence officer. They told him to either serve in the army or earn a degree in law, so he went to university for law at Leningrad State University, where he earned his degree in 1975. After graduation he joined and studied as a junior officer at the KGB 101st Intelligence School and later attended the Yuri Andropov Red Banner Institute. The spy craft programs he attended were designed to give the officer basic training including foreign language, surveillance, specialty photography, wiretapping, breaking and entering, small arms assassination, and how to manipulate people to become spies against their own nation. The school's curriculum also included a heavy dose of indoctrination in Marxist-Leninist philosophy and an emphasis on service to the state above all else.[1] Here Putin would learn the organization's unofficial motto: "Once KGB, always KGB."

"Fairly quickly, I left for special training in Moscow, where I spent a year," Putin said. "Then I returned again to Leningrad, worked there in the First Main [Chief] Directorate—the [foreign] intelligence service."[2]

From 1985 to 1990 Putin was assigned to No. 4 Angelikastrasse, the KGB offices in Dresden, located in what was then East Germany. There he ran East German academics and businessmen across the Iron Curtain and helped them spy or recruit sympathetic West Germans for the KGB. Most interestingly, he used agents with the East German computer company Robotron as cover stories for agents to steal computer technology secrets from the West with the help of the East German secret police, the Stasi. Putin's pattern of theft using advanced information systems would come up again and again in his future. For this assignment, the KGB awarded Major Putin a Bronze Medal.

During the fall of the Berlin Wall in 1989, a crowd of East German protesters gathered outside Putin's office and threatened to storm the building. Putin received orders to conduct emergency destruction of his field site's files. The beginning of the end had come for Communism in Germany, and the KGB needed to sanitize its many satellite offices before they abandoned them.[3] For a short period he was also assigned to Directorate K, the KGB's counterintelligence division. This unit was designed to hunt spies, and his experience would build on a natural mistrust of people, a tendency that would come to serve him well in his future. Putin officially resigned from the KGB in August 1991 after the KGB old guard attempted to overthrow the government and keep Communism in place. He went to work at a university in Leningrad, now called St. Petersburg.

Anatoly Sobchak, mayor of St. Petersburg, launched Putin's political career. Vladimir was made deputy mayor of the city and appointed chair of foreign economic relations. The innocuous-sounding body was actually a gold plated prize in the immediate post-Soviet era. It was Putin's job to liquidate Soviet assets and real estate in St. Petersburg and control the buying of foodstuffs and assets for a population that was just feeling freedom for the first time in seventy years. His position brought in billions of dollars to the mayor and his friends in the second largest city. Needless to say this job required the toughness and guile of a former spy, but it also showed him how to work the new class of oligarchs that would make money hand over fist.

In the post-Soviet period, St. Petersburg became known as the "Gangster Capitol." During that period under President Boris Yeltsin, Putin was alleged to have been stealing food and siphoning funds off from the sale of assets and reconstruction. However when corruption accusations hit Mayor Sobchak and Yeltsin, Putin showed loyalty and stood behind those who backed him up when he was rising. Sobchak, a reformer, would later die in suspicious circumstances, some say poisoning, after returning to St. Petersburg to stump for Putin in February 2000.[4]

Yeltsin, suffering from ill health and alcoholism, and under threat of removal due to the massive corruption in Russia, kept the strong young Putin by his side. Here Putin cultivated the public image of an unabashed KGB officer who mastered judo and politics. Putin even created his own public relations videos. In 1998 he became director of the FSB, the Office of State Security, now centralizing all power both foreign and domestic. In August 1999 Boris Yeltsin appointed Putin to the office of prime minister, and the Duma approved his appointment shortly thereafter.

Once he was appointed prime minister he would find a reason to quickly launch a second brutal war in Chechnya that would eventually kill more than fifty thousand people—terrorism. As the political campaign started, terrorists detonated four apartment complexes in Russia and Dagestan, killing more than three hundred citizens. When Putin hit the stumps and came out as a pitbull on a Russian nationalist platform against terrorism, he rose in popularity. When Yeltsin resigned the presidency, Putin became president in accordance with the Russian constitution.

American journalist David Satter, who investigated the apartment bombings, believes that a failed Hexogen bomb with advanced military detonators found in the city of Ryazan used technology and materials exclusive to the Russian army. The men caught planting them were FSB officers.[5] In response, Satter, author of a book on Putin's rise to power—*Darkness at Dawn*—was expelled from Russia in January 2014. Virtually all other high-profile activists who investigated this attack ended up assassinated, including the ex-KGB officer Litvinenko, who was poisoned with an extremely rare Polonium-210 radionuclide while drinking tea. The substance could only have originated in Russian nuclear reactors. He died three weeks later.

School of the Second Profession

During Putin's time at the KGB, "active operations"—shorthand for direct espionage—drew on a rich history. Russia had a long tradition of court espionage and intrigue among the European kingdoms. As far back as anyone could remember, the ancient methods of spying formed the basis for every thought and action of the Tsars. It was far more sophisticated in some ways than today, due to its heavy reliance on solid tradecraft and observation techniques in a world limited by foot and horse. The KGB taught its officers the traditions of using manual codes and ciphers, slow surveillance, concocting poisons, reading secret inks, and forging false handwriting as skills to master and to appreciate.

Most importantly, learning to read people, their wants, dreams, likes, dislikes, and desires—all to get them to betray their own country—was the most basic and oldest of all lessons in the Russian intelligence foundations.

Every one of the Russian Emperors and Tsars established secret intelligence collection; maintaining court influence required advanced information on plots and betrayals, as well as the occasional murder. The Oprichnina, established in 1565 by Ivan the Terrible, was the first known Russian intelligence agency. They were six thousand horse guard uniformed in all-black cavalry clothes, and their coat of arms was "The Broom and The Dog"—to sniff out and sweep up anyone opposed to Ivan.[6] Their duty was simple. They were the police, bodyguard, and spies tasked to detect, hunt down, and kill Ivan's enemies.

When the Oprichnina outlived their usefulness, Ivan dissolved the organization in 1572, but in seven years they set the pace for state terror and espionage.

In 1697 Peter the Great established the Preobrazhensky Office; Empress Anne established the Chancellery for Secret Investigations in 1731, and Peter III had an organization called the Secret Bureau. All of these state organs opened illicit letters, listened to whispers at keyholes, assassinated enemies, and intercepted couriers. But it was Emperor Nicholas I who set up the Third Section. This group went far further than any of the previous amateurish gendarmerie. They did not just open letters from mistresses; the Third Section was the first agency to truly train, maintain, and deploy professional Russian foreign intelligence officers for missions targeting foreign countries.

As rulers gained power they used increasingly brutal secret police tactics. Nicholas I's successor, Alexander II, established the Okhrana, an organization that set the precedent of being completely above any law while acting in the defense of the realm. They carried out mass surveillance, arrests without warrant, summary executions as they saw fit—all in the name of the Tsar. They operated as deep cover spies in the European courts and ran spy networks in France, Switzerland, and Britain. While they watched and killed revolutionaries and anti-government plotters of all stripes, the Okhrana's specialty was to infiltrate and suppress dissidents living abroad. Somehow these agencies could not stop the spread of ideologies and none had a great impact on the coming Communist uprising. Tsar Nicholas II was well informed of the Communist unrest in his armed forces, but his secret police were either unable or unwilling to stop the Russian Revolution, or his death—along with his family—at the hands of the Bolsheviks.

In February 1917, more than four hundred thousand industrial workers in St. Petersburg revolted and, with the aid of the Russian army, overthrew Tsar Nicholas II. Vladimir Ilyich Lenin gave them that revolution, and in 1917 he knew, better than most, the necessity for a secret agency to prevent a Royalist counter-revolution. One of his first acts was to establish the All Russia Extraordinary Commission for Combating Counter Revolution and Sabotage, known simply as the Cheka, from the Cyrillic acronym.[7]

The first director of the Cheka was Felix Dzerzhinsky. The coat of arms for the Cheka organization was the Sword on a Shield. Dzerzhinsky organized his agency to be an absolutely ruthless internal security tool. To Dzerzhinsky the Cheka "stood for organized terror. . . . Terror is an absolute necessity during times of revolution. . . . We terrorize the enemies of the Soviet government in order to stop crime at its inception." That philosophy permeates the belief system of every Russian secret service officer up to today. So famed was Dzerzhinsky that a statue known as the Iron Felix stood in in Lyubyanka square—also known as Dzerzhinsky Square—in front of the Moscow headquarters of the KGB for almost seventy years. Although the statue disappeared after the failed coup of 1991, the KGB's successor organization, the FSB, still occupies the offices at that location.

With the death of Lenin in 1924, Joseph Broz Stalin took over. During this time Stalin used the secret police forces to arrest and execute an estimated 50 million people in order to maintain order among citizens. In 1930 the NKVD appeared, and later established the Administration of Special Tasks. Their job was to infiltrate agents and convert socialist supporters of the revolution in Western and fascist countries, in addition to exterminating dissent among potential NKVD backsliders. During the 1930s some of the great successes would be to develop spies in British and American universities and recruit members of the Cambridge Five spy ring, including Harold Adrian Russell "Kim" Philby, an officer of the British Secret Service MI6, Guy Burgess, and Don McLean.

After more than a decade of tumultuous leadership, Lavrenti Beria expanded the NKVD, which was under the OGPU, to the point where a separate organization needed to be created. This became NKGB, in charge of internal security, espionage, and guerilla activities in World War II. When Stalin died in 1953, Beria tried to replace him, but the politburo arrested, tried, and executed Beria in 1953. Nikita Khrushchev would head the new soviet government and on March 13, 1954, formally established the Komitet Gosudarstvennoy Bezopasnosti ("Committee for State Security") or KGB. It would be responsible for all facets of state security including internal security, police, and border patrol, and for the next four decades would operate a ruthless campaign against the West—as well as the citizens of the Soviet Union.

Ivan Serov was named the first chairman of the KGB. Its first task was to eradicate Beria supporters. With reorganization under Khrushchev, the Soviet Union relaxed censorship, reduced the size of prison camps, and became more active in foreign affairs. In 1958, Aleksandr Shelepin became KGB chairman. "Shelli" sought to enhance the USSR by destabilizing "enemy" nations including the United States, Britain, and Japan. This led to almost three decades of Soviet-sponsored anticolonial terrorism in the Middle East, Europe, Africa, and Latin America.

By 1967 Yuri Andropov, the longest-serving KGB chairman with fifteen years in the post, headed the KGB. Andropov headed the KGB's "golden age," continuing Khrushchev and Shelepin's organizational restructuring, while stepping up intelligence gathering and foreign espionage. He helped build an organizational structure to fund and supervise technological advancements in Russian defense while actively suppressing any government dissidence. Andropov stepped down in 1982, to lead the Politburo.

After a short series of leaders, Vladimir Kryuchkov became the last chairman of the KGB in 1988, leading a failed coup August 18, 1991, to overthrow Mikhail Gorbachev. The Communist Party was effectively dissolved December 25, 1991, ending the bloody seventy-year legacy. What was left was a nascent post-Communist Russian state, and every state needs an intelligence agency; the KGB would survive after the Soviet Union expired.

Putin's New Nobility

After the Soviet Union's collapse, the KGB became the FSK (Federalnaya Sluzhba Kontrrazvedki), Federal Counterintelligence Service. It was designed to be similar to Britain's MI5. In 1995 FSK turned into the FSB—the Counterintelligence "K," being replaced with the Security (Cyrillic "B") Bezopasnost—effectively becoming the Federal Security Service.

In December 2000, FSB Director Nikolai Patrushev, the successor to Vladimir Putin, spoke to the Russian daily tabloid *Komsomolskaya Pravda* on the founding anniversary of the Cheka secret police. He described the role and stature of the new FSB:

> I don't want to give a fancy speech, but our best colleagues, the honor and pride of the FSB, don't do their work for the money. When I give government awards to our people, I scrutinize their faces. There are the highbrow intellectual analysts, the broad-shouldered, weather-beaten Special Forces men, the taciturn explosives specialists, exacting investigators, and the discreet counter-espionage operational officers. . . . They all look different, but there is one very special characteristic that unites all these people, and it is a very important quality: It is their sense of service. They are, if you like, our new "nobility."[8]

The founders of the Soviet Union and now Russia harnessed this rich history of the dark arts, and where necessary, applied them precisely and ruthlessly. The modern techniques of electronic intelligence collection, planting listening devices, and using computers to conduct break-ins, lives up to its centuries of spy pedigree. In fact Putin's life-long worldview stems from maintaining faith with a long tradition of Russia's agencies dedicated to spying, assassination, and political influence. Now as leader of Russia, he is a master of applying espionage as well as a consumer of its fruits.

The Illegals Take Manhattan

A recurring theme in FSB operations in the United States is real estate. From the end of the Soviet Union to the rise of the oligarchs, Russian state money has been buying property and making real estate deals all over the United States. It was a flush market for Russians and a good place to hide illicit cash. Real estate was the perfect investment instrument for the FSB to also introduce its officers into the United States.

In the old KGB, the First Chief Directorate also was known as the Foreign Directorate or the *INU*. This Directorate was responsible for overseas operations related to foreign intelligence collection and active measures performed by KGB officers, cultivating the KGB's competence of infiltrating spi nte foreign countries as well as recruiting and maintaining source of intelligence.[9] Although it is unlikely that Putin is directing United States external intelligence operations, one can be sure he gives them his opinions based on his own experience. In a British government inquiry about the murder of ex-KGB officer Alexander Litvinenko, Sir Robert Owen stated:

> While all academics, media commentators and reporters make much of Putin's earlier careers in the KGB and the FSB, there have appeared no substantial revelations about his routine of working relations with the intelligence agencies since the start of his first Presidential term. The usual assumption is that he keeps a close eye on their activities and gives them strategic guidance. But the exact extent of his oversight of active operations is veiled in secrecy. It is one of those matters that no one has yet managed to uncover.[10]

The answer to that question would be solved in 2010 when the US Department of Justice arrested a network of ten Russian spies operating in the United States. All of them were non-official cover (NOC) agents, The Illegals.

With the fall of the Soviet Union and the rise of Vladimir Putin, several structural changes came to the agency. The INU functions were detached and became the Foreign Intelligence Service (SVR), responsible for intelligence activity.[11] Underneath First Directorate was Directorate S—home of The Illegals. They were the deepest of deep cover spies to infiltrate foreign countries and conducted background operations in preparation for other active operations.

According to Justice Department documents, federal law enforcement agents began surveillance of a key Russian SVR officer named Anna Chapman in January 2010, across various locations in New York City. Surveillance uncovered regular interactions between Chapman and a Russian official operating out of the Russian Mission to the United Nations in Manhattan. Using network surveillance equipment, the federal agents were able to observe that the Russian official and Chapman would connect to the same private wireless ad hoc network and covertly communicate electronically.

Their secret communications would often take place in coffee shops, book stores, other public places, across the street or nearby one another, rather than communicating directly person to person. On multiple occasions, using network-surveillance equipment, federal agents observed the transfer of data between the two. An undercover agent posing as a Russian official from the Russian Consulate in New York City, arranged with Chapman to have a fake passport delivered to an undercover Russian operative who was using a false name, also working in New York. [12]

After the meeting with the undercover US federal agent, Chapman was observed purchasing a temporary Verizon cellphone from a Verizon store in Brooklyn, New York. She used the cell phone to call her father, a Russian intelligence officer in Moscow. Her lawyer later revealed that she was wary of the passport assignment and was calling her father for advice. Her father instructed her to turn the passport into a police station, where the Federal Bureau of Investigation arrested her for espionage, along with nine others.[13] [14] The Department of Justice charged them with conspiring to act as unlawful agents of the Russian Federation within the United States.[15]

Chapman was born Anna Vasil'yevna Kushchyenko on February 23, 1982, in the industrial city of Volgograd, Russia, to math teacher Irene and Russian diplomat Vasily. She suffered from scoliosis as a child and lived with her grandmother as her father was sent to work in the Russian embassy in Kenya. She briefly attended a creative studies school in Volgograd from 1996 to 1997. She went on to study economics at the People's Friendship University in Moscow, graduating at the top of her class in 2004.

In 2001 and 2002 she spent her summers visiting London, where at the age of nineteen she met twenty-one year-old student Alex Chapman. The two were married in Moscow in 2002. Soon after, now with the name Anna Chapman, she received a British passport. According to Alex Chapman, Anna's father never took a liking to him and seemed to trust no one. Alex reported that Anna told him her father was a former KGB operative.

After eventually settling in London, Anna began habitually lying about her work experience, claiming to sell private jets to Russians on behalf of Net Jets and working closely with owner Warren Buffet. Alex began to observe her becoming increasingly secretive around this time, often meeting with other Russians in private, boasting about influential people she was meeting, and suddenly having large sums of money. The two eventually divorced in 2006.[16]

When Anna Chapman arrived in New York, she moved into an apartment one block south of the New York Stock Exchange. She also claimed on her LinkedIn page to run an internet real estate company valued at $2 million.[17] The *Daily News* reported that she likely became involved with then-sixty-year-old millionaire Michael Bittan, who made his money in the restaurant industry, real estate, jeans manufacturing, and pharmaceuticals.[18]

After she was arrested by US federal agents in June of 2010, the US and Russian governments arranged a swap in July of the same year, exchanging the ten arrested in the US for four former Russian spies who were detained in Russia for helping the US. One of them was instrumental in arresting former US FBI Agent Robert Hansen, who had been providing the Russians with information for years.[19]

Upon returning to Russia, Chapman received national celebrity status, modeling for the Russian version of *Maxim* magazine and appearing in multiple fashion shots. She has also met and has been praised by Putin and made appearances in Russian military recruitment and propaganda videos. The British tabloid magazine *Daily Mail* reported that Chapman posted a picture to her Instagram account this April expressing support for 2016 GOP presidential nominee Donald Trump. In her account she wrote "Trump will 'get along with Putin,' he approves of the Russian operation in Syria and is surprised why the USA supports Ukraine. Changes in America are closer? What do you think?" An additional post also mocked Trump's Democratic rival, Hillary Clinton.

Chapman's return as a conquering hero, even if she was a failed spy, is not surprising in Putin's Russia. Putin values loyalty to the nation above all else, and an attractive, loyal FSB officer is propaganda gold. His sense of loyalty to the spy service propelled him to national fame under Yeltsin and keeps his position safe today. In fact, in order to be put under Putin's "roof" of protection, it is nearly essential for that individual to have a prior association with the KGB/FSB. An estimated 78 percent of Russia's top one thousand leading political figures worked for FSB or its predecessor the KGB or GRU.[20] When asked about a book written by a dissident Putin said, "I don't read books by people who have betrayed the Motherland."[21]

This deep history of espionage, intrigue, and murder shaped Vladimir Putin's worldview toward the West. Forged between decades of a poverty-stricken Soviet Union and tantalized by the riches of US and European economic dominance, Putin's actions and public statements hint at a world where he and his nation receive the respect and preeminence they deserve. Apparently, Putin surmises that America and NATO are waning, with the US military stretched thin beyond capacity due to two failed wars costing trillions of dollars.

Russia is changing Russia's face and not towards democracy. Karen Dawisha, a professor at Miami University, told PBS Frontline that "Instead of seeing Russia as a democracy in the process of failing, see it as an authoritarian system that's in the process of succeeding."[22] Putin is that authoritarian. For him to succeed at the mission of damaging the United States he will use all tools of the Russian statecraft such as forging alliances, but also blackmail, propaganda, and cyberwarfare.

To Putin, the best of all possible worlds would be an economically crippled America, withdrawn from military adventurism and NATO, and with leadership friendly to Russia. Could he make this happen by backing the right horse? As former director of the KGB, now in control of Russia's economic, intelligence, and nuclear arsenal, he could certainly try.

4

TRUMP'S AGENTS, PUTIN'S ASSETS?

There are no morals in politics; there is only expedience.
A scoundrel may be of use to us just because he is a scoundrel.
—VLADIMIR ILYICH LENIN

DONALD TRUMP HAS LONG SOUGHT TO establish real estate relationships with Russia's wealthy elite. In 2013 he got his chance. He was invited by one of the richest families in Russia to cohost the 2013 Miss Universe Pageant in Moscow.

It would not be Trump's first visit to Russia. Trump's interest in Russia predated the fall of the Soviet Union. Long before the pageant, in 1987 Soviet Ambassador Yuri Dubinin convinced Trump to visit Moscow and St. Petersburg to develop a Trump Tower for Russia. Trump went on an exploratory trip but the business and construction conditions were not optimal for him to take advantage of the Soviets or make a profit. He returned home without any projects in hand.[1]

Trump didn't have to wait long for conditions to change. The fall of the Soviet Union in 1991 led to an extreme concentration of wealth in Russia. With Putin at its helm, the money went straight to his cronies, and the oligarchy developed—a premier class made up of

Putin loyalists. Russian oligarchs must have very deep, personal ties to Russian strongman Vladimir Putin to get anything accomplished or even to hold onto their wealth. Having a "roof" over one's head—a Russian euphemism for sponsorship by the politically powerful—is a tradition as old as Russia itself.

Twenty years after Trump's initial visit, there was a huge demand for more luxury and higher quality brands in Russia. Trump's son Donald Jr. visited Moscow in 2008, looking to expand the Trump real estate brand beyond America to Europe and the Middle East. According to the Russian newspaper *Kommersant*, Trump had considered aiding the reconstruction of the city's Moskva and Rossiya hotels.[2, 3]

But it wasn't hotels or the golden Trump name that won Russians over. It was his popularity as a finger-pointing, quick-firing boss in the NBC television show *The Apprentice*. His fame on that show brought him into contact with the wealthy Agalarov family. Their money, lavishness, and flattery won Trump over. Aras Agalarov, a billionaire Russian real estate mogul, and his son Emin, the rich pop singer, were big fans of his—Emin even had Trump appear in one of his music videos "In Another Life," to "fire" Emin at the end of the video as he daydreamed about luxury houses filled with hot women. Emin has been called the Donald Trump of Russia due to his popularity, wealth, and personal relations with Vladimir Putin.[4]

Aras was born in Azerbaijan in 1956. His *Forbes*-estimated net worth is roughly $1.3 billion in real estate development. His company, Crocus Group, received Kremlin contracts for two World Cup 2018 stadiums. Putin even gave Aras a medal of honor in 2013. As with all things Putin, the medal itself wasn't important or even valuable—it was Putin's imprimatur in front of the nation that sealed Aras's status as a personal benefactor to the president.

"I have always been interested in building in Russia," Trump said in an interview with the *New York Post* after returning from Moscow in 2013. He was also proud that "almost all of the oligarchs were in the room."[5]

Trump negotiated the deal that brought the Miss Universe pageant to Moscow with the blessing and support of the Agalarovs. "We just had a meeting . . . we all seemed to like each other, shook hands and signed our contract within a week's time," Emin said in his *Forbes* interview, adding that the pageant would cost $20 million to host. Trump first announced Moscow winning the bid in June 2013. "Moscow right now in the world is a very, very important place. We wanted Moscow all the way."[6]

After being turned away by American banks due to bankruptcies, Trump has been getting considerable investments from Russian sources, including many with known criminal ties. At one point he even turned to Muammar Gaddafi, the terrorism-loving Libyan dictator who blew up American soldiers at a discotech in Germany, funded the Irish Republican Army, and destroyed Pan Am Flight 103 over Lockerbie, Scotland, and the French UTA Flight 772 over the Sahara. Those airline attacks alone killed 413 total passengers and crew.[7]

Trump certainly must have been thrilled to be in the presence of the super nouveau-riche of Moscow, a city where Mercedes-Benz was selling more cars than anywhere else in the world. Even Putin's personal counter-assault teams from the KGB rode in armored stretch Mercedes G-Wagons. The money was spilling from Russia and Trump was now associating himself with some of the most powerful people in the eastern hemisphere.

The beauty pageant would be held in the Crocus City Hall, a 7,500-seat concert hall just four years old. Trump was dazzled, and desired the attention of the only oligarch who mattered, Vladimir Putin. He tweeted with gleeful apprehension, "Do you think Putin will be going to The Miss Universe Pageant in November in Moscow—if so, will he become my new best friend?"[8]

When Trump met with the Agalarovs in November 2013, Alex Sapir and Rotem Rosen were also in attendance. The Russian developers helped construct the Trump SoHo hotel and condominium project in Manhattan.[9] Sapir's father was alleged to have had close ties to ex-KGB officers. This should hardly be surprising, as the KGB, now FSB, is a deeply entrenched part of the new Russia, where ex-KGB hands reach out to make deals and take advantage wherever they can to the benefit of Putin's regime.

Sapir told New York's *Real Estate Weekly* that Russian visitors to the Trump SoHo "have been telling us they wish there was something modern and hip like it in Moscow. . . . A lot of people from the oil and gas businesses have come to us asking to be partners in building a product like Trump Soho there." Russian money would be enough for Trump. "The Russian market is attracted to me," Trump said. Upon returning to the United States Trump gave his experience in Russia glowing reviews. "I just got back from Russia—learned lots & lots," Trump tweeted upon his return to the US. "Moscow is a very interesting and amazing place! U.S. MUST BE VERY SMART AND VERY STRATEGIC."[10]

Trump did not say whether or not he met Putin but was fond of his reputation in the country. Putin "has a tremendous popularity in Russia," Trump told Fox News. "They love what he's doing. They love what he represents."[11]

The pageant experience left Trump with a newfound "understanding" of Russian society. Trump explained in an interview with Fox News May 6, 2016, "I know Russia well," Trump said. "I had a major event in Russia two or three years ago, which was a big, big incredible event." Asked whether he had met with Putin there, Trump declined to say, though he added: "I got to meet a lot of people." "And you know what?" he continued. "They want to be friendly with the United States. Wouldn't it be nice if we actually got along with somebody?"[12]

The man Trump so enamored, whom Trump was so desperate to meet and impress, was not just the ruler of Russia. He was a man steeped in the most dangerous of experiences—he was a master of espionage and an expert at manipulation and exploitation. He could do to Donald Trump what he did to the oligarchy of Russia; make him or break him with a single sentence of approval or insult. Trump, knowing he was culling favor with a powerful man—he had nuclear weapons and beautiful women—responded with obsequiousness that must have pleased such a spy king. Putin must have recognized this showman as a target who could be developed into a political asset friendly to Russia.

Putin's Candidate Development Strategy

If Putin were to consult the spy-handling experts at the FSB or recall his lessons from the Yuri Andropov School of Intelligence, he would not be hard-pressed to find a more suitable candidate who shared his values and could "Make America Great Again."

Putin has successfully manipulated people from when he was a junior spy, parlaying his ascent to the premiership of Russia. The new FSB methods are exactly the same as the old KGB methods he learned but harness technology to speed up operational timelines. Not only has Putin used human intelligence and espionage asset management to great effect, but he has also led the way in using the computer information systems technology he was tasked to steal in the 1980s. The creation of new perceptions through propaganda to secure the state has always been a mainstay of the Soviet systems, now it just protects the assets and standing of the oligarchy. Russia fully understood the potential of the internet age to mold perceptions and create its own reality, and information warfare is a central tenet of Russian political, diplomatic, and military operations. The internet age has just sped up the time that propaganda—both innocent and malicious—can infect the global information flow and corrupt whatever target Vladimir Putin desires.

A defector from the KGB, Yuri Bezmenov, gave a series of lectures on KGB recruitment strategies and precisely whom the organization targeted for recruitment by its officers. Bezmenov's information was confirmed by other former Russian officers as standard fare for recruitment of spies worldwide, particularly in the West.

To some it may come as a surprise that the KGB considered extremist leftists, communists, and so forth ill-suited to divulge the secrets the KGB wanted, or to gain the highest levels of government clearance. After the 1950s it was KGB policy to always try to recruit the highest level spies from circles that were unexpected; they specifically targeted Westerners from conservative ideological profiles. Bezmenov said:

> My KGB instructors specifically made a point. Never border with leftists. Forget about these political prostitutes. Aim higher. Try to get into wide circulation, established conservative media. The rich. Filthy rich movie makers. Intellectuals. So-called academic circles. Cynical egocentric people who can look into your eyes with an angelic expression and tell you a lie.[13]

If there were ever a candidate for recruitment by hostile intelligence agency then Trump would be moved to the head of the class. When he came onto the political scene, FSB officers must have surely remembered this lesson about recruiting the rich, the egomaniacs, and the liars. The record is patently clear that Donald Trump misleads and deceives with impunity. Trump's methodology of denial, deception, misdirection, tacit victim-blaming, and outright fabrication has come to permeate every aspect of his campaign.

Trump has proven time and again he cannot keep the truth straight when it comes to claiming prestige and high level associates. During a planned trip to the USA by Russian President Mikhail Gorbachev, Trump claimed he would be showing him a $19 million dollar apartment during a visit to Trump Tower. This was one in a long list of false stories that Trump seeded in the press. To add insult to injury, a Gorbachev impersonator was brought to the tower and shepherded around by Trump, who was completely fooled, despite later denials.[14]

At the end of the year the political fact-checking group POLITIFACT categorized virtually everything the Trump campaign

THE PLOT TO HACK AMERICA

said in 2015 as "Lie of the Year." It was bold and audacious to just let lies, innuendo, and fabrications be the main thrust in seizing a nomination, but it was a strategy the spies of the Kremlin could appreciate. To them, Trump would not only fit the bill of a potential asset, but he seemed to have adopted—or learned through guile—the fundamental tenets of Russian psychological and information warfare's "active measures": Deny, Deceive, and Defeat.

Play and Manipulate the Subject's Ego

In discussions with confidential sources, I have learned that the FSB still maintains the policies and techniques that have worked for over a century in recruiting agents to be unwitting suppliers of information. They will either find a willing asset who voluntarily works with them for personal, financial, or ideological reasons, or they will find a suitable candidate and "develop" him or her into a useful asset, whether that asset discovers his or her role. This is called an "unwitting" asset or agent.

When recruiting spies or other types of useful propaganda assets (which could include apologists, sympathizers, and even opponents) the officer is trained to observe and hone in on the personal and psychological flaw or flaws that make the asset vulnerable: flattery for the vain, cash to the indebted gambler, adventure for the thrill junkie, sex for the hideous; it is the officer's job to size up the potential subject and make him or her eager to work for the officer.

The skilled intelligence officer would have applied one of the universal agent recruitment evaluating tools on a potential recruit like Trump. The US government uses a system called MICE. It is an acronym used by the CIA which stands for Money, Ideology, Coercion (or Compromise), and Ego or Excitement.[15] Although a more in-depth alternative to this system called RASCLS (Reciprocation, Authority, Scarcity, Commitment/Consistency, Liking, Social proof) exists, we shall use MICE for this assessment.

The FSB's chief spy-recruiting officers assigned to the SVR—the foreign intelligence collection directorate (or the GRU if it was military intelligence operation)—are trained to play to the desires of their potential assets. They watch carefully before ever making the approach. If the subject wants to feel important, then importance is stressed in all discussions.

Money is an incredible inducement for a potential recruit. If the subject wants to be impressed by promises of wealth and opportunity, then the oligarchs will be rolled out to make him feel as if he is or could be one of them. In Trump's case, he may in fact have been unwittingly steered into positions sympathetic to Russia, such that he now thinks they are deeply-held beliefs, due to the flattering conversations with his Russian supporting friends and staffers concerning his heart's desire: to be an oligarch playing on the global playfield on par with Putin.

The ideology of the individual can be a self-driving motivator for those who may offer their services to a foreign power, or who find their fortunes have great similarities. The FSB's SVR recruiters will always attempt to enhance the subject's prestige if that's what it takes to keep him personally motivated. The craft of nudging a person to espouse a political position that is against the interests of the person's birth nation requires the officer to be able to read the subject's ideological belief system, and subtly maneuver them into agreement, or to at least be neutral to another, less-palatable belief system that just happens to be the path to treason.

Compromise (or coercion) is generally not a desired process, but where it is clear that a potential recruit has a secret that can be used against them, such as secretly embezzling government money, or sexual liaisons of an illicit nature, it can be useful for the purpose of blackmail. Compromise in these terms would be photographs or videos of "honeypots"—sexual traps laid by the hostile intelligence service—and then coercing the individual to begrudgingly betray their country. No one has ever publically accused Donald Trump of being susceptible to coercion, but there is the possibility of being personally compromised or finding oneself in a compromising position at, let's say, a beauty pageant, in a nation where the intelligence service routinely uses beautiful women as sexual traps. Retired KGB General Oleg Kalugin once famously said "In America, in the West, occasionally you ask your men to stand up for their country. There's very little difference. In Russia, we just ask our young women to lie down."

Ego or Excitement (or both) is the last of the categories of basic recruitment. Bezmenov emphasized that there is an archetype of potential asset in the West that the service desired most of all – Egocentric narcissists, like Trump.

"Ego-centric people who lack moral principles—who are either too greedy or who suffer from exaggerated self-importance. These are the people the KGB wants and finds easiest to recruit."[16]

If Putin so chose to develop him, only the highest-level state agents would be involved in a potential cultivation of Trump as an exponent of Russian interests. Putin himself, under advisement of the FSB management and SVR's top human intelligence experts, would have to assess the suitability of the candidate and his potential to assist Russia, whether the candidate knew it or not. In Trump's case, it would be very easy. At almost every turn, his "bromance" with Putin would potentially stand on a foundation of his desire for their riches, and to be universally recognized as a man of substance and stature. It would cost Russia nothing to entertain his desires while furthering their own.

A skilled autocrat such as Putin would easily understand how to play and manipulate Donald Trump's ego. Putin would want Trump to feel as if he is truly qualified to be President, over the opposition of his American detractors who ridicule Trump as not being remotely qualified. Putin would know this from his intelligence collection apparatus that Trump would need strategically-timed compliments in an effort to foster his image and massage his easily-bruised ego.

Putin's strategically-placed endorsement of December 2015 is

a classic example of a "hands-off but actually hands-on" supporting statement to make the asset feel special. On Trump, Putin said:
"[Trump] wants to move to another level of relations, a closer, deeper
level of relations with Russia. . . . How can we not welcome this? Of
course we welcome this."[17]

"He is a bright and talented person without any doubt. He is the
absolute leader of the presidential race . . ."[18]

This statement and many others, as well as the largesse of attention
and support from even average Russian citizens, would make Trump
feel indebted to Putin. Such indebtedness could even have contributed to Trump's mistrust of the American system of government. The
sentiment that Putin's kind words were somewhat responsible for vali-
dating Trump on a world stage could explain Trump's gushing admiration for Russia almost every time he speaks on the subject, much to the
consternation of Trump's staff. In his own mind, Trump may feel he
received more support from Moscow than he did from the Republican
Party, when Putin paid the compliment ("My friend [Putin] likes
me."). This may be more than enough to maintain the bond between
an active-measure handler and an unwitting asset.

The Kremlin Crew

A group of Russian-backed associates orbit Trump and have become
known in some circles as "The Kremlin Crew." It is not a problem for
Trump to commune with money; the problem is his associates' many
disturbing connections to the Russian oligarchy and officers of the
KGB/FSB. A wise businessman may seek out cash in the nouveau
riche parts of the world. But add Russian oligarchy cash managed by
FSB spies, and it adds up to the kind of relationships the FBI counterintelligence division routinely arrested people for during the Cold
War—as espionage assets.

The Bayrock Group

One of Trump's most troubling intelligence connections was to the Bayrock Group. Trump first aligned with them to build a hotel in Moscow in 2005. When that didn't happen, he partnered with them to build the Trump SoHo. Bayrock was chaired by Tevfik Arif, originally a Soviet Union commerce apparatchik from Kazakhstan, who worked to introduce Trump to Russian investors. Trump saw it as a chance to open Trump Hotels and Towers in Moscow, Kiev, Warsaw, and Istanbul.[19]

Felix Satter also worked for Bayrock. He has been implicated in ties with Russian Mafia. Satter is also known for "using mob-like tactics to achieve his goals," and was convicted of a stock fraud scheme. Satter made arrangements with Trump to develop projects in Russia and the US. He bragged in 2008 testimony, "I can build a Trump Tower, because of my relationship with Trump."[20] Trump denies knowing Satter. However, the relationship was significant enough that condo buyers in Trump International Hotel and Tower mentioned it in a lawsuit filed over construction.[21] Trump sought to disassociate himself from the project, claiming he simply lent his name and denied knowing Satter. During his depositions, Trump said he knew neither Arif nor Satter.[22]

Satter is described as having threatened Bayrock employees with violence. Even after he left Bayrock, Satter kept a relationship with Trump including an office. AP reported that Satter used business cards that claimed he was a "Senior Advisor to Donald Trump."[23]

Donald Trump announced his plans for Trump SoHo, a 46-story condominium-hotel in New York, on a 2006 episode of *The Apprentice*. For the project, Trump partnered with development companies the Sapir Organization and the Bayrock Group. The Sapir Organization was founded by the late Tamir Sapir, an émigré from the former Soviet republic of Georgia who quickly made millions on New York real estate in the 1990s. In 2006 his son Alex assumed the reins of the company. Of the elder Sapir, Charles Bagli wrote in the *New York Times*:

> He landed in New York in 1976, where he drove a cab for three years before borrowing $10,000 against his taxi medallion to open a small electronics store. The store, at 200 Fifth Avenue in the Flatiron neighborhood, became a wholesale outlet for Soviet diplomats, K.G.B. agents and Politburo members.[24]

Tamir Sapir's son-in-law, Rotem Rosen, was also involved in the SoHo project. Ben Schreckinger wrote in *Politico*:

> During the Cold War, Tamir Sapir, an émigré from the Soviet Union, sold electronics to KGB agents from a storefront in Manhattan. Alex Sapir's business partner Rotem Rosen is a former lieutenant of the Soviet-born Israeli billionaire Lev Leviev, an oligarch with longstanding ties to Vladimir Putin who counts the Russian president as a "true friend."[25]

From the start, Trump SoHo had a hard time attracting buyers, in part because zoning laws restricted owners to living in the units 120 days of the year. When the owners weren't there, units would be used as hotel rooms and owners would share part of the profit. It was soon revealed, however, that potential buyers were told inflated estimates of the number of units sold. Within months of the opening, a group of condo buyers filed a lawsuit alleging fraud against Trump, the Bayrock Group, and the Sapir Organization. According to *Reuters*:

The complaint said the defendants in sales pitches and to the media during the first eighteen months of marketing advertised that the building was "30, 40, 50, 60 percent or more sold." Instead, when the offering plan went effective, buyers learned that just 62 of the 391 units, or 16 percent, had been sold, the complaint said. A minimum of 15 percent was needed for the plan to be effective.[26] Then, in November

2011, Trump agreed to a settlement, without admitting wrongdoing. The buyers received 90 percent of their deposits. Mike McIntire of *The New York Times* writes:

> The backdrop to that unusual denouement was a gathering legal storm that threatened to cast a harsh light on how he did business. Besides the fraud accusations, a separate lawsuit claimed that Trump SoHo was developed with the undisclosed involvement of convicted felons and financing from questionable sources in Russia and Kazakhstan. And hovering over it all was a criminal investigation, previously unreported, by the Manhattan district attorney into whether the fraud alleged by the condo buyers broke any laws, according to documents and interviews with five people familiar with it. The buyers initially helped in the investigation, but as part of their lawsuit settlement, they had to notify prosecutors that they no longer wished to do so. The criminal case was eventually closed.[27]

The property was foreclosed on and put up for sale in 2014.[28]

The Americans in the Pocket

Once Trump took on the Presidential campaign he also managed to acquire the most controversial of all the Putin-associated characters: Paul Manafort.

Before becoming Trump's campaign manager, Manafort was known as the leader of the "Torturer's lobby" while working for the law firm of Black, Manafort, Stone and Kelly.[29] They represented some of the worst dictators in the world, including Mobutu Sese Seko of Zaire, The Filipino President Ferdinand Marcos, and the brutal Angolan warlord Jonas Savimbi. Manafort has also been an advisor to the Trump kingdom since the mid-1980s.

Manafort's shadowy dealmaking could best be described in a

bribery caper in France known as "The Karachi Affair." Manafort was hired to advise Edouard Balladur, a mentor to former French Prime Minister Nicholas Sarkozy, with payments from a Lebanese arms dealer, Abdul Rahman al-Assir, chairman of Interstate Engineering.[30]

The case was part of the failed 1995 French presidential campaign.[31] Al-Assir paid Manafort to advise Balladur in the campaign. At the core of the controversy was the sale of three French Agosta 90 class submarines, which Al-Assir helped to sell to Pakistan for $950 million. A French probe speculated that Balladur's campaign was being funded in part by bribes from those weapon sales. He also received a $250,000 loan from a Middle East arms dealer.[32] This was a pretty typical deal for Manafort; seemingly unscrupulous but legal.

Manafort took on the unenviable task of replacing Corey Lewandowski. Initially it was smooth sailing for Manafort before he was removed as the chief advisor. Then the revelations about the Ukraine deals surfaced. Manafort was coming under fire for his work with past clients in Ukraine, including work for Viktor Yanukovych in a 2010 campaign.[33] Manafort's efforts with Yanukovych included getting him to stop speaking Russian in public statements. Manafort worked for Serhiy Lyovochkin, former chief of staff to Yanukovych. Also part of the focus on Manafort relates to his involvement with shell companies that he has profited from.

In 2005, Manafort was working for mining tycoon Rinat Akhemetov along with Manafort partner Rick Gates, Konstantin Kilimnik, and the "International Republican Institute" of Moscow.[34] Manafort represented Dmytro Firtash, a gas "tycoon" who is wanted by the US. Manafort was also named as a defendant in a civil racketeering case with Firtash filed by Yulia Tymoschenko, the golden-haired leader of the Orange Revolution. According to US Ambassador William Taylor, in cables released by Wikileaks, Firtash admitted having ties to Seymon Mogilevich, an organized crime boss in Russia.[35, 36]

Manafort was sued in a Cayman Island court over abusing his investment money. The plaintiff was the president of the largest aluminum company in the world, Oleg Deripaska, who said Manafort has not accounted for the use of the funds or returned them.[37] Russian investors filed a petition that claimed they invested $26 million into buying a Ukrainian cable company. Surf Horizons was trying to reclaim its investment from Pericles. Manafort was ordered to be deposed in that case in 2015.[38] The US government revoked Deripaska's US visa in July 2006, and he sought to have it restored. In 2007, Manafort and Deripaska sought to establish "Pericles Emerging Market Investors," investing in Russia and Ukraine. Manafort helped to arrange meetings between Senator John McCain and Deripaska.

Manafort was a close paid advisor to Trump. On August 14, 2016, The *New York Times* published a story "Secret Ledger in Ukraine lists cash for Donald Trump's campaign chief," which detailed Manafort's relationships with Viktor Yanukovych, the deposed president of the Ukraine and close Putin loyalist. Before his abrupt departure and exile in Russia, Yanukovych was a master manipulator of Ukrainian politics. He hired Manafort to help with some of that manipulation. When he escaped a popular uprising against him it was a severe blow to Russia, as the people had been agitating to get closer to the Europe and NATO.

Manafort's dilemma following the disclosure of the ledgers, numbering around four hundred pages, was that he claimed to have never worked for either the Russian or Ukrainian governments. The handwritten ledgers reflect large projects including sales of a Ukrainian cable company under the Pericles banner.[39] They show cash payments for Manafort over a period ranging from 2007 to 2012. The article also claims that Manafort never registered his work as a "foreign agent" as required with the US Department of Justice.

According to investigators, Manafort's name appears twenty-two times. He was allegedly paid $12.7 million in cash or untraceable investments over a span of five years. The investigator did note that there is nothing in the ledger that indicates Manafort ever received payments, just that they were issued.[40]

All of these were drops in the bucket that could easily have been overlooked, but on August 17, 2016 the London *Times* released a bombshell report from Ukrainian prosecutors that Manafort had been paid by pro-Russian parties in the Ukraine to organize anti-NATO protests in Crimea, leading to the withdrawal of forces for a planned NATO exercise. The prosecutors wrote,

> It was his political effort to raise the prestige of Yanukovych and his party—the confrontation and division of society on ethnic and linguistic grounds is his trick from the time of the elections in Angola and the Philippines. While I was in the Crimea I constantly saw evidence suggesting that Paul Manafort considered autonomy [from Ukraine] as a tool to enhance the reputation of Yanukovych and win over the local electorate.[41]

Two years later Crimea would be invaded and seized by Russia.

Howard Lorber is the Trump campaign's economic advisor. The president of Vector Group, he is a Trump campaign donor and investor in Russia.[42] He's given $100,000 to the "Trump Victory fund." When Trump went to Moscow in 1996 to consider branding projects, Lorber worked to help Trump open a building in Moscow, but the venture failed. Visits with Lorber include one in November 1996. The trip focused on a project under development in Moscow like Ducat Place.

Carter Page joined Trump's campaign in March 2016. In July 2016, Page went to Moscow and delivered a series of speeches on establishing a better relationship with Russia. His recommendations included easing of economic sanctions imposed after the invasion of Crimea in 2014. As the Trump campaign talks about ending TPP and other trade deals, the unelected candidate's spokespeople are out inviting business with Russian partners, especially in industries that are known to have crime bosses and Russian mafia ties.

Senators John McCain and Lindsey Graham were staunch advocates of arming the government of Ukraine in their fight with Russian separatists and Putin. During the Republican National Convention, the party platform committee proposed language to the effect that Ukraine needed US weapons and NATO support to defend itself, in support of a long-held Republican position. Carter Page, now on the Trump campaign team, used to work in the Merrill Lynch's Moscow office and has personal investments in Gazprom, a Russian state oil conglomerate. He told Bloomberg that his investments have been hurt by the sanctions policy against Russia over Ukraine.[43] He has characterized the US policy toward Russia as chattel slavery.[44]

Page was the Trump campaign's representative to the party platform committee. Trump wanted a more Russian-friendly platform, and his team, led by Page, insisted on removing any language that would demand the arming of the Ukraine. Shortly after Page's visit to the committee, the platform was modified to do just that—all language to support arming Ukraine was removed. RNC officials told the Huffington Post that it was the "only major revision the campaign demanded."[45]

Richard Burt was the former US ambassador to Germany under President Ronald Reagan from 1985 to 1989. Mr. Burt is the Chair of the advisory council for the *National Interest*. He joined the Trump campaign at the request of Paul Manafort. Burt sits on the board of the largest commercial bank in Russia, Alfa-Bank. He also has a role in an investment fund that controls Gazprom, the same company where Carter Page has deep investments. He has been a vocal critic of the need for NATO and has written position papers on the future of Russia-Ukraine relations.[46] The *Nation* speculated that Richard Burt wrote Trump's April 27, 2016 Russia-friendly speech on foreign policy.[47]

Dmitri Konstantinovich Simes was born in Moscow in October 1947. He moved to the US in 1973. He's the former director of Soviet studies at the Center for Strategic and International Studies and former chair of the Carnegie Endowment for Peace's Center for Russian and Eurasian Programs. He is the publisher of the *National Interest*, a renowned foreign policy publication.[48]

The Center for the National Interest is close allies with the Institute for Democracy and Cooperation, a Russian-funded organization led by Adranik Migranyan. It was revealed in State Department documents leaked via WikiLeaks that Migranyan was given the position by Russian Foreign Minister Sergei Lavrov.[49] Migranyan has called Russian president Putin "Russia's Reagan" and has advocated for an ease of sanctions on Russia.

Michael Caputo lived in Russia in the post Soviet 1990s. Caputo worked for Gazprom Media, and has done work under contract to improve Vladimir Putin's image. He took on the role of Trump's adviser for the New York primary in 2016.

Trump's Spy, Putin's Ally?

General Michael Flynn. In 2015, retired Army General and former Director of the Defense Intelligence Agency, Michael Flynn, attended a Russia Today (RT) anniversary gala, where he sat at a table with Vladimir Putin. Since retiring from the Pentagon, Flynn has become a regular contributor for RT, the state-sponsored and Kremlin-controlled news outlet. Flynn has been critical in recent years of President Obama's foreign policy, especially during Hillary Clinton's term as secretary of state. He was forced to retire after clashes within the intelligence community over his vision for the DIA.

Most surprisingly, Flynn has also expressed desires to develop a stronger relationship with Russia and has been an adviser to Donald Trump and his 2016 presidential campaign on matters of national security. Flynn accompanied Trump on his CIA intelligence briefings before the election.

According to Flynn's writings, Russia is a potential ally against an "Enemy Alliance," whose members include Iran, Venezuela, North Korea, and . . . ISIS. Nowhere in his writings does he identify Russia for facilitating the destabilization of Syrian civil war or meddling elsewhere. In fact, General Flynn is proud of his associations with Russia. In an interview with the *Washington Post*'s national security writer Dana Priest, he bragged about being the only US officer allowed into the headquarters of Russian Military Intelligence, the GRU.

Flynn does not see the relationship with Russia as adversarial, but necessary to fight Islamic extremism. When asked him about that:

PRIEST: You saw the relationship with Russia as potentially good for the US?

FLYNN: No. No. I saw the relation with Russia as necessary to the US, for the interests of the US. We worked very closely with them on the Sochi Olympics. We were working closely with them on the Iranian nuclear deal. We beat Hitler because of our relationship with the Russians, so anybody that looks on it as anything but a relationship that's required for mutual supporting interests, including ISIS, . . . that's really where I'm at with Russia. We have a problem with radical Islamism and I actually think that we could work together with them against this enemy. They have a worse problem than we do.[50]

When the subject of a former Director of military intelligence being a paid pundit on Russian state TV, he took a hands-off approach; it wasn't his fault, it was his agent's.

PRIEST: Tell me about the RT [state-run Russian Television] relationship?

FLYNN: I was asked by my speaker's bureau, LAI. I do public speaking. It was in Russia. It was a paid speaking opportunity. I get paid so much. The speaker's bureau got paid so much, based on our contract.

PRIEST: Can you tell me how much you got for that?

FLYNN: No.[51]

Priest asked him about why he went on Russian Television, which is a propaganda mouthpiece for the Kremlin.

PRIEST: Have you appeared on RT regularly?

FLYNN: I appear on Al Jazeera, Sky News, Arabia, RT. I don't get paid a dime. I have no media contracts. . . . [I am interviewed] on CNN, Fox . . .

PRIEST: Why would you go on RT, they're state run?

FLYNN: Well, what's CNN?

PRIEST: Well, it's not run by the state. You're rolling your eyes.

FLYNN: Well, what's MSNBC? I mean, come on . . . what's Al Jazeera? What's Sky News Arabia? I have been asked by multiple organizations to be a [paid] contributor but I don't want to be.

PRIEST: Because you don't want to be hamstrung?

FLYNN: That's right. I want to be able to speak freely about what I believe. There's a lot of people who would actually like to be able to do that but, for whatever reason, they can't. . . . I feel pretty passionate about what's happening to the country.[52]

The most disturbing optics for Flynn is how he was invited to the Russian Television tenth anniversary gala in Moscow. Flynn was seated at the right hand of Vladimir Putin. When asked how he felt being sat next to Putin himself, in a position of favor, he said he didn't have any problem sitting next to a nuclear-armed autocrat—it was all about him getting paid.

Flynn's acceptance of money from RT, speaking his mind in forums he feels are less state controlled than MSNBC and CNN, and visual association with Putin (certainly in the eyes of the Russian leadership and people) raised the eyebrows of not just the national security elite of the United States, but practitioners in the US intelligence community. Some wondered if Flynn was not adopting the same method of speaking out the way that Edward Snowden did, by using the national platform of a former communist autocrat as his shield from criticism.

Some members in counterintelligence said that twenty years ago this would have resulted in an extensive investigation to see if his "tail was dirty," a euphemism indicating that he was being handled without his knowledge, due to cash inducements. One could easily apply the MICE recruitment principle to his behaviors when added with his complete distain for President Obama and admiration for Putin, and come up with an interesting profile that might make the GRU want to do more for him than serve coffee.

Though Flynn said he was standing up for the principles of the United States, to the Russian public, having the director of defense intelligence seated at the right hand of the most powerful ex-director of the KGB implied that the old spymaster had him under Putin's "roof" . . . in America it would translate to "He's my bitch."

Putin's Strategy to Compromise an American Election

The revelations of the Kremlin Crew's proximity to Putin and Moscow are stunning in their depth. They reveal how easily some Americans will accept money to work against their own national interest whether in business, government, or propaganda. Precisely as the KGB had discerned over seventy years ago. They also show how easily money and business relations are now the new currency of former and current Russian intelligence officers. Such riches would surely be issued with invisible strings, allowing the FSB to gain access to the highest level players in a new American administration.

These pro-Russian players apparently were so close to Trump that they could literally be chosen as his campaign manager and placed at essentially at arm's length to a potential president. At best their ties are tenuous and ill-advised, at worst they could be the grounds for an FBI espionage investigation. That remains to be seen.

If Trump's acolytes did have real ties to Russia's center of power, and if they were successful in electing Trump, they would be in a position to handle a potential president's most intimate secrets. They would also be able to advance Russia's objectives, desires, and activities—fully in-line with their own personal fortunes—above America's interests, with the full force of the Oval Office.

In the framework of the conflict between former Secretary of State Hillary Clinton and Russian President Vladimir Putin, angered by US intrusion in his wars in Georgia, Syria, Ukraine, the military seizure of Crimea, and pressures on NATO allies Latvia, Estonia, and Lithuania, Putin may be unleashing Trump's challenge as a way to exact revenge on the United States. Putin Biographer Masha Gessen, author of *Man Without a Face: The Unlikely Rise of Vladimir Putin* told CNN, "There's a really aggressive posture to both men. Putin respects fighters and he respects aggression and he doesn't respect sort of calm and deliberation. . . . He wants a manly adversary. He wants somebody he can understand."[53] Putin would also want a president of the United States who would work with Putin to attain Russia's goals above all. Trump's bluster and bravado is breezily transparent. He is exactly as they taught in KGB school: an egoist, a liar, but talented—he knows the mind of the wrestling-loving, under-educated, authoritarian-admiring white male populous. This is raw material Vladimir could use. Trump would just need to be coddled, supported, flattered, and indirectly tasked by the oligarchy and the conservative Americans who see Russia as a model for American authoritarianism. It would not be hard to believe that Trump could be convinced he could reestablish US–Russian relations. In Putin's favor, of course. Trump wants money and Russia has money, prestige, and the kind of women Trump likes. Trump's worldview on subjects is dear to Russia's heart, including a hands-off policy on the former occupied nations of Ukraine, Latvia, Estonia, Lithuania; as well as tough talk about not supporting NATO. These would all be hallmarks of Trump's campaign, almost as if Putin himself had written these goals. Needless to say, Putin did not have to—everyone who works for him and who desires Russian cash understands that these are the political minimums to even start to discuss any arrangement with the East.

Putin could not do this with just smiles and comments. He would need to create an operational organization that would manage the US elections. It could be based on the same Information Warfare Campaigns that degraded the Baltic States using the new Russian strategy of Hybrid political warfare. Hybrid war is an ever-shifting mélange of media propaganda, cyberwarfare, and touches of military adventurism that could help elect Trump and lead to the break-up of the European Union and NATO. Putin's vision would be to use the sycophant Trump as president to subordinate America to the role of junior partner to a rising Russia.

How to make him the political frontrunner? No problem. Russia has quite a bit of experience in this field.

Master Class in "*Kompromat*"

In 1948, American diplomat George Kennan wrote a paper called "On Organizing Political Warfare," where he defined Political Warfare as:

> The employment of all the means at a nation's command, short of war, to achieve its national objectives. Such operations are both overt and covert. They range from such overt actions as political alliances, economic measures (as ERP [Economic Recovery Plan, i.e. the Marshall Plan]), and "white" propaganda, to such covert operations as clandestine support of "friendly" foreign elements, "black" psychological warfare and even encouragement of underground resistance in hostile states.[54]

His writings were taken very seriously by many in defense and academia but not so seriously as the Soviet Union's KGB. The KGB was so adept at political warfare that Russians used a word for exploiting situations where blackmail can be applied, embarrassment can stifle activism, and words or images can defame those in power and limit their ability to respond to threats or even warfare. That word is Kompromat—which translates as "compromising material." This can include both real and fabricated information, but it is always applied judiciously and maliciously. When hit with Kompromat, you have entered the big leagues of Putin's animosity.

The Kremlin has harnessed the power of this tool to defeat its enemies both domestically and abroad. Amanda Taub wrote a brilliant primer on the subject in the *New York Times*. She explained the simple processes that can have a huge impact:

> First, Kremlin insiders or other powerful individuals buy, steal or manufacture incriminating information about an opponent, an enemy, or any other person who poses a threat to powerful interests.

Then, they publish it, destroying the target's reputation in order to settle public scores or manipulate public events.[55]

Taub writes that after the DNC email leak—if Russia is indeed responsible—"we may be seeing one of the most sordid tools of its domestic politics deployed as a hostile weapon in foreign policy."[56] She argues correctly the same position held by the US intelligence community: that the DNC hack is materially different from other hacks the US has experienced. She wrote, "Rather than using the information seized for intelligence purposes, the hackers selected damaging excerpts from the cache of stolen data, and then leaked them at a pivotal moment in the presidential election."[57] In other words, a classic case of Kompromat.

Collecting and exploiting information in political warfare is so common among Russian politicians that there is a series of websites dedicated to tracking the incidents, such as kompromat.ru. This site is run by a Russian blogger who sells salacious stories gathered from the steamy political underbelly by Russians who use it to their own advantage on a local scale.

David Remnick, editor-in-chief of the *New Yorker*, writes that whether or not Russia was responsible for the DNC hack and subsequent leak to WikiLeaks, "what's undisputed is that the gathering of Kompromat—compromising material—is a familiar tactic in Putin's arsenal. . . . For years, the Russian intelligence services have filmed political enemies in stages of sexual and/or narcotic indulgence, and have distributed the grainy images online."[58]

In a previous article for the *New Yorker*, Remnick described one infamous case of Kompromat:

In 1999, on the eve of a national election, a prosecutor named Yuri Skuratov was investigating corruption at the Kremlin and among its oligarch allies. Now all that anyone remembers about Skuratov is the grainy black-and-white film of him attempting, without complete success, to have sex with two prostitutes; the film was broadcast nationally on state television, and that was the end of Skuratov and the investigation. (The head of the secret services at the time was Vladimir Putin.)[59]

Franklin Foer writes in *Slate*, "There's a clear pattern: Putin runs stealth efforts on behalf of politicians who rail against the European Union and want to push away from NATO."[60] In an interview on *Slate*'s podcast "Trumpcast," *Washington Post* columnist Anne Applebaum also mentioned Russia's "pattern" of interfering in elections of Western democracies, citing as one example Russia's funding of Marine Le Pen, president of France's National Front, a far right political party.[61] Computer hacking adds another dimension to Kompromat. Applebaum said that the events unfolding in the 2016 presidential election seem to follow a pattern that other European countries have experienced when Russia has exerted its influence:

> But I hadn't thought through the idea that of course through hacking, which is something they're famously very good at, that they could try and disrupt a campaign. And of course the pattern of this is something we've seen before: There's a big leak, it's right on an important political moment, it affects the way people think about the campaign, and of course instead of focusing on who did the leak and who's interest it's in, everyone focuses on the details, what's in the emails, what did so-and-so write to so-and-so on Dec. 27, and that's all that gets reported.[62]

Paul Roderick Gregory argues in an opinion piece in *Forbes* that a former KGB officer like Putin could capitalize on Clinton's use of a private email address and server while secretary of state to either blackmail her into dropping out of the presidential race, or leak information that "would weaken the United States' hand in world affairs throughout a Clinton presidency."[63] Furthermore, he notes the Kremlin doesn't even need to have hacked or be in possession of Clinton's emails to exert this influence, writing, "Those who follow Kremlin propaganda understand that *it is not necessary for Putin to have Clinton's e-mail*s to cause serious damage to a Clinton presidency. All he needs is that many *believe* he has Hillary's e-mails."[64] He continues:

> The Kremlin specializes in fabricating narratives (such as the US intent to steal Siberia) that are false but may contain a small kernel of truth. Putin's army of "information technologists" (propagandists) can release fabrications to its numerous clandestine sources throughout the world. Clinton might ignore or deny those narratives (which cannot be traced to the Kremlin), but the mere idea that Putin has her e-mails will lend the necessary credibility to the story.[65]

Professional Assessments of Putin's Recruitment

The Putin Strategic Kompromat & Recruit strategy is so scripted and so clearly a FSB/KGB styled political warfare operation that members of US intelligence quickly saw through it. The current members, including the Director of National Intelligence James Clapper, and Director of the CIA John Brennan, danced around the subject on the DNC hacks, as they are sworn to secrecy about the origins and sources.

Former acting Director and former Deputy Director of the CIA Michael Morell has served six presidents—three from each party—and has voted for both Democrats and Republicans. He has kept his politics to himself throughout his thirty-three year intelligence career, until now. He takes a dim view of the entire Russian constellation of "coincidences" that surrounds Donald Trump. We may recall the US intelligence community's observation that "coincidences take a lot of planning." The Trump coincidences seemed to bear the hallmarks of the sword and the shield of the FSB.

In August 2016 Morell wrote an op-ed for the *New York Times* in which he explained why he will no longer remain politically silent

during this election. It had little to do with Trump and more to do with
his professional intelligence assessment of the threat to the United
States:

> President Vladimir V. Putin of Russia was a career intelligence offi-
> cer, trained to identify vulnerabilities in an individual and to exploit
> them. That is exactly what he did early in the primaries. Mr. Putin
> played upon Mr. Trump's vulnerabilities by complimenting him. He
> responded just as Mr. Putin had calculated . . . In the intelligence
> business, we would say that Mr. Putin had recruited Mr. Trump as an
> unwitting agent of the Russian Federation.[66]

OPERATION LUCKY-7: THE KREMLIN PLAN TO ELECT A PRESIDENT

How to Organize an Election Theft

To help elect Donald J. Trump president of the United States, the Russians would need to draw from their experience in the art of compromising the integrity of a selected person or political party that they wanted to influence or deter through the Russian strategy of Kompromat. If Vladimir Putin, the Russian intelligence apparatus, and its underground global hacking wings sought to destabilize the West, break up NATO, and reestablish the global order, they would need to lay out a strategic hybrid warfare plan.

Hybrid warfare is the new Russian model to harness the strength of all aspects of Russian intelligence, propaganda, cyber operations, and Kompromat to support battlefield preparations before ordering terrorism, special operations, and full-scale military warfare. In this case, the FSB would be tasked to plan a cyberspace-based strategic political warfare operation to influence the US elections though the theft of emails and materials from the Democratic Party and make selective releases through a third-party surrogate, called a cutout, that does not know or care that the source is the FSB.

With this election, Vladimir Putin, the former director of Russia's intelligence agency, sees the election of Donald Trump as the fastest way to destabilize the United States and damage its economy, as well as fracture both the European Union and NATO. These events, which start with the election of Trump, would allow Russia to become the strongest of the world's three superpowers and reorder the globe with a dominant Russia at the helm.

Operation Plan LUCKY-7
(Operatzia Paveslo Sem—Операция Повезло Семь)

For the purposes of this analysis we will refer to the Russian operation as LUCKY-7. Seven is the international calling code for Russia. To pull off such an enormous political warfare operation successfully would require at least seven phases. The number is not only a universal symbol of luck, but it is also consistent with Russian superstition and harnesses the iconography of the seven sacraments in the Russian Orthodox Church.

To conduct an operation at this level would require a level of organization far greater than any that had been done before anywhere in the world. A political and cyber mission of this magnitude would require every component of the Russian cyber and intelligence arsenal. The mission would seem daunting at first, until one recognized that it would simply resemble a Kompromat-style political warfare operation, but with far greater delicacy.

The 2011 treatment of Trump by President Obama at the White House correspondents' dinner sent him out in humiliation. A powerful man like Trump would need to be handled carefully, like all of those old East German academics Putin recruited to infiltrate West

Germany. They were all the same: full of themselves and possessing an unquenchable thirst for recognition and fortune. For the spymaster-in-chief it must surely have flickered across Putin's mind that this was an asset that could be recruited, groomed, and handled. To what end originally, we may never know. But it would not hurt to have a powerful, rich, American blowhard who could inspire the common man in one's pocket. This was a man who enjoyed being a showman on the wrestling entertainment circuit, who had a wildly popular show in which he behaved exactly like a Russian oligarch. To the FSB spies it must have been especially enticing to use their skills for the spy-in-chief to bring this man into a position of favor; a man like this in the White House could be very helpful indeed. But that would take a great measure of work, care, and feeding. Trump would need to first feel at home with Russia. The runway for this approach would require the first word of the MICE recruitment strategy be dangled before his eyes, and to which he was particularly susceptible: money. The FSB could easily arrange for a billionaire wanting to earn money in Russia to meet the Kremlin's own mutli-billionaires. Like all intelligence operations, it comes down to a Go–No Go decision by a top spy. It would involve so little effort that Putin would have to think, why not?

The Strategic Objectives of the Kremlin for LUCKY-7

The first objective for the covert operations officers of the FSB's SVR division to meet the goals initiated by Vladimir Putin would be to bring the selected candidate into a position of favor in the American media. With almost minimal effort the Russian state could harness its own global media machine and collect strategic intelligence, in an effort to determine faults in the opponent's policies in advance. Additionally, acquisition of the Clinton opposition research would be the highest priority. This research would not only give insight into the candidate from the opponent's perspective but would also be able to contribute to the overall assessment as to the suitability of the preferred candidate to meet Moscow's goals. For an old spy, all information is good information. Information from other Republicans or Democrats could help LUCKY-7 adjust their strategy and deploy new tactics as needed. All dimensions of political and intelligence knowledge that could help meet the Kremlin's goals would be of value, when the stakes for Russia are so high. The effusive praise that Donald Trump heaps upon Putin and the Kremlin may have been seemingly innocent in his eyes, but to the spymaster and the LUCKY-7 operations team, every utterance, every positive commentary, would put Russian objectives in a position of dominance over current and potentially future US policy.

Objective: Damage Hillary Clinton & Obama
If Possible, See Her Lose the Election

Putin would have a clear motive to push for Trump to be the vessel to attack their mutual enemy: Hillary Clinton, and by extension, President Barack Obama's policies. Trump's spy General Flynn himself noted how he perceived that Putin does not respect American leadership and apparently changed his policy to suit that disdain. It would be well within Putin's interest to take advantage of his now well-honed political and information warfare apparatus to show his preference and steer Trump to do his bidding.

Applying the Russian global media and information warfare structure to attack the critics of his campaign would be the first step, and there is no greater threat to Putin's policies than Hillary Clinton. The objectives of LUCKY-7 would be to focus all efforts of the Russian cyberwarfare information operations directorates to damage her election by stealing as much internal information as possible and smacking her with a full-scale Kompromat operation. If the materials existed, they would be judiciously released. If not, then the forgery masters of the FSB would be able to produce whatever dirt would be necessary.

The deep personal animosity between Clinton and Putin is long and sordid, but a few events between them are noteworthy. In March 2014, former Secretary Clinton gave a speech at the Boys and Girls Club annual fundraiser where she compared Putin's actions seizing Crimea to the actions of Hitler and the Nazi party:

> Now if this sounds familiar, it's what Hitler did back in the '30s . . . All the Germans that were . . . the ethnic Germans, the Germans by ancestry who were in places like Czechoslovakia and Romania and other places, Hitler kept saying they're not being treated right. I must go and protect my people and that's what's gotten everybody so nervous.[1]

Putin responded to these comments to French TV March 4, 2014. Dripping with sexism and disdain, he claimed her comments were not befitting a woman.

> It's better not to argue with women . . . But Ms. Clinton has never been too graceful in her statements. Still, we always met afterwards and had cordial conversations at various international events. I think even in this case we could reach an agreement. When people push boundaries too far, it's not because they are strong but because they are weak. But maybe weakness is not the worst quality for a woman.[2]

Clinton was having none of it. She apparently had Putin's number and understood what CNN Masha Gessen noted when she said "[Putin] sees himself as someone who doesn't mince words and who gets into verbal fights, as well as knife fights. And in fact Russians see him like that."[3]

So Clinton gave him a knife fight but using a verbal putdown that even Russian women could understand.

"He is very difficult to read personally," she said. "He is always looking for advantage. So he will try to put you ill at ease. He will even throw an insult your way. He will look bored and dismissive. He'll do all of that."

"I have a lot of experience with people acting like that," she said. "Go back to elementary school. I've seen all of that, so I'm not impressed by it."[4]

Objective: Candidate Should Damage NATO Alliance and Push for Its Realignment

Leon Aron, writing in *Foreign Affairs*, believes that the Putin Doctrine is to reestablish the Soviet state with modern Russian norms instead of communist doctrine.[5] Aron believes that the Russian state after Putin's election in 2000 has accepted the overarching goal of remaining a global superpower that will harness all aspects of military, political, and economic power to maintain hegemony and dominance in Eastern Europe.

Every six years Russia creates a strategy document to assess and guide its strategic policy. At the end of 2015 they submitted the National Security Strategy of the Russian Federation until 2020. This document is multidimensional in that it reflects not only the risks Russia faces in defense, foreign affairs, and geopolitical challenges but also internal security, cultural, and economic risks. The first major takeaway was that above all, Russia views the United States and NATO as a threat to their global position.[6]

The security of Putin's Russia is not just a matter of military prowess; it reflects on Putin himself and the position he sought to carve out in the post-Soviet world. Putin views Russia as a nation that must acquire and maintain a newfound respect from its opponents. National prestige and deep pride in the new Russian nation has been a consistent theme since he became president. Anything that challenges this is a security threat, be it loss of economic status, the impression that its defenses are weak, or that Russia is not in control of its own destiny.

If one watches how Putin has ruled since 2000, almost every move has been to gain international status and to impress Russia's rising dominance upon the world. Anything that can be done to bolster that prestige is quickly adopted. Putin sought aggressiveness in foreign policy, economic negotiations, and military affairs, particularly if it helped the Russian public see Putin as steering the ship of state to its destined greatness.

When Russia flies relatively obsolete Tu-22m BACKFIRE jet bombers from its military base at Engels in Southern Russia to drop unguided gravity bombs indiscriminately on Aleppo, it meets the strategic goals of impressing its allies, adversaries, and the Russian people. Even if militarily such a strike mission has little to no effect on the war effort except killing innocent civilians, it looks good on Russia Television.

The nationalistic Russia-goes-it-alone fever wasn't always a cornerstone of their defense policy. Until the invasion of Georgia in 2004, Russia was integrating its national defense goals into NATO via various sub-organizations. The North Atlantic Treaty Organization (NATO), established in April 1949, is a military alliance between twenty-eight states to create a system of collective defense for member nations. Russia leaned towards the alliance when it joined the North Atlantic Cooperation Council in 1991, and the Partnership for Peace program in 1994. This culminated in the 1997 NATO-Russia Founding Act, providing a formal basis for relations. In 2002, the NATO-Russia Council (NRC) emerged as consultation on security issues, leading to more direct cooperation. Formal NRC meetings and cooperation in a few areas were suspended because of Russia's military action in Georgia in August 2008. Talk show host Charlie Rose summed it up this way:

> I think Vladimir Putin, because of all of his experiences, has a real fear about being—about NATO being on his borders. He's always had that. They had that with respect to Georgia and with respect to Ukraine. I think he probably worries that if a government in Ukraine

was . . . leaning to the West—it might one more time entertain the idea of NATO membership, which he really, really—that's probably the thing that he dislikes the most.[7]

Anna Vassilieva noted that Russia under Putin was fundamentally changing. "Russians feel that they have the right to an equivalent of the Monroe doctrine and the right of foreign political noninterference in their domestic politics."[8] At the St. Petersburg international Economic Forum in 2015, Putin blamed NATO for the crisis in Crimea, and by extension Georgia and Ukraine, due to its insistence on expanding into territory he views as his domain. Putin said,

> Why is there a crisis in Ukraine? I was quite confident after the bipolar system went into oblivion and after the collapse of the Soviet Union, certain Western partners of ours, particularly the United States, were in a kind of euphoria, and instead of trying to create a new situation, good neighborly partner relations, they started to explore new free geopolitical spaces—well, free in their view. And that is why we are witnessing the expansion of NATO eastwards.[9]

Senators Lindsey Graham and John McCain were some of the loudest Republican voices opposed to Russia's aggressive dominance of territories. All cooperation, military and civilian, under the NRC was suspended in April 2014 following the Russia-Ukraine conflict. NATO's stance: "The Allies continue to call on Russia to reverse its recognition of the Georgian regions of Abkhazia and South Ossetia as independent states."[10]

At the Wales Summit in September 2014, NATO leaders condemned Russia's aggression in the Ukraine, demanding that the nation comply with international law and end its illegal "annexation" of Crimea. Russia effectively ignored President Barack Obama's warnings, invaded Crimea, and annexed it within thirty days under armed occupation. Under Putin, Russia also backed separatist groups. NATO was keeping a close eye on Russia's increasing military activities along NATO's borders, realizing that the new aggressive growls by the bear would threaten Euro-Atlantic security and stability.

Following Russia's seizure of Crimea, President Obama announced economic sanctions on Russia and Crimea in March and December 2014. According to the BBC, the president said "The executive order is intended to provide clarity to US corporations doing business in the region and reaffirm that the United States will not accept Russia's occupation and attempted annexation of Crimea."[11] The European Union soon followed suit.[12] In response to the various sanctions, Russia called the actions "meaningless, shameful, and disgusting." Russia imposed its own sanctions by halting the export of agricultural products to North America, Norway, Australia, and the European Union. In July 2015 he extended the sanctions.

Trump was having none of it. As far as he was concerned, if the policy affected Russia, and was implemented by President Obama—or any president since 1947 for that matter—then he wanted to be rid of it. Trump gave the *New York Times* a wide-ranging interview in which he remarked that he saw a major change for the seventy-year old NATO alliance. He said that if Russia attacked any NATO nation, he would first consult and determine if they had "fulfilled their obligations to us" before coming to their aid.[13] Trump set forth a policy of extortion never before heard or seen in American politics:

> If we cannot be properly reimbursed for the tremendous cost of our military protecting other countries, and in many cases the countries I'm talking about are extremely rich. Then if we cannot make a deal, which I believe we will be able to, and which I would prefer being able to, but if we cannot make a deal, I would like you to say, I would prefer being able to, some people, the one thing they took out of your last story, you know, some people, the fools and the haters, they said, "Oh, Trump doesn't want to protect you." I would prefer that we be able to continue, but if we are not going to be reasonably reimbursed

for the tremendous cost of protecting these massive nations with tremendous wealth . . . Then yes, I would be absolutely prepared to tell those countries, "Congratulations, you will be defending yourself."[14]

The statements rang alarms all across Europe and instantly damaged the credibility of the US nominee worldwide . . . except in Russia.

Objective: Advocate for and/or Repatriate Ethnic Russian Regions

Like Hitler, Putin uses a form of Post-Soviet appeal to a virulent Russian ethno-nationalism in former Soviet states. With his stoking of the nationalist fervor he and his intelligence agencies fund and direct ethnic Russian populations to agitate to the point where Russian military forces can seize territory that was lost. To effect this, it is necessary for the SVR and GRU to covertly fund and mobilize popular political support in the affected areas and build a public outcry to "defend" ethnic Russian populations. It is particularly acute in nations that were former Soviet satellite states, but are now closely aligned with NATO.

Hitler carried out a similar strategy in 1938 when he exhorted Germans to validate his annexation of the Sudetenland, the ethnic German-speaking region of what was then Czechoslovakia. Hitler saw the immense power of rallying the German people to repatriate those he characterized as poor ethnic Germans to the greater Reich. Putin has adopted this strategy of ethnic "rescue" to justify political operations in Eastern Europe. Usually this was a slow process of creating Russian political parties, infusing them with cash and illicit weapons. Waiting for them to form a popular uprising with the help of the SVR and then diplomatically protesting greatly that ethnic Russians were in danger. Hillary Clinton noted this when she said Putin was a man "who believes his mission is to restore Russia's greatness. . . . When he looks at Ukraine, he sees a place that he believes is by its very nature part of Mother Russia." [15]

Trump himself was aware of Putin's designs, but unlike most Americans, he applauded. In his 2011 book *Time to Get Tough* he wrote, "Putin has big plans for Russia. He wants to edge out its neighbors so that Russia can dominate oil supplies to all of Europe." Elaborating, Trump wrote "I respect Putin and Russians but cannot believe our leader (Obama) allows them to get away with so much. . . . Hats off to the Russians." [16]

Objective: Keep America Out of the Ukraine in Particular

To meet his goals for hegemony in the Ukraine and the Baltics, Putin would require a total realignment of the priorities of NATO. It would also be most favorable to Russia if the United States could be convinced that it was not in their interest to respond to Baltic States' requests for article 5 of the NATO Charter. Article 5, which requires all member states to respond militarily if one nation is attacked, has only been invoked once, by the United States after the 9/11 attacks. How would the Americans ever abandon NATO? They created it. Only a president who shared the same viewpoint or who was in league with Putin's desires would ever even consider such treachery. Certainly not a nominee from the conservative American Republican Party led by Senators John McCain and Lindsey Graham; they were the war hawks.

It is widely believed that the issue of the Ukraine is a solid red line for Moscow. This may explain why he and his surrogates made serious efforts to hire and put in place Americans who could advance their interests. Veteran journalist Marvin Kalb notes that the entirety of the national security elites in the West hold the view that to Putin, Eastern Europe is a Russian sphere of influence or "Russian backyard." [17] Anna Vassilieva, of the Middlebury Institute of International Studies at

Monterey told NBC News that "Ukraine is a big issue . . . a red line that Putin is not going to compromise."[18]

Hillary Clinton's own words must have struck fear into Putin's heart because it encapsulates the Western school of thought on how to deal with him in the future:

> I am in the category of people who wanted us to do more in response to the annexation of Crimea and the continuing destabilization of Ukraine. . . . I do think we should do more to help Ukraine defend its borders. New equipment, new training for the Ukrainians. The United States plus NATO have been very reluctant to do that, and I understand it completely because it's a very sticky, potentially dangerous, situation. But I think the Ukrainian army and the Ukrainian civilians who've been fighting against the separatists have proven that they're worthy of some greater support.[19]

Such pronouncements would give Putin every impetus to find alternatives to her worldview. And surprisingly, seemingly out of nowhere, Putin managed to find and ally himself with the one man in the United States who believed precisely as himself: Donald J. Trump. Trump himself believed that NATO was obsolete and should be disbanded, that Crimea should be given to Russia, and that America should adopt an isolationist foreign policy. In the interim, NATO member states that didn't pay their full share of the alliance financial commitments would be ignored if they had a military crisis. Who would have ever thought that Russia could be so lucky to find that a major party nominee in America would align himself so closely with the new Russian worldview? Who could have dreamed that a potential American president would imply that the United States would corrupt NATO's mission to a protection racket that essentially extorts its members? Forty percent of the American electorate indirectly approved this high-stakes international racketeering.

Trump's positions on NATO would also meet the strategic political objectives of the Kremlin simply by mainstreaming ideas and concepts that were far afield of hawkish Republican positions since the beginning of the Cold War. To the Republican Party, NATO was the United States. Until the rise of Trump there had never been any discussion as to the viability, militarily or financially, of the United States' position in that alliance. It was unthinkable for the potential US president to actually enunciate a position in which the necessity of the alliance was questioned.

It was bad enough that Trump was essentially giving assurances to Putin that Crimea was off the table, but he also appeared to not be the best surrogate, since he did not seem to understand the timeline of Ukraine's crisis, either. In an interview with George Stephanopoulos Trump said, "he's not going into Ukraine, OK, just so you understand. He's not going to go into Ukraine, all right? You can mark it down. You can put it down. You can take it anywhere you want."

"Well, he's already there, isn't he?" Stephanopoulos responded, in a reference to Crimea, which Putin took from Ukraine in early 2014.

Trump replied, "OK—well, he's there in a certain way. But I'm not there."[20]

If NATO wasn't coming to the rescue in Georgia, Ukraine, or Crimea, then a Donald Trump administration could almost be relied upon to validate or even explain away a Moscow invasion of the NATO Baltic republics. For Putin, it must surely be a dream come true to put a major party candidate espousing these policies into the White House.

LUCKY-7: The Information Warfare Management Cell (IWMC)

Russia would need to task out the Kremlin staff, the SVR, GRU, FSB, and all aspects of the state propaganda organs to meet the spymaster-in-chief's goals. We may never know the actual discussions of how an operation like LUCKY-7 started, but it must have developed in a circumstance where Vladimir Putin used his instincts and information from his acolytes and spies to see something in Donald Trump that virtually no one was seeing in 2012.

Once the candidate was positively handled by the office of the president and his allies in the oligarchy, the intelligence community would form an information warfare management cell (IWMC). The LUCKY-7 joint task organization would be needed to directly respond and advise the Kremlin on how to best support a mission of this sensitivity. Though each agencies' staffs would be compartmented from the rest of the FSB and GRU, such an operation would absolutely require a joint information operations office.

Centered in a secret location the IWMC would be a hub where the specialties of each agency could be brought to bear. The collection of data and its dissemination would be necessary to quickly influence the news cycles, be supported by state media, and send tips and advice to their candidate though direct, official comment by Putin or indirectly through specially tasked senior SVR case officers.

Putin, his chief of staff, and the director of the SVR would be the only senior staff to be aware of what outcome the president desired. Based on past strategic intelligence missions, only a few—perhaps no more than five or six case officers—would be assigned to manage a mission of this political magnitude. By virtue of the clandestine nature of their work, these would be the most trusted intelligence officers in the FSB; officers who work for Putin personally.

An overall IWMC commander would be the controller for the entire mission. He would have a subordinate executive officer from the Special Communications and Information Service of Russia (SCISR), Russia's version of the National Security Agency, to ensure the fusion of HUMINT and CYBER into the operation went smoothly. For the FSB side, there would be a senior manager to oversee the SVR contribution to the IWMC. An FSB-SCISR cyberwarfare officer would manage the SVR's FANCY BEARS cyber hacking team and a second officer would control the GRU's COZY BEARS cyber commandoes as an alternate, sometimes parallel collections team. A third cyberwarfare officer from the Scientific & Technology directorate would be the operations manager to run a black propaganda support team. When necessary, a fourth liaison officer could task and collect from the Russian mafia-run CRIMINAL BEARS. At the Kremlin level, all liaison with state media and statements by the president himself would be handled by the Russian Foreign Ministry.

To advise the president on the behaviors and opportunities to manage their candidate, the SVR's political activities branch would assign perhaps three or four of the best field officers in the SVR and GRU. They would be read into the program and isolated at the IWMC. These officers would have to possess a proven track record on turning the unwitting into active spies, whether they wanted to be or not. Due to the nature of the mission, the officers would need to be fluent in American English with experience working as "illegals,"—deep cover covert operations officers—who served in the United States and understand both business and the political process. Perhaps one political warfare advisor would be allowed to know the full scope of this mission, remotely evaluate the target of the mission, and advise the cell operations managers as to the day-to-day effects of the entire process. If events required other officers to be brought in, they would be assigned compartmented tasks from the pool of the IWMC staff.

Phases of Operation LUCKY-7

Until a friendly American administration was elected all of these goals would be pies in the sky. Nothing could be effected without risk, and the launch of this operation would be the least risky of all operations. The right man was running for president, he was managed by a close ally, and his foreign policy/intelligence chief was literally on the Kremlin payroll of *Russia Today*.

PHASE 1: Make Contact, Befriend, and Encourage the Asset

PHASE 2: Make Asset Feel Indebted to Russia

PHASE 3: Conduct Covert Cyber-Intelligence Preparation of the Battle Space

PHASE 4: Prepare the Political Battle Space

PHASE 5: Develop and Sustain Supporting Political/Propaganda

PHASE 6: Fund and Manipulate a Cutout Asset to Disperse Kompromat Information.

PHASE 7: Execute Kompromat Operations

Phases 1 through 4 had already been put in place. Phase 5 would be the easiest. By using Russia Today TV to blast Hillary Clinton on an international scale and tacitly express support for Trump, Putin has been able to get Donald to tout his connections to Russia as a positive for America.

Trump and his surrogates have helped the Kremlin as well by making exclamations that Putin doesn't respect Obama, and that Russia doesn't like "crooked" Hillary because she helped spark political protests in Russia in 2011 and 2013, and by convincing formerly anti-Russian Americans that Putin is an ally to be assisted in the war against ISIS. It was a master stroke that would require considerable planning and precision to execute if it had been done by spies. However, it was executed by a carnival barker. To his followers, Trump has successfully spun the line that "Putin respects me and would work with me, he won't work with Hillary," and they love it.

Launching the CYBER BEARS

The FSB CYBER BEARS strategy was to steal critical political intelligence data from all wings of the US Democratic Party, the Democratic National Committee, the Democratic Congressional Campaign Committee, the Hillary Clinton Campaign, and donors and supporters. Republican Party enemies of Russian defense policy would also need to be hacked in case they became too opposed to the operation. A little side activity to guarantee the silence of the risk-averse politicians would generally be found in the hidden corners of a laptop or nude photos that were deleted from the hard drive but still recoverable by one or more of the CYBER BEARS.

For old-school officers trained under the KGB, conducting a political and cyberwarfare operation would be a lifelong dream. It would create the space and environment to realign Russia as the preeminent power in the world. Even though most Russians who know Putin believe that this would be a very long shot, the fortunate emergence of a self-absorbed and servile Donald Trump coupled with Putin's long hatred of Hillary Clinton meddling in his Eastern European plans would make this a tempting opportunity to severely damage the United States. Winning battles in Cyberspace are a matter of influencing the global perception thought output of "opinions" and "voices" to "trend" a perception that the producer wishes. Whether it's the number of hits on the latest trending kitty playing with yarn video or the location of a Pokémon GO character, if an organization with a large enough computing system and secret operatives so wishes they can steal, smear, influence and quite possibly select a US president with little pushback from the media. This is apparently the terminal mission objective of Operation LUCKY-7: Direct the CYBER BEARS to collect enough damaging information on Hillary Rodham Clinton and the Democratic Party to damage them in the mind of the American public.

Russian intelligence would spare no effort to elect Donald J. Trump president of the United States. However, the IWMC needed to disseminate the information publically. A cutout could be found, but the group needed its own "legend"—espionage terminology for a false backstory to protect the identities of the case officers. The Cyberspies decided to create their own legend and to honor a hacker who was already well known: Guccifer.

The original and only Guccifer was the Romanian eccentric Marcel Lehel Lazar, who was arrested and extradited from Romania to the US after breaking into dozens of emails that belonged to officials like both George Bush Sr., George W. Bush, Colin Powell, and Sidney Blumenthal, long-time friend of Hillary Clinton. He used the name Guccifer as his handle for his attacks. He had claimed that he successfully hacked a private server belonging to Hillary Clinton, but during the House hearing on the FBI decision not to prosecute Clinton for use of private server or other crimes, Representative Blake Farenthold asked FBI Director James Comey if there was any truth to the claims made by Guccifer that he breached the server. Comey stated unequivocally that Guccifer lied about the breach and there was no indication that any such breach ever occurred, even if the concerns or threat may have existed.

What better way to cause mayhem, confusion, and mischief than to release the stolen emails under the same name? Google searches would only add to the confusion as the original Guccifer would always come up first. Since this was a new entity, a second generation, it was only fitting that he be version 2.0. Hence, Guccifer 2.0 was born.

6

BATTLES OF THE CYBER BEARS

Putin's CYBER BEARS

In late July 2016, after the news of the DNC hack hit the headlines, two groups came to the center of attention after nearly a decade of engaging in attacks on perceived adversaries of the Russian government. These two groups carried the names given to them by the American cyber security firm CrowdStrike and thus the world would be introduced to two designations for Russian hackers: "FANCY BEAR" and "COZY BEAR." These cryptonyms were assigned to hacking threats under the term "Advanced Persistent Threats" or APTs. APTs are often associated with nation-state actors because of the level of sophistication and resources needed to conduct persistent attacks on a given target. The weapon of choice for APTs is malware. Malware is malicious computer software, such as viruses or tools that can be inserted or introduced to a target's computer. There are estimated to be just over a hundred APTs working hostile missions through cyberspace as of August 2016. APTs include attacks by nation-state actors, cyber criminals, hacktivists (activists who use hacking as a tool of protest), and cyber mercenaries.

CYBER BEARS are what we will call the conglomeration of several Russian intelligence agencies, nationalist militias, criminal contractor cyberwarfare units, and the malware weapons these groups use in cyberwarfare. The CYBER BEARS—so called due to Crowdstrike's BEAR designation for the DNC hackers—have conducted numerous hacking and black political propaganda operations in states that came into conflict with Russia, including Estonia, Georgia, Lithuania, Kyrgyzstan, Crimea, and Ukraine. COZY BEAR, FANCY BEAR, and VENOMOUS BEAR are specific cyber-infection threats that have been traced to Russian intelligence, whereas CRIMINAL BEAR is the collective name for all Russian criminal hackers. MILITIA BEARS are pro-Russian nationalist hackers who pile onto Russian intelligence attacks that become public.

Clusters of CYBER BEAR attacks occurred most often alongside tense geopolitical backdrops associated uniquely in line with the interest of one country, Russia. Whether it was retaliation in Lithuania or Estonia, data blinding operations in Georgia, or flipping the switches on power plants in Ukraine in an attempt to undermine confidence in the government, the CYBER BEARS, attacks leave plenty of marks and footprints for cyber security companies and intelligence agencies to examine.

The history of the attacks of the CYBER BEARS demonstrates advanced abilities to create code on the fly and to adapt to the security environment of their target in a way that few independent or lone attackers would be able to maintain due to the complexity of the attack alone. They are also believed to be associated with thousands of attempted penetrations of US defense and industry computers as well as cyber theft and internet fraud operations. Collectively, the BEARS are the definition of a national cyber threat.

The Advanced Persistent Threats

The key characteristics of classifying an entity an APT are that they are:

- **Advanced**: The development skill for APTs is advanced enough to both develop their own tool kit and capable of using existing advanced tools with ease.
- **Persistent:** The Adversary is goal-oriented in the attack and is driven to achieve the mission. This can often indicate a nation-state actor who has been given orders to acquire specified information.
- **Threat:** The Adversary is organized, funded, motivated. There is a high level of intent to these attacks. Unlike malware that simply seeks to find any vulnerability and is cast like one would throw a fishing net, APTs are focused on a target until a mission is attained.

APTs are not actually groups of people but a description of the malware tool kits used by hackers. By examining the malware samples and correlating the metadata (the background information embedded in code) of the attacks you can discover much about the real world people on the other end in a way that code cannot tell you. By scrutinizing when malware kits are compiled, you can discover where development operations leading up to an attack occur. In most tool kits attributed to Russian hacking groups, the timecodes on their digital metadata occur in one of the two Eastern hemisphere time zones of UTC+3 or UTC+4, indicating Eastern Europe and/or Western Russia as a likely development zone. Then there are sometimes tags in the code that indicate a similarity only found in a batch of malware like the "Sandworm" group, whose attacks were identified by a cyber security firm who noticed the code was laced with references to Frank Herbert's book *Dune*.

These clues help forensic investigators piece together not only the story of a particular infection, but the trajectory of development by hackers who reveal themselves not by name but by deed.

For example, CyberBerkut, a group of pro-Russian hackivists almost wholly focused on anti-Ukraine activity, includes subgroups who will announce their attacks as well as their ideology. CyberBerkut's methods, tools, and remnants can be examined in the open, allowing investigators to attribute CyberBerkut's contribution to the known attacks as they look for additional threats by groups who have aims beyond Ukraine. The same has been true for the APT29 malware sets known as COZY BEAR (aka "The Dukes"). The Finnish cybersecurity firm F-Secure found a series of malware sets that varied according to their version of development and improvements over time.

For example, private Russian hacker Dmytro Oleksiuk created a set of malware called BlackEnergy1 in 2007 to stop up networks through DDoS (distributed denial-of-service) attacks, where millions of pieces of emails or data to a single IP address create a massive internet traffic jam that stops all data flows.[1] This malware was used by a group of Russian hackers in 2008 to overwhelm the Georgian internet. In 2010 a second variant, BlackEnergy2, emerged, containing more advanced malware tools inside. Finally, Russian intelligence took it and developed BlackEnergy3. Sandworm used a malware kit named BlackEnergy3 (the 3rd variant, or 3.0) to attack power plants in Ukraine.

In order to keep track of APTs cyber firms designate the APTs with easily remembered names associated with clustered behavior. They are also known by a variety of other names depending on the firms who have detected and catalogued their malware and activities. According to Richard Bejtlich of Mandiant, a cyber security firm associated with FireEye, and a former USAF information warfare agency operative, the practice came from US Air Force analysts who were working with civilians and needed a way to discuss the attacks with civilians.[2]

APTs work by using a combination of code, social engineering (asking innocent questions and getting secrets), and common human errors to achieve their goals. They are capable of adapting to the most up-to-date security systems. As a persistent threat, they require constant vigilance on the part of security firms, developers, governments, institutions, and private enterprise. The tools these groups use are constantly evolving, even as security firms track their development and create patches to protect from their intrusion.

Zero Day

A Zero day (or written 0day) is a vulnerability in code that has remained undetected until it becomes active, giving a target zero days to manage the effects of the vulnerability. If discovered first by hackers, then the target organization is at risk unless the hacker is friendly and working for them (called a White Hat hacker). If the hacker is from a malicious group (Black Hat hackers) the hacker can exploit the vulnerability until they are detected by cyber security experts.

Many hackers develop "0day exploits" and can either use them directly or sell them. Sales of 0day exploits are lucrative business on the black-market via the Dark Web. In order to find these holes in security, hackers have to develop a comprehensive profile of the target to include what email systems are used, what operating systems are in play, and what proprietary computer systems are in use. For the Democratic National Committee hack they used a custom computer system created by NGP VAN, a specialist computer company that helps progressive non-profits. Malware samples discussed in the CrowdStrike report on the hack showed that the attackers were custom coding components to be used for that specific attack on that specific software to get a very specific result—Watergate 2.0.[3]

After detecting hacking activity, the victim often helps security companies and government agencies to determine the attacker's origin or backers. APTs from China tend to focus only on Chinese government interests, which could include activities of its neighbors, or as seen in the past few years the Chinese buildup in the South China Sea. Some well-documented APTs developed by China include Blue Termite, The Elderwood Platform, Hidden Lynx, Deep Panda, and

Putter Panda (APT2). Computer security authorities have identified APT1 as departments of the Chinese People's Liberation Army (PLA) and also carries the APT name, "PLA Unit 61398." It is well known for its focus on US technology firms.

The Iranians are often labeled under APT names associated with Kittens. Rocket Kitten, for instance was credited in August of 2016 for cracking the Telegram encryption, constituting a threat to dissidents in or related to Iran. Other groups included Flying Kitten, Magic Kitten, and Clever Kitten just to name a few.

The Russians, similar to the Chinese, focus on Eastern Europe, NATO forces, the United States, and opposition to Russian interests. These attacks range from hits on a power station in Ukraine to an attack on the World Anti-Doping Agency in August 2016. While many firms do not directly attribute attacks to nation states capriciously, they do reveal the metadata patterns that indicate Russian or Chinese involvement, including examples of the OS the hackers used to compile the malware, IP ranges associated with spear-phishing-waterhole attacks, to the domain names used to spoof the target into clicking on hot links. Unlike Russian cyber criminals, Russian government APTs are focused almost purely on cyber espionage.

Criminal APTs or CRIMINAL BEARS, like Anunak/Carbanak and BuhTrap clearly focus on banking institutions across the world. First detected in December 2013, Carbanak stole well over $1 billion in strikes against US retailers, including office retailer Staples. They use very similar methods to other APTs, such as spear-phishing campaigns. Spear-phishing is a malicious, fraudulent email that appears to come from a trusted source. It generally contains a hyperlink to a false sign-in page to enter your passwords, credit card, or other information. It could also be a direct link to a virus.

Like the nation-state actors, the Carbanak method of stealing financial data exploits malware with a backdoor that replicates itself as "svhost.exe" before it connects to a command-and-control server to download more files and begin probing for more vulnerabilities.

The APT can then download additional tools to take control over the infected computer, including keylogging, as well as capturing data from screen captures, microphones, and video cameras. Carbanak has even documented their operations in video form to evaluate the process and train others. The data that this group seeks to exfiltrate may go beyond financial information alone, but the primary goal has been to steal funds via fraudulent transactions.

From Mechanical Hacks to Cyber Theft

In the height of the Cold War, Russia learned to make the leap from manual intercept of printed media to the computer age well before the internet existed. Between 1978–1984 the KGB carried out an audacious electronic intelligence operation that preceded the CYBER BEARS antics. A select group of special technicians had intercepted a shipment of American IBM Selectric II and Selectric III electrical typewriters en route to the American embassy in Moscow and the US Consulate in St. Petersburg. The KGB inserted devices called the Selectric Bug into sixteen of the typewriters.[4] The special electrical device was embedded in a hollow aluminum bar that would capture the impact of the rotating print ball as it struck the paper. As a typist struck the keys, the bug would transmit each keystroke to a nearby listening post via a short-distance radio signal. The NSA countered this by deploying a special team to Moscow and inspected all of the Embassy's computers, encoding machines and typewriters. Code named GUNMAN, the NSA team eventually found the bugs and replaced the typewriters with secure ones in secret.[5] Still, the KGB's early awareness of the advance in print technology led them to implement one of the very first keystroke detection systems before computers became commonplace. With this corporate knowledge in hand, the KGB was well ahead of the curve in intercept technology, an aptitude they would soon come to command in the computer age.

Cyber intelligence collection operations didn't start in the twenty-first century; they preceded the rise of Putin. During the period where Vladimir Putin was just taking the reins from the former KGB under the leadership of Boris Yeltsin, the NSA and the Department of Defense's Information Operations Response Cell noted a series of sophisticated computer penetrations, accessed through research university servers. The hackers were stealing sensitive information, but what was noteworthy was the seemingly random nature of the hacks and the peculiar nature of the sensitive information. Author Fred Kaplan detailed this hack, called MOONLIGHT MAZE, and numerous others in his brilliant book *Dark Territory: The Secret History of Cyber War.* The hack was tracked back to Russia after decrypts found that the hacker was using a Cyrillic, Russian language, keyboard. The classified materials stolen about obscure scientific programs perfectly matched discussion topics at recent conferences in the United States attended by Russian scientists. The Russian would attend a conference, realize that it held more secrets, and task the CYBER BEARS to steal the research. The Russian Academy of Sciences in Moscow submitted hack requests and the KGB, now FSB, acquired the 5.5GB of classified materials.[6]

Russia didn't sit on its laurels by stealing American scientific data. For more than ten years, volunteer militia hackers and cyber criminals carried out limited, and on occasion, full-scale cyberwarfare on its neighbors in Europe. There is an arms race in the cyber weapons world as nation-states and freelance hackers seek to push the technology envelope. By 2016 the history of Russia's attacks showed proficiency at destroying enemies with cyber strikes.

First Steps in Cyber Campaigns

The first step is to establish a target organization or individual. Second is to find out how and where to compromise the target's IT systems with the least amount of effort possible and without being detected. This most often starts with examining the publicly posted employee rosters at a company, organization, or government office. Next is a scour on social media sites like Facebook, LinkedIn, Twitter, Google, or even simply within the agency of the target.[7]

The target or targets are subjected to an email spear-phishing campaign. Spear-phishing is a technique that seeks to fool a target into clicking on links or opening email attachments in emails the target would expect to receive. For example, if a State Department official was expected to attend a conference on a UN refugee program, they might receive an email with the title "Schedule for the Refugee Committee" with an attached document or link. If it is a link instead of an attachment, the target might take a look at the link before clicking, but the reasonable-looking link will lead to a spoofed site that has just returned malware back to their computer. Once that malware is installed, it may do a number of things depending on the intent of its coding. The first function it is likely to perform is to breach.

The APT countermeasure system tracks not only the malware tool kits themselves, but the source of origin and related resources, including IP addresses of the remote command-and-control servers (C2), or in some cases metadata found in the compiled tools used by the threat actors. In addition, a pattern of behavior in what the hackers steal can help indicate further distinctions on the group behind the malware infection. For instance, nation-state hackers acting on behalf of Russia and China do not typically engage in financial theft but focus on espionage targets, even if that target is a private enterprise.

In the case of the attacks on the DNC, the company CrowdStrike identified two actors in separate breaches on the servers used. The two found were identified as "FancyBear" and "CozyBear" by CrowdStrike, but elsewhere they have other names depending on the security firm who encounters their activities. FancyBear is also commonly known as APT28 or Sofacy. CozyBear is commonly known as APT29.

APT28—FANCY BEAR
Russian State Security/Covert External Intelligence (FSB/SVR)

APT28 is a group that goes by many names, depending on who has discovered them. In order to learn the character of this group it helps to look at all the cases investigated on the range of names the group gets assigned. Along with the naming of the group, different firms also name the malware and conflicting names can occur for the same toolset. FireEye calls them APT28, CrowdStrike named them FancyBear, Trend Micro has called them Operation Pawn Storm, Microsoft Security Intelligence Report calls them STRONTIUM,[8] Secure Works tagged them as TG-4127. They've also been called Sednit (by Eset), Tsar Team (iSight) and Sofacy Group. Despite these names the methodology and toolset is distinct and shows a deployment sophistication that truly qualifies as an advanced persistent threat; it is considered one of the most potent threats in the list of known APTs.

Security authorities first discovered the group in 2007. Their attacks have included a range of Eastern European countries including Ukraine, Georgia, Poland, to the south at Pakistan, and further west to the United States and France. They have been linked to the GRU. They were even tied to attacks on the Russian all-girl band Pussy Riot.[9]

Typosquatters and Watering Holes

Many hackers establish typosquatting websites. These are where a false "squatter" website is installed on the actual location of a known website or where they buy a URL that is nearly identical to a well known website but where fat-fingered "typos" occur (e.g. Microsift.com, Amaxon.com). Hence "Typosquatter." Another technique to gather login, password, or financial information from a targeted victim is to establish or insert malicious viruses into a targeted site. Many typosquatters are *Watering Hole* sites—decoy or fraudulent websites that are loaded with malware and used to lure targets via spear-phishing emails to download their payload. To fool computer users into following these links, the site would need to look relevant or identical to the target's working interest, and include very up-to-date information, whether it be a bombing attack in Iraq mentioned in an email to the Vatican Embassy in Iraq, or schedule and coordination information sent to Hungary. In many cases, the malicious domain is very similar to the real domain.

Trend Micro examined four cases in the "Operation Pawn Storm" attacks and found these examples.

Hackers sent a series of emails to the Hungarian Ministry of Defense supposedly inviting them to the world's largest defense exhibit held in Paris each year, Eurosatory. The hacker's email included links to *"eurosatory2014.com."* The link led to a false site that stole the user's information. So the technique is to deceive the employee into thinking the website is legitimate if they have attended the conference before or are aware of upcoming participation.[10]

A staff member of the Organization for Security and Cooperation in Europe in Vienna was victim of an attempt at phishing. A link in an email sent to employees was to "vice-news.com" even though Vice News is found at "news.vice.com." To lure an employee at SAIC, hackers used a link aimed at "Future Forces 2014," which pointed to "natoexhibitionff14.com" when the real exhibition website is "natoexhibition.org"[11] The purpose was to lure the personnel to give up their webmail log-in credentials so the hackers could walk through the front door. For instance, the OSCE's real OWA domain is "login-in.osce.org" an extension of "osce.org." The phishing account purchased to steal credentials was "login-in-osce.org" In the case of SAIC, the OWA domain was "webmail.saic.com" related to "saic.com." The phishing account purchased was "webmail-saic.com."[12]

Fancy Bear also targeted Academi, the infamous company formerly known as Blackwater. The link sent to them was meant to look like it came from "tolonews.com," when in fact it came from "tolonevvs.com," which was infected and part of the phishing campaign. As with the pattern above, the real email server was a very close misspelling that may have passed a casual glance, "academl" instead of "academi.com."

In the case of a German company, attackers went so far as to buy an SSL certificate to mask their heist. SSL certificates are sold to allow a vendor to establish a secure connection to the buyer's browser. Trend Micro says they were able to warn the target and avoid attack only because of early detection.[13] Trend Micro engaged the attackers by sending fake credentials through these webmail login pages. Attackers responded "within minutes" of the intentional "leaking" of these fake accounts and began attempting unauthorized access. After an initial login check came from the site itself, they noticed additional login attempts that came next from Latvia (46.166.162.90) and the United States (192.154.110.244).[14]

Once the hackers are in they deploy a range of tools to take control of the infected computer and begin efforts to gain data to download—credit cards, photos, or bitcoins, they steal it all.

In a Trend Micro assessment from August 2015, APT28, aka "Pawn Storm," focused 25 percent of its targeting efforts on the Ukraine, followed by the United States at 19 percent. When it came to attacks by sector, the emphasis shifted depending on the country. In Russia 23 percent of attacks targeted media, followed by 17 percent on diplomacy, then activism at 15 percent. By contrast, the Ukrainian sectors struck were 18 percent military, 18 percent media, 16 percent government. For the United States the sectors were even clearer, with military at 35 percent, defense at 22 percent, and government at 8 percent. Attacks on American media were at 7 percent.[15]

APT29 COZY BEAR—Russian Military Intelligence (GRU)

Like its companion Russian cyber groups, APT29 has its own tool set and methods of attack. In operation since 2008, CrowdStrike named the group COZY BEAR. It is also known as Cozy Duke by

Mandiant. Before it struck the DNC, targets of APT29 included the US State Department, US Joint Chiefs of Staff, and the White House. The group has developed a tool kit commonly labeled "The Dukes." One tool set, called Hammertoss or Hammerduke, even uses steganography (encrypted data or messages within a photograph) via images posted on Twitter. They usually gain access to computers through Spear-phishing.

In a September 2015 study on APT29 attacks, Finnish cyber security firm F-Secure found several samples of APT29 activity in Chechnya between 2008 and 2015.[16] Though F-Secure calls them "The Dukes," other firms have also named and tracked these tool kits. For example, the one tool kit has been named "SeaDaddy" as found in the DNC breach. Similarly, "HammerDuke" is the same tool kit as "HammerToss" tracked by FireEye. Their targets have been Chechnya, the Ukraine, and the United States. Most of their operations occur in the UTC+3, UTC+4 time zones, so they too indicated Russian origins.

According to F-Secure's analysis of PinchDuke, the first samples were found in November 2008 on Turkish websites hosting Chechen materials. One of the sites was labeled as a "Chechan [sic] Information Center;" the other site contained a section on Chechnya.[17]

Venomous Bear[18] was identified by Crowdstrike (and nicknamed Uroburous (Snake), Epic Turla, SnakeNet, Waterbug, and Red October) first in 2008.[19]

This group is best known for the notorious cyberattack on US Central Command in 2008. This attack was called the "Worst Breach of US Military Computers in History." Though the Pentagon says no data was lost because the transmission of data was interrupted, it transformed how the military would use thumb drives as well as its defensive posture.

The attack was likely due to an infected USB flash drive inserted into a US military laptop. In order to engage the rest of its programming, the malware had to communicate to a C2 server. When it tried to do so, NSA's Advanced Network Operations (ANO) team detected the malware. As a result, DOD issued a worldwide ban on thumb drives. Another result of this breach by Agent.btz was the creation of the US Cyber Command. DOD also responded with the launch of "Operation Buckshot Yankee,"[20] which aimed to both clean all infected machines and protect the "digital beachhead," as Deputy Defense Secretary William Lynn III called it. The breach was so severe that NSA's famous Tailored Access Operations (TAO), the elite cyberattack squad team, worked to counter the threat.[21]

Like the other APTs, this group uses spear-phishing to trick the target into opening a PDF attachment with malware or into clicking a link to a waterhole site. Like the APT28 and APT29 attacks, the Venomous Bear attacks used attachments to emails that were carefully targeted and worded to get the target to open either the attached PDF that then activated "Trojan.Winpbot" and "Trojan.Turla" according to a Symantec report examining the group's attack.[22] The "Trojan.Turla" is used to exfiltrate data.

According to CrowdStrike's Global Threat Report, Venomous Bear has been targeting government agencies, NGOs, energy firms, tech firms, and educational organizations.[23]

Attacks of the CYBER BEARS

Estonia: Unleashing the CYBER BEARS

Russia views the Baltic states, the countries that border it on the Western frontier, as nations that should be in their sphere of political and economic influence rather than oriented toward Western Europe. The nations of Lithuania, Estonia, and Latvia felt left behind to suffer for more than five decades under Soviet domination. When they got the chance, they quickly aligned themselves with America and the rest of Europe and joined NATO. The pain of this was especially sharp in Estonia.

Estonia sits just to the southwest of St. Petersburg on the Baltic, and Russia has long considered it, along with Lithuania and Latvia, as rogue satellites. Reclaiming them would give Putin a bridge to its enclave of Kaliningrad, a small province of Russia north of Poland that is separated by the Baltic States. A Russian-dominated Baltic region would also push NATO back to the Polish frontier. Many believed that the 1940 seizure of Estonia and its "liberation" by the Soviet Union in 1944 was part of Russia's tsarist desire to control the satellite states in its backyard. As many as 320,000 Estonians are ethnic Russians, and 40 percent of the population is considered "foreign." The Russian populations of Estonia came during the Soviet occupation or were born there. Upon independence, the Estonians decided that Russians and other non-Estonian peoples would be considered émigrés and not nationals. Putin's Russia took a dim view to the treatment of their ethnic brothers that would turn dark in 2007.

The Estonian break with Russia would come to a head when the government attempted to remove a bronze military monument to Russian soldiers lost in World War II. This dark grey statue of a young, chisel-chinned, highly-decorated Russian soldier, rifle slung over his back, helmet in hand, head lowered out of respect to the dead, once stood in the center of the Estonian capital of Tallinn. It was a beautiful piece of artwork, but ever since the Soviets reoccupied in 1944, the monument stood as a hated symbol of their Communist and post-Communist hegemony. After independence in 1991, Estonia sought ways to remove the monument without antagonizing the local Russian population.

In 2007 Estonia was one of the most wired countries in the world. Its 1.3 million inhabitants fully integrated the internet into their daily lives using computers, tablets, and smartphones, which made them the highest per capita users of online technology in Europe and the Middle East regions. Estonia wired itself for global access to make it favorable to European markets. Marketing campaigns touted Estonia's global

interconnectedness, its small but growing economy, and its 2004 acceptance into NATO.

When the protests broke out, the bronze statue was vandalized.
Bloodred paint was routinely thrown on it. The new imperial Russia
was not amused. The opposition to the monument culminated in a
series of riots that led to a greater, even more monumental event in
the history of European political warfare. Estonia was attacked, but
not one bullet was fired and not one person was injured. The CYBER
BEARS were tasked to punish the nation as a whole. They did so by
sending an entire European nation back to the pre-internet age.[24]

On April 26, 2007 a massive, covert barrage of cyberattacks struck
the computers of Estonia. A series of "denial-of-service" attacks
blocked up the servers that distributed web traffic and completely
shut down all internet access to the nation. The sites targeted included
the Estonian president, the parliament, the ministries, three news outlets, political party sites, and two banks.[25] In order to stop the attack,
countermeasures blocked all international traffic, which allowed the
site traffic to return to normal levels.

Estonia conducted an investigation and later charged a twenty-
year-old Estonian, Dmitri Galushkevich, for his role in the DoS attacks.
He stated that his attack was inspired as a protest against removing
the bronze soldier. He pleaded guilty. As he had no previous criminal record he was fined €110 and released.[26] Despite his admission of
starting the first DoS hack, many firms have concluded that cyber militias working under the direction of the Russian government quickly
jumped onto the initial DoS attack and expanded it to the extent that
it shut down the country's internet.

The Bears Went Down To Georgia

Since 1988 when the people of Ossetia, an enclave in Southern Georgia
asked for more autonomous authority, the independent central

government asserted its control in a tug of war with Russia. Georgia had declared its independence from the Soviet Union in 1991, and shortly after South Ossetia declared its independence from Georgia. Ossetians had been seeking to increase their autonomy for years, but under the new Georgian President Zvaid Garmskhurdia it was clear Georgia was not going to give up this territory as it sought independence for itself. Ossetia had been an oblast, or province, under the Soviet system since 1923.[27] After Garmskhurdia was deposed in December 1991, Eduard Shevardadze became the new Georgian leader, and by mid-1992 a ceasefire agreement accompanied another agreement to leave Georgia in substantial control over South Ossetia.[28]

However, the South Ossetians are supported largely by Russia, and this tension boiled up over Georgian control in 2004 and again in 2008. In August 2008, Russia and Georgia clashed in South Ossetia and Abkhazia after years of tensions. When Georgian troops sought to enter South Ossetia, they were outmaneuvered and outflanked by the Russian-backed forces. In five days, the combined Ossetian and Russian forces defeated the Georgian forces.[29]

During the clash Russia hit Georgia with a campaign of hybrid warfare that included massive cyberattacks on the websites of the officials, ministries, and others. Their campaign against Georgia started three weeks before the August 7, 2008, assault on Ossetia.[30] On July 20, 2008, the Georgian president's office suffered a denial-of-service attack that shut down the website. As the conflict ensued, Russia used its cyber assets to both send pro-Russian messages aimed at the former soviet state and render the online resources of the Georgians useless. On August 8, 2008, hackers used an early variant of BlackEnergy malware to conduct distributed denial-of-service (DDoS) attacks against Georgian government websites as Russian forces invaded.[31] This is perhaps the first time combat has joined with cyberwarfare operations. The aim of the attacks was to shape public opinion and control Georgian communications.

The coordination of the attacks was well planned and well targeted to gain the maximum effect of creating a digital outage for Georgian authorities, including stopping the ability to get their messages out to seek support. Georgia was blindsided and blinded at the same time. Analysts later determined that Russian nationalists who had received advanced warning conducted the attacks. Russia recruited these hackers via social media forums. The use of patriot hackers in this operation would set the pace for future hands-off operations. Russia's use of hackers and cyber militias under a nationalistic banner proved effective over the Georgian authorities.[32]

Pro-Russian websites were launched during the war in South Ossetia. Unlike the attacks on Estonia, the attacks on Georgia's cyber systems used botnets, waves of self-replicating cyber agents, to engage in a distributed attack. As of 2016, the CYBER BEARS APT28 and APT29 continue peripheral attacks on Georgia with spear-phishing campaigns aimed at the administration and military.[33]

Lithuania Under Attack: June 2008

In 2008, the Lithuanian parliament passed a series of amendments that aimed to prohibit the display of symbols of both Nazi Germany and the Soviet Union. This would include depictions of Nazi or Soviet leaders and Nazi or Soviet symbols, including the swastika and the hammer and sickle.[34]

In response to this law, more than three hundred websites suffered both vandalism and DoS attacks.[35] Most of the sites were co-located with the server host.[36] Hackers defaced the websites with anti-Lithuanian messages and images of the Soviet hammer and sickle.[37] The sites affected included Lithuanian Socialist Democratic Party, the Securities and Exchange Commission, government agencies, and private enterprises.

Though officials in Lithuania said they could not prove the attacks were conducted or orchestrated by Russia, it was clear the attacks were tied to the laws passed banning Soviet symbols. The government said the attacks came from an array of computers from outside the country.

Kyrgyzstan: January 18, 2009

On January 17, 2009, an official of the Kyrgyzstan government informed the United States that the Manas Air Force Base outside of Bishkek would close. The United States had been using the base since December 2001 as part of the effort in Afghanistan. The official said that the base closure would come in days as a result of Russian pressure. Just a month before, Russia's top general Nikolai Makarov accused the United States of planning to expand its number of bases in the region.

To drive their point home, a series of DoS attacks hit the country's two main internet service providers in Kyrgyzstan, essentially knocking out the internet, websites, and email for the country.[38] Though there are no conclusive reports that definitively name the responsible party, many firms state the attack appeared to be tied to the decision to let the US use the Bishkek base as a logistics center for the war in Afghanistan. The attacks were attributed to "cyber militias" much like the attacks in the Russo-Georgian conflict just a few months before.

Despite the base having been in operation for nearly eight years, on February 3, 2009, Kyrgyzstan President Bakiyev announced it would close. This was a major victory for Russian control over Central Asia. After Kyrgyzstan complied with Russia's demands it received a multimillion-dollar aid package.[39]

Ukraine Power knocked out by Sandworm: December 23, 2015

Three Ukrainian power companies came under attack by the Sandworm tool set after employees downloaded BlackEnergy3 malware packages. According to an investigation by Robert M. Lee, former US Air Force cyberwarfare operations officer and cofounder of Dragos Security, the infections started in spring of 2015.

Attackers engaged in a spear-phishing campaign using infected Word documents aimed at system administrators and IT staff at the facilities. The targets who opened the Word document saw a prompt asking them to click to "enable macros," which installed the

BlackEnergy3 malware. It is notable that macros had been in decline until the time of this attack but were now on the rise.[40] After the malware successfully installed, it began to scan around for paths to the supervisory control and data acquisition networks, SCADA, which would allow them to take control of the plant's control systems.[41] All of this would be exceptionally risky at many power plants, but it turned out the Ukrainian security was above average and even outclassed many US facilities. The networks were all very well segregated via firewalls but the CYBER BEARS stole in anyway.[42]

One of the plant operators stated he saw the attackers control one of the computer terminals and successfully search for the panel that would control circuit breakers. The attacker began to take down the power grid in front of his eyes. Though he tried to take control of the computer it was too late. The attackers locked him out and continued its task of shutting down around thirty electrical substations.

After the breach, the attackers used an eraser program called "KillDisk," which wiped out major sectors of files, corrupted master boot records, and essentially rendered the systems useless without taking them offline and replacing them. The attackers reconfigured the backup generators in a manner that disabled them so the repair crew had to tough it out in the dark.

To top this off, they didn't do this just once; the attackers hit three power stations simultaneously belonging to the Ukrainian power company Kyivoblenergo in the Ivano-Frankivsk Region.[43] They also struck Prykarpatyaoblenergo with an outage that affected 80,000, as well as the Chernivtsioblenergo station.[44] In total, an estimated 225,000 people were affected for nearly six hours. The companies restored power by going back to manual control. Power had to be restored manually since many systems were fried by the "KillDisk" deletions.

To make all of this more complicated, a telephone denial-of-service (TDoS) attack on the telephone system flooded the circuits with bogus calls, which prevented citizens from alerting the power companies about outages.

The Warsaw Stock Exchange, aka The Cyber Caliphate False Flag Attack #1: October 24, 2014

After the website for the Warsaw Stock Exchange went offline for two hours, a Pastebin message screamed to the world, "Today, we HACKED Warsaw Stock Exchange!" and "To be continued! Allahu Akbar!" Authorities initially credited the Cyber Caliphate, a hacker group that claims its allegiance to ISIS and works in association with the United Cyber Caliphate groups. The message posted on Pastebin, an online bulletin board, said the hack was in retaliation for Polish bombing of the "Islamic State."[45]

Initially, many accepted that ISIS-affiliated hackers were responsible, but the techniques, tools, and more importantly digital footprints suggested the attackers came from Russia. This is old spycraft technique called a False Flag operation: a deception where one entity is blamed for the actions of another. The false flag cover didn't last, as forensic analysts demonstrated that Russian hackers had posed as ISIS and let them take the blame.[46] It was later revealed that the hackers stole details on investors and the stock exchange's network, including credentials for authorization to access customer accounts.[47]

The TV5 Monde Attack, aka The Cyber Caliphate False Flag #2

On the evening of April 9, 2015, at 10:00 PM the French TV channel TV5 Monde experienced a cyberattack that resulted in the suspension of their broadcast, as hackers infiltrated their internal systems and social media profiles. First, the website crashed, then emails went down.[48] Helene Zemmour, digital director for the station said it all went down in a "synchronized manner." CNN reported, "Shortly after the beginning of the attack our internal computer system fell and other programs followed."

The defaced pages were relabeled by the Cyber Caliphate with "Je Suis ISIS" tagged on them, recalling the pro-Charlie Hebdo rally cry, "Je Suis Charlie." However, the fake Cyber Caliphate website was in fact on a server with an IP belonging to APT28. Security firms picked up on this and the consensus began to develop that suggested the attack was that of a nation-state actor. Due to a combination of notable similarities to APT28, Cyber Caliphate was ruled out as the attacker. The threat was beyond the capabilities of ISIS's hacker wannabees.

In more practical terms, Wassim Nasr, on France24, noticed the Arabic of the claims was barely real Arabic. On France 24, he pointed out improper use of the language in several areas, notably in the *Bismillah* phrases common from ISIS where "and" was used in a manner no Arabic speaker would.[49] They most likely came from Google Translate. Unwitting ISIS-affiliated groups still took credit for the attack and their fan boys attribute it to the Cyber Caliphate Army.

The channel and social media accounts were reclaimed by the next afternoon. TV5 director Yves Bigot said the security had been recently checked. One CNN anchor even said, "once again terrorism has targeted freedom of expression."

No One Is Immune

On May 20, 2015, APT28 hit the German Bundestag and started to steal data from servers after launching the Sofacy malware on the systems. After the attack, the Bundestag director Horst Risse advised the other staff to avoid opening files or links via email.[50] In August 2015, APT28 launched a spear-phishing effort at EFF, the Electronic Frontier Foundation. The group attempted to use email to lure targets to a spoofed site at "electronicfrontierfoundation.org". The official site for EFF is at "eff.org". Oracle fixed the Java zero day.[51]

On July 21, 2016, on the eve of the Olympic games in Rio De Janiero, the World Anti-Doping Agency or WADA recommended banning the entirety of Russian athletes from the 2016 Olympic games.[52] WADA believed that there was a systematic national effort to use and conceal illegal doping agents from the agency. WADA reached a compromise with the Russian Olympic team in which 70 percent of Russian athletes could participate, though 110 could not. Although it appeared that the matter was resolved, the CYBER BEARS unloaded on WADA with a massive FANCY BEAR spear-phishing campaign.

On August 15, 2016, stakeholders in WADA were notified of an email campaign aiming to spear-phish the members by getting them to click bogus websites that looked like official WADA portals. The watering hole domains had been recently purchased on August 8, 2016, along with additional domains not used in the strikes but perhaps held for future targeting. The domains were registered to the users as if they were in Riva, Latvia. The URLs were "wada-awa.org" and "wada-arna.org," which were not affiliated with the organization.

FireEye and ThreatConnect[53] have tied APT28 to the WADA attack.[54] However, as with the DNC, the TV5Monde, and the Warsaw Stock Exchange hacks, this one was suddenly claimed by someone else. In this case the claim emanated from a Twitter account named "Anonymous Poland" and the handle @anpoland. Like Guccifer 2.0, this new Twitter channel had no back history, suggesting it was a sock puppet account created just for the operation.

Targets of the attack included athlete Yuliya Stepanova, who had her emails hacked after she stepped forward as a whistleblower on the Russian doping scandal. She personally drew the ire of Putin, who referred to her as a "Judas." It wasn't surprising that Russian authorities would want to retaliate as they have long shown a state interest in the success of their athletes, even if by banned or controversial methods. Grigory Rodchenkov was director of an anti-doping lab that helped Russian athletes cheat WADA controls. Rodchenkov claims that a Russian intelligence officer was assigned to observe his lab to find out what happened to athlete urine samples.[55]

Numerous other Russian hacks struck government, diplomatic, and civilian websites in the United States as well. In December 2014, Russian hackers breached the account of a well-known US military correspondent. As a result, the attackers took the contact information from that breach and went on to attack fifty-five other employees of a major US newspaper.[56] In **January 2015** three popular YouTube bloggers interviewed President Barack Obama at the White House. Four days later they were targets of a Gmail phishing attack.

The Office Monkeys Campaign

In October of 2014, some White House staffers received an email with a video attachment of a zip file with an executable file. "Office Monkeys" was the title and it featured not only a video clip of a chimpanzee with suit and tie but also the CozyDuke tool kit from APT29 equipped to open up the exploits necessary to get to the intended data.

The White House attack came as a result of a similar breach at the State Department just weeks before. In that case a staffer clicked on a fake link in an email referring to "administrative matters."[57] The resulting data gained at the State Department allowed attackers to map out an approach to White House attack vectors. The White House breach resulted in unclassified but perhaps sensitive information being compromised, including emails of President Barack Obama's schedule.[58]

The CYBER BEARS also conducted a spear-phishing campaign on the US Joint Chiefs, aimed at the US military's joint staff. The entry malware was disguised as coworker emails. The resulting breach shut the system down for ten days, during which time four thousand staffers were offline.

OPERATION WATERSNAKE

An example of the extent of the FSB and GRU covert cyber collection and exploitation was the exposure of what was most likely a Russian State Security & Navy Intelligence covert operation to monitor, exploit, and hack targets within the central United States from Russian merchant ships equipped with advanced hacking hardware and tools. The US Coast Guard boarded the merchant ship SS Chem Hydra and in it they found wireless intercept equipment associated with Russian hacking teams. Apparently the vessel had personnel on board who were tasked to collect intelligence on wireless networks and attempt hackings on regional computer networks in the heartland of America.[59]

The Criminal Bears, Militia Bears, and Others

Berzerk Bear, VooDoo Bear, Boulder Bear: CrowdStrike identified a group that has been active since 2004 as "Berzerk Bear" and tied the group to Russian Intelligence Services. The aim of this group is information theft,[60] and it has shown a flexibility to write tools appropriate to its mission. Berzerk Bear was active during the 2008 Russo-Georgian conflict, acting against Georgian websites. However, without extensive reports detailing the attacks, it is hard to tie these names to a larger matrix of attacks that are chronicled by malware tracking firms.

CyberBerkut: The group known as CyberBerkut is different than the APT threats from the Russians. These Pro-Russians from Ukraine have been launching their anti-Ukrainian DDoS attacks since 2014. In addition to DDos attacks, CyberBerkut employs data exfiltration and disinformation to attack its target.[61] Although the group's attacks have largely been aimed at discrediting the Ukrainian government, it has also been noted that CyberBerkut only aims its attacks at members of NATO. They have a website and have been quasi-public in a manner resembling Anonymous. They have even engaged in conspiracy theories related to the murder of James Foley by posting a staged video meant to resemble the famous video with Jihadi John and Foley.

Putin's Professional Troll Farm

Several internet hoaxes spread on social media and caused panic in around the United States in the fall and winter of 2014. The first came after an explosion at a Louisiana chemical plant in September, then later an Ebola outbreak, and a police shooting of an unarmed black woman in Atlanta in December. None of these events, however, actually happened.[62] But this was not immediately clear in any of the cases. During the chemical plant hoax, for example, posts inundated social media, residents received frantic text messages, fake CNN screenshots went viral, and clone news sites appeared.[63] In each instance, reporter Adrian Chen discovered, a Russian group known as The Internet Research Agency concocted the elaborate hoaxes. Online, these pro-Russia, anti-everyone paid staffers are known as the "Trolls from Olgino."[64]

Chen traveled to the Russian city of St. Petersburg and reported extensively on the so-called troll farms for a June 2015 article titled "The Agency" in the *New York Times* magazine. He wrote that the agency had become known for "employing hundreds of Russians to post pro-Kremlin propaganda online under fake identities, including on Twitter, in order to create the illusion of a massive army of supporters."[65]

Analysts suspect that Putin business associate Engeny Prigozhin runs the agency. Chen identifies him as "an oligarch restaurateur called 'the Kremlin's chef' in the independent press for his lucrative government contracts and his close relationship with Putin."[66] The *Times* quoted former employees as saying that the agency had "industrialized the art of trolling."[67] Chen wrote, "The point was to weave propaganda seamlessly into what appeared to be the nonpolitical musings of an everyday person."[68] In an interview with PBS NewsHour, Chen said the purpose was "to kind of pollute the Internet, to make it an unreliable source for people, and so that normal Russians who might want to learn about opposition leaders or another side of things from the Kremlin narrative will just not be able to trust it."[69]

A year before Chen reported on the Internet Research Agency, Max Seddon reported for BuzzFeed about leaked emails that showed the agency had begun a project to flood social media and the "comments" sections of popular American websites such as *Politico*, *Huffington Post*, and Fox News, pushing themes such as "American Dream" and "I Love Russia." BuzzFeed reports one project team member, Svetlana Boiko, cited fears that news organizations and internet commenters were not writing positively of Russia. In a strategy document, Boiko wrote that non-Russian media were "currently actively forming a negative image of the Russian Federation in the eyes of the global community."[70]

After the Ukrainian crisis began, followed by the Russian annexation of Crimea from Ukraine in March 2014, BuzzFeed reported an increase in Pro-Kremlin internet activity, which Seddon writes, "suggests Russia wants to encourage dissent in America at the same time as stifling it at home."[71] The documents show that each day, the "trolls" were expected to comment on news articles fifty times, tweet fifty times from ten accounts, and post three times on six Facebook accounts.[72]

After WikiLeaks released the leaked DNC emails in July, Chen, now a staff writer at the *New Yorker*, wrote that since his original article there appeared to be decreased activity at the Internet Research Agency. But he did notice a trend in some of the Twitter accounts that continued to post. He writes, "But some continued, and toward the end of last year I noticed something interesting: many had begun to promote right-wing news outlets, portraying themselves as conservative voters who were, increasingly, fans of Donald Trump."[73]

WIKILEAKS: RUSSIA'S INTELLIGENCE LAUNDROMAT

FOR PUTIN'S LUCKY-7 OPERATION TO BE successful, the CYBER BEARS teams would need a dissemination platform once the information had been recovered. The hacking teams would store the main flow of data and assess the data for the most damaging files. FSB *Kompromat* disinformation campaigns rely on the theft of politically explosive data, then secretly leak it out to the global news media though a third party in order to protect the actual source. This third party is known in intelligence parlance as a cutout.

The LUCKY-7 information warfare management cell would distribute documents stolen by the CYBER BEARS in a manner that would meet the results the Kremlin desired. This would require serious control of the data release scheduling, constant monitoring of the political landscape, and analysis of the contents of the documents so that the most damning could be released. Emails of immediate value could be released to the public via a trusted "cutout." Files that could harm Trump, such as the opposition file, would be made public to dilute their power and allow him to respond.

The cutout for these operations would be a globally known person whose organization's mission is to daylight secret documents. The FSB chose Julian Assange, a British citizen who is a vocal and vehement enemy of Hillary Clinton and the founder of the online organization WikiLeaks. Assange has described WikiLeaks as a "giant library of the world's most persecuted documents."[1] By the end of 2015, the site claimed to have published more than 10 million documents, many of which have been controversial or classified. The site has drawn both praise and scorn since its inception.[2]

Assange founded WikiLeaks in 2006 with the purpose of providing an outlet for leaked documents. "WikiLeaks is developing an uncensorable Wikipedia for untraceable mass document leaking and analysis," the website's "About" page read in 2008, "Our primary interest is in exposing oppressive regimes in Asia, the former Soviet bloc, Sub-Saharan Africa, and the Middle East, but we are of assistance to people of nations who wish to reveal unethical behavior in their governments and corporations."[3]

Born in Australia in 1971, Assange had inconsistent homeschooling during a childhood marked by constantly being on the move. His family moved thirty-seven times by his fourteenth birthday.[4] By the time he was a teenager, Assange had developed an interest in computers, and in 1987, at age sixteen, he received his first modem, which he hooked up to his Commodore 64 to connect to a network that existed four years before the World Wide Web came into use.[5]

Julian quickly discovered the world of hacking and "established a reputation as a sophisticated programmer who could break into the most secure networks," including that of the US Department of Defense.[6] In 1991, Assange was under arrest and charged with thirty-one counts of hacking and related charges stemming from his infiltration of telecommunications company Nortel; he pled guilty to twenty-five charges—the remaining six were dropped—but a judge ruled he only had to pay "a small sum" in damage, citing his "intelligent inquisitiveness."

It wasn't until 2010 that WikiLeaks entered the mainstream consciousness when the site published a video, dubbed "Collateral Murder," showing two US helicopters opening fire in Baghdad, killing at least a dozen people, including two Reuters journalists, and wounding two children.[8] Reuters had been attempting to get the footage released under the Freedom of Information Act for years before WikiLeaks released it in April 2010. The *New York Times* wrote:

> The release of the Iraq video is drawing attention to the once-fringe Web site, which aims to bring to light hidden information about governments and multinational corporations—putting secrets in plain sight and protecting the identity of those who help do so. Accordingly, the site has become a thorn in the side of authorities in the United States and abroad. With the Iraq attack video, the clearinghouse for sensitive documents is edging closer toward a form of investigative journalism and to advocacy.[9]

WikiLeaks then began publishing unprecedented numbers of classified documents related to the wars in Iraq and Afghanistan—and later the Guantanamo files—leaked by Army private Bradley Edward Manning, a US Army soldier assigned to an intelligence unit in Iraq. Manning had access to the US Army's sensitive intelligence network and managed to copy and pass on to Assange hundreds of thousands of pages of classified documents. Authorities caught Manning, prosecuted her in a court martial, and convicted her of the Espionage Act and abuse of government computer networks. She was sentenced to thirty-five years in prison for the leak.[10] Assange referred to Manning's prosecution as "an affront to basic concepts of Western justice."[11] World leaders and the public had mixed reactions to Assange's actions. The US government response, however, was decidedly anti-WikiLeaks. The Defense Department wrote:

> We deplore WikiLeaks for inducing individuals to break the law, leak classified documents and then cavalierly share that secret information

with the world, including our enemies. We know terrorist organizations have been mining the leaked Afghan documents for information to use against us, and this Iraq leak is more than four times as large. By disclosing such sensitive information, WikiLeaks continues to put at risk the lives of our troops, their coalition partners and those Iraqis and Afghans working with us. The only responsible course of action for WikiLeaks at this point is to return the stolen material and expunge it from their Web sites as soon as possible.[12]

Assange again drew fire from US officials after the release of approximately 250,000 diplomatic cables in November 2010. The White House called the release a "reckless and dangerous action."[13] Then-Secretary of State Hillary Clinton referred to the leak as "an attack against the international community."[14] The international community and the American public were less sure of what to make of the one-time hacker who facilitated the mass leaks. The *New York Times* wrote, "The Russians seemed to take a special delight in tweaking Washington over its reaction to the leaks, suggesting that the Americans were being hypocritical." Russian Prime Minister Vladimir Putin criticized the US response. "You know, out in the countryside, we have a saying, 'Someone else's cow may moo, but yours should keep quiet,'" Putin said, using a Russian proverb the *New York Times* described as roughly equivalent to "the pot calling the kettle black."[15] Meanwhile, Assange won *Time*'s readers' choice for Person of the Year in 2010 but lost Person of the Year to Mark Zuckerberg.[16]

WikiLeaks worked with a number of media organizations during these leaks. As executive editor of the *New York Times*, Bill Keller wrote he "would hesitate to describe what WikiLeaks does as journalism" in an article in January 2011 detailing his dealings with Assange. Keller wrote, "We regarded Assange throughout as a source, not as a partner or collaborator, but he was a man who clearly had his own agenda."[17] This was not the first time—and wouldn't be the last time—the site's founder would be accused of having an agenda. WikiLeaks sprang from Assange's belief in scientific journalism, an idea he elaborated on in an interview with Raffi Khatchadourian, who was profiling Assange for the *New Yorker*:

> I want to set up a new standard: 'scientific journalism.' If you publish a paper on DNA, you are required, by all the good biological journals, to submit the data that has informed your research—the idea being that people will replicate it, check it, verify it. So this is something that needs to be done for journalism as well. There is an immediate power imbalance, in that readers are unable to verify what they are being told, and that leads to abuse.[18]

Assange, however, over time has strayed far away from the traditional journalistic principle of striving for objectivity, and instead has focused on the idea of justice. Khatchadourian writes, "Assange, despite his claims to scientific journalism, emphasized to me that his mission is to expose injustice, not to provide an even-handed record of events."[19] Assange would later write in his 2014 book *When Google Met WikiLeaks*, "I looked at something that I had seen going on with the world, which is that I thought there were too many unjust acts. And I wanted there to be more just acts, and fewer unjust acts."[20]

It is this very idea that has gotten WikiLeaks into hot water. The site and Assange have been criticized as openly having an agenda while claiming to be a journalistic enterprise. In his column for *Slate*, author Christopher Hitchens had critical words for the WikiLeaks founder:

> The man is plainly a micro-megalomaniac with few if any scruples and an undisguised agenda. As I wrote before, when he says that his aim is "to end two wars," one knows at once what he means by the "ending." In his fantasies he is probably some kind of guerrilla warrior, but in the real world he is a middle man and peddler who resents the civilization that nurtured him.[21]

When WikiLeaks held off publication of the DNC emails until just before the Democratic National Convention, WikiLeaks came under renewed criticism for having an agenda, for not being objective, and for straying from its original purpose: "It's become something else," John Wonderlich, executive director of the non-profit Sunlight Foundation, told *Time*. "It's not striving for objectivity. It's more careless. When they publish information it appears to be in service of some specific goal, of retribution, at the expense of the individual."[22]

Even those critical of Assange and WikiLeaks, however, have acknowledged the value of some of the site's revelations. Still, critics worry about the ideological motives behind the operation. German journalist Jochen Bittner wrote in a February 2016 opinion piece in the *New York Times* that the "idea behind WikiLeaks is simple, and ingenious." He continued:

> Whistle-blowers submitted material that proved corruption of the former Kenyan president, tax-avoidance strategies employed by big European banks, and indiscriminate killings of civilians by an American attack helicopter in Iraq. News outlets, including *The Guardian*, *Der Spiegel* and *The New York Times*, helped Mr. Assange spread the scoops. Yet, even back then, observers and media partners felt that Mr. Assange had more in mind than transparency, that there was an ideology behind his idea. Over time, that ideology has become increasingly apparent, through his regular public statements and his stint as a host for a Russian state-controlled TV network.[23]

In August 2010, just months after the first Manning documents were published, two women accused Assange of rape and sexual assault in Sweden. Assange denies the allegations, and he has not been charged. Assange was arrested in London in December, and a British court ruled he should be extradited to Sweden, a decision he appealed to the UK Supreme Court, which upheld the extradition decision in May 2012.

To prevent extradition to Sweden after the sexual assault accusations, Assange went to Ecuador's embassy in London and appealed for political asylum, a request Ecuador granted in August of 2012. However, since leaving the building would entail his leaving Ecuador's diplomatic immunity he is effectively residing in the Ecuadorian Embassy in London on house arrest.[24] In August 2016, Sweden and Ecuador reached an agreement to interview Assange at the embassy, although the statute of limitations expired on all crimes but the rape allegation.[25]

Ricardo Patiño, Ecuador's foreign minister, cited fear of political prosecution as a reason for granting his asylum request. "There are serious indications of retaliation from the country or countries that produced the information published by Mr. Assange; retaliation that could endanger his safety, integrity and even his life," Patiño said at a news conference.[26] Patiño further suggested Assange would not receive a fair trial if extradited to the United States, adding that it was "not at all improbable he could be subjected to cruel and degrading treatment and sentenced to life imprisonment or even capital punishment."[27]

Russia's connections to Assange and WikiLeaks have been the subject of discussions and internet conspiracy theories, but tangible evidence of a real connection has started to accrue only recently.[28] The misgivings about Assange developing an agenda, coinciding with his embassy imprisonment, were drawn in much starker relief when his relationship with the Russians grew closer.

In the Soviet era, all Russian media was considered tainted and ideologically controlled from a central communications authority. *Tass*, *Pravda* (Truth!), and the *Izvestia* distribution networks acted as mouthpieces for the Soviet politburo. Today Putin's Russia has diversified that portfolio and added BBC-style media of Russia Today to introduce negative propaganda by adopting sloppy Fox News–style reporting ("Some people say . . .") to air conspiracy theories or further their anti-US propaganda. For example, "Islamic State operative confesses to receiving funding through US: report." They then link to and "investigate" unscrupulous or deliberately false news stories from "blogs" or unnamed sources.

Julia Ioffe, a journalist who has written extensively about Putin and Russia, wrote in the *Columbia Journalism Review* that the RT network began in 2005 "as a soft-power tool to improve Russia's image abroad, to counter the anti-Russian bias the Kremlin saw in the Western media."[29] However, Ioffe wrote, today the network has "become better known as an extension of former President Vladimir Putin's confrontational foreign policy."[30]

Powerful Russian financial backing has given RT the legitimacy of many international news agencies. They use it to pay American contrarians to appear on their RT America channel and offer an air of debate, frequently on Kremlin-directed themes. Not surprisingly, Assange hosted his own twelve-episode television show called *The World Tomorrow*, or simply *The Julian Assange Show*. It ran from April to June 2012, airing from the Ecuadorian embassy in London.

The *Guardian* journalist Luke Harding, who was the paper's Moscow correspondent from 2007 until 2011, referred to Assange as a "useful idiot" in a review of the show.[31] Assange's first interview was with Hassan Nasrallah, leader of Lebanon's militant Hezbollah group who hadn't spoken to the media for six years, but Harding writes it "wasn't quite the incendiary event that Russia Today had promised." He continues, "The questions were clearly agreed in advance. Some were softball, others fawning, with Nasrallah's answers unchallenged."[32] In a preview posted by RT on April 16, 2012, Assange said he imagined forthcoming criticism: "There's Julian Assange, enemy combatant, traitor, getting into bed with the Kremlin and interviewing terrible radicals from around the world."[33] In response to this expected critique, he said, "If they actually look at how the show is made: we make it, we have complete editorial control, we believe that all media organizations have an angle, all media organizations have an issue.[34]

A year and a half earlier, events unfolded that indicate a connection between Assange and Russia. Princeton University professor of American history Sean Wilentz writes in the *New Republic*:

> In October 2010, just before WikiLeaks reached the acme of its influence with the release of the State Department cables, Assange vowed that WikiLeaks would expose the secrets not just of the United States but of all repressive regimes, including that of Russia. In an interview with Izvestia, a formerly state-controlled daily, he explained, "We have [compromising materials] about your government and businessmen." The same day, Kristinn Hrafnsson of WikiLeaks told a reporter, "Russian readers will learn a lot about their country."

Unlike the Americans, though, the Russians put WikiLeaks on notice. The day after Hrafnsson's interview appeared, an anonymous official from Russia's secret police, the FSB, told the independent Russian news website LifeNews.ru, "It's essential to remember that given the will and the relevant orders, [WikiLeaks] can be made inaccessible forever."

Then, something strange happened: A few days after Assange was arrested on sexual assault charges, Kremlin officials emerged as his most vocal defender. The *Moscow Times* reported that Vladimir Putin himself had condemned Assange's arrest: "If it is full democracy, then why have they hidden Mr. Assange in prison? That's what, democracy?" Putin's indignation was echoed by other top Russian politicians, including State Duma Deputy Gennady Gudkov, who observed, "The real reason for his arrest is to find out by any means who leaked the confidential diplomatic information to him and how."[35] But journalist Jochen Bittner observed in a *New York Times* op-ed:

> It's curious that one of the world's most secretive governments has gotten a pass from WikiLeaks. Why, in all its time online, has WikiLeaks never revealed any Russian intelligence scandal? Because

there is none? Or because Mr. Assange doesn't want to embarrass Mr. Putin?[36]

Assange has also said that he is the one who encouraged NSA whistleblower Edward Snowden to seek asylum in Russia. According to the *Guardian*, Assange said, "He preferred Latin America, but my advice was that he should take asylum in Russia despite the negative PR consequences, because my assessment is that he had a significant risk he could be kidnapped from Latin America on CIA orders. Kidnapped or possibly killed."[37]

Hillary Derangement Syndrome

Assange has made no secret of his dislike of Hillary Clinton. In an article titled "A Vote Today for Hillary Clinton Is a Vote for Endless, Stupid War" published on WikiLeaks in February 2016, Assange wrote that Clinton "certainly should not become president of the United States." He continued, "I have had years of experience in dealing with Hillary Clinton and have read thousands of her cables." And, "Hillary lacks judgment and will push the United States into endless, stupid wars which spread terrorism. Her personality combined with her poor policy decisions have directly contributed to the rise of ISIS. She's a war hawk with bad judgment who gets an unseemly emotional rush out of killing people."[38] Assange has also accused Clinton of pushing to indict him after WikiLeaks release of more than 250,000 diplomatic cables, which Clinton condemned at the time.[39] Assange has claimed more leaks related to the former secretary of state are to come. "We have a lot of material, thousands of pages of material," Assange told Megyn Kelly on Fox News.[40] "It's a variety of different types of documents from different types of institutions that are associated with the election campaign, some quite unexpected angles that are, you know, quite interesting, some even entertaining."[41]

Clinton's campaign manager, Robby Mook, drew a connection between Russia and the DNC hack in a July 24 interview with CNN. "What's disturbing to us is that experts are telling us that Russian State actors broke into the DNC, stole these emails, and other experts are now saying that the Russians are releasing these emails for the purpose of actually helping Donald Trump," Mook said. "I don't think it's coincidental that these emails were released on the eve of our convention here, and I think that's disturbing."[42]

Assange affirmed that WikiLeaks did time the release to come before the start of the DNC. "That's when we knew there would be maximum interest by readers, but also, we have a responsibility to," Assange told CNN's Anderson Cooper. "If we published after, you can just imagine how outraged the Democratic voting population would have been. It had to have been before."[43]

As for the allegations that Russia was involved in the leak, Assange told CNN, "I think this raises a very serious question, which is that the natural instincts of Hillary Clinton and the people around her, that when confronted with a serious domestic political scandal, that she tries to blame the Russians, blame the Chinese, et cetera, because if she does that when she's in government, that's a political, managerial style that can lead to conflict."[44]

He said, "What we have right now is the Hillary Clinton campaign using a speculative allegation about hacks that have occurred in the past to try and divert attention from our emails, another separate issue that WikiLeaks has published."[45] Assange held that the organization liked to "create maximum ambiguity" about the identities of its sources, saying, "Obviously, to exclude certain actors is to make it easier to find out who our sources are. So we never do it."[46]

A month and a half before the publication of the DNC emails, Assange teased the release during an interview with Britain's ITV. "We have upcoming leaks in relation to Hillary Clinton, which is great."[47]

With that said, Operation LUCKY-7 had its cutout. The FSB's Information Warfare Management Cell (IWMC) would create a false flag source to feed Assange the data taken from the DNC and any subsequent hacks through Guccifer 2.0. Assange was desperate to be relevant, and the IWMC was going to create a new era where his own hatreds and agenda could be skillfully manipulated by the FSB's active measures officers, while the cyber teams would keep him well fed. Assange was primed to do LUCKY-7's bidding and now only needed the data they had stolen. WikiLeaks was now a wholly owned subsidiary of the FSB and essentially the cyber equivalent of a laundromat, a Russian laundry—ready to clean and give a white appearance to the dirt.

8

WHEN CYBER BEARS ATTACK

Once is happenstance. Twice is coincidence. Three times is enemy action.
—IAN FLEMING

CYBER BEARS! Attack!

At some point early in fall of 2015 the National Security Agency and the FBI cyber division had indications of unusual activity related to Democratic National Committee servers. The signature of the attempts was familiar, since this had not been the first time that foreign entities had attempted to penetrate related to the US political parties' networks, high-profile persons, or US government agencies. Individual hackers would attempt these penetrations for personal notoriety and bragging rights among the tight and secretive hacking community, but this practice had long since expanded into a global business worth billions in stolen data. Some hacking thieves stole Social Security numbers, credit cards, and identity theft information belonging to ordinary people, in sophisticated exploits that skimmed cash at the blink of an eye. Other groups specialized in stealing large-volume banking data or attempting large-scale fraud.

It has long been a dictum of warfare that forewarned is forearmed. In business and politics as well, the strengths of an opponent can be exploited, their weaknesses taken advantage of and manipulated. To this end a small, elite network of individual hackers or hacker gangs specialize in stealing corporate secrets to sell or use for blackmail. A hacker of this ilk will sell the stolen data to business rivals. Whether it be the size of the bid on a contract or the nude photos of an opposing CEO's mistress, such data that could never have been previously available without physically breaking and entering a file or safe could now safely be extracted from a third party that often does it for a reasonable fee. Throughout the 1990s hacking groups performing these services had formed in Eastern Europe, then West Africa, China, and South Asia. Foreign intelligence agencies often subcontracted their services to see what they could find on targets in America as well.

It was always advisable for the FBI and cyber security companies to give the political parties warnings before the run-up to an election season. Clearly, a history of hacks had occurred before, and the FBI told the DNC to be on the lookout for "unusual activity."[1] Director of National Intelligence James Clapper said that the Department of Homeland Security and FBI had been working "to educate campaigns against potential cyber threats." Clapper added, "I anticipate as the campaigns intensify, we'll probably have more of those [attempts]."[2]

Given the size and scope of their systems, IT divisions have to deal with many different and routine hacks, and exploits occur on a regular basis, including nuisance messages, offensive and malicious emails with links to archaic viruses, or offers from Nigerian princes. A more critical method of attacking the servers is to flood the networks with a massive email tsunami of spam, all at once, and from multiple sources. This is called a Denial-of-Services or DoS attack. The vast amount of data filling the entryways to the server slows down or blocks authorized messages from entering the system, akin to an internet brownout. As each bit of valid data competes with the massive quantity of hacker-fed data, the entire system grinds to a halt in a cyber traffic jam. Hence, service is denied.

Though the DNC IT security staff did not receive warnings about specific activity, they should have been well aware of previous political exploits. At a minimum, all of the security personnel and their subcontractors should have received briefings about the previous hacks and signatures that could indicate a real threat coming down the pike. In the end, they were left to fend for themselves. The hackers most likely knew that, since the DNC is a private political organization, they would only be as good as the local IT security, a human factor weakness to be exploited. The National Security Agency and Cyber Command were not responsible for political security outside of government agencies. For all of their vast protective power, the federal agencies gave what was minimally required . . . a bit of advice.[3]

The DNC took what precautions they thought were appropriate for the level of risk. Yet others were watching with greater interest. In October 2015, InfoSec Institute, an information security training center, carried out a protective hack known as advanced penetrative testing. White Hat hackers at IT security companies performed these defensive hacks to test the perimeter of the network's security walls and reveal the holes in the security system. Such tests sometimes reveal minor vulnerabilities, but most of the time these tests expose holes so extensive that a cyber-tractor trailer could pass through without any chance of detection.

It is important to identify and share information on threats as they have developed and as they currently operate. There are also ways to detect the location of adversaries by examining the available metadata found in the files captured, by accessing the C2 (command-and-control) servers, and by finding where data is routed or retrieved, by examining timestamps in the meta to determine build times, and by examining the deployment of files and routine check-ins conducted by the attackers. IPs found in C2 servers, locations where files are retrieved for operations, and IP info in emails can help determine the source of the attack.

InfoSec Institute's tests revealed the DNC servers had massive security flaws, setting themselves up for a hack the exact same way the Chinese exploited the Obama and McCain campaigns in 2008. The best defense to these threats is a regular security update at the client end, so the developers could stay on top of the latest exploits and 0day vulnerabilities. Sometimes all of these efforts can be overlooked, not shared, or just fall by the wayside. That is how the DNC got hacked: The sum efforts of sharing, comparing, and preparing was like a small rainstorm and the CYBER BEARS managed to dance between the raindrops.

The Bears Arrive

In April 2016 DNC chief executive officer Amy Dacey contacted DNC lawyer Michael Sussman. Dacey called him to let him know that the DNC's IT department noticed strange behavior on their system. Sussman was a partner at Perkins Coie, a firm focused on cybercrimes. Sussman contacted Shawn Henry, president of cybersecurity firm CrowdStrike, to conduct an assessment and determine if there was a breach and how deep it went.[4] CrowdStrike revealed that the DNC computers had been breached and that data on contributors, opposition research on candidates, and even the day-to-day inter-office chats and email had been stolen. The whole system had been professionally compromised.

CrowdStrike assessed that COZY BEAR had breached the system in 2015 and had been engaged in gathering data for a year. They then found that a second group, FANCY BEAR had breached the server in April of 2016. They managed to penetrate through spear-phishing, the technique of sending a false email to a victim, who would subsequently click on a link in the email, connecting them to a hacker's server. In this case, one of the spear-phishing attacks used a fraudulent site with the deliberately misspelled URL "misdepatrment.com." The link was supposed to connect the target to the MIS Department. Instead sent the user to an identical, but fake site called a watering hole, that downloaded a malware kit on the victim's computer. The malware contained additional modules to disseminate the computer virus widely throughout the DNC's servers.

CrowdStrike discovered that COZY BEAR used a malware kit identified as "SeaDuke" (also called "SeaDaddy"), a backdoor module that was installed in the file "pagemgr.exe."[5] It was noted by F-Secure that SeaDuke was written in the Python coding language, which indicated that COZY BEAR knew the operating system might be based on Linux.

In order to evade the security systems, the attackers would update their modules or the location of their C2 servers. The report said the second attack group was APT28, FANCY BEAR. It used a module named "X-Agent" to enable it to send remote commands, watch every keystroke through keylogging, and transfer files via the C2 server. The group also used "X-Tunnel" malware to give them the ability to send even more remote commands to the servers. The X-Tunnel was set to 45.32.129.185, revealing that it was built specifically for this hack, giving it the ability to extract passwords and create its own encrypted private network to operate covertly.

Several cyber security firms have examined the related metadata to the ATP28 FANCY BEAR infections. They have nearly unanimously found that several combinations of factors tie this group to a large group of similar infections since 2007. In particular, the Internet Protocol or IP address like 176.31.112.10, used for its command-and-control-server (C2), shows up repeatedly in other cyberwarfare campaigns.[6] This IP was linked to the breaches at the German Bundestag, the DNC, and the DCCC. Additionally, both IPs are associated with the watering hole attacks and the C2 servers on the DNC and DCCC hacks, revealing their past associations. Another key indicator is the time zone associated when compiling the malware. Russian threat actors like APT28 work most commonly at UTC+4 time zone. While compiling the data about the hack, several firms noted that the operating system used to develop the malware was set to Cyrillic, Russian language text, during some of the development, but not in all.

The firms also noted Russia's association with the APT29 COZY BEAR malware, also called "SeaDaddy" or "SeaDuke," because it had already been extensively tracked by several cyber security firms and associated with Russian Intelligence. As with APT28, indicators embedded within the metadata pointed to Russia as the source of this malware. This also included the C2 server IPs reused from past operations known to be Russian. The operational time of module compilation and the targets they struck were beneficial only to Russian interests.

Another indicator of professional intelligence agency involvement was the way they performed OpSec or Operational Security. OpSec was the methodology the operators used to evade detection and cover their tracks. CrowdStrike was impressed and called it "superb." They noted that they demonstrated a "live off the land" approach to evading security. In fact, just one year before the DNC hack was revealed, the firm found COZY BEAR responsible for hacks of the White House, the State Department, and the US Joint Chiefs of Staff.

"We have identified no collaboration between the two actors, or even an awareness of one by the other," Dmitri Alperovitch wrote in a blog post. "Instead, we observed the two Russian espionage groups compromise the same systems and engage separately in the theft of identical credentials."[7] Alperovitch wrote this is "not an uncommon scenario" in Russia, where the primary domestic and foreign intelligence agencies—the FSB and SVR, respectively—have a competitive and even adversarial relationship.

The hackers frequently cleared out the logs that would reveal their activities or reset the timestamp of files so it appeared that they were never opened or tampered with.[8] However, some additional breadcrumb trails lead many cyber security firms and intelligence agencies to conclude that this was the work of the CYBER BEARS or one of its hired hacker hit squads.

Another critical bit of evidence was the use of a specific command-and-control server in the attack. It was traced back to the IP address of 176.31.112.10, and it had been seen before. This same IP came up during the investigation on the German Bundestag spear-phishing. That attempt was believed to have been carried out by Russian intelligence.[9]

By May 18, 2016, the director of national intelligence, James R. Clapper Jr., spoke at the Bipartisan-Policy Center in Washington and said there were "indications" of attempted cyberattacks in the 2016 presidential campaign without specifying either attempted intrusions or suspected foreign or domestic hackers.[10] Brian P. Hale, director of public affairs for the Office of the Director of National Intelligence, backed Clapper up stating, "we're aware that campaigns and related organizations and individuals are targeted by actors with a variety of motivations, from philosophical differences to espionage, and capabilities, from defacements to intrusions," and, "we defer to FBI for specific incidents."[11]

On June 15, 2016 a Wordpress page appeared with links to the stolen DNC documents. It was posted by Guccifer 2.0 and came with a list of Frequently Asked Questions.

"Hello! I received lots of questions from journalists and other people who are interested in my doings. Many thanks to all of you, it's a pleasure for me!

Unfortunately, I couldn't reply to each of you personally, especially given that you often asked the same questions. That's why I decided to answer the most frequently asked questions here.

I divided them into three groups:

1.   About me

2.   About my activities and publications

3.   About my political views

As you can guess, all special services are doing their best trying to locate and catch me. And I have absolutely no desire to help them. So, if your curiosity isn't satisfied after reading this post, you may have my apologies. It's a matter of life and death. But I can assure you that everything I do corresponds to my beliefs.

Let's get it started!

1.   A glimpse of me

Many people ask me where I'm from, where I live and other personal information.

You see, I can't show you my IDs, it would be stupid of me.

I can only tell you that I was born in Eastern Europe. I won't answer where I am now. In fact, it's better for me to change my location as often as possible. I have to hide.

But generally, it's not that important for where I live. I can work wherever there's an Internet connection. So I feel free in any free country.

A lot of people are concerned if I have any links to special services and Russia?

I'll tell you that everything I do I do at my own risk. This is my personal project and I'm proud of it. Yes, I risk my life. But I know it's worth it. No one knew about me several weeks ago. Nowadays the whole world's talking about me. It's really cool!

How can I prove this is true? I really don't know. It seems the guys from CrowdStrike and the DNC would say I'm a Russian bear even if I were a catholic nun in fact. At first I was annoyed and disappointed. But now I realize they have nothing else to say. There's no other way to justify their incompetence and failure. It's much easier for them to accuse powerful foreign special services.

They just fucked up! They can prove nothing! All I hear is blah-blah-blah, unfounded theories and somebody's estimates.

Specialists from Eastern Europe, Russia, China, India work for the leading IT-companies such as Google, IBM, Microsoft, Apple. There's no surprise that many hackers are descendants from these regions."

Guccifer 2.0, who claimed to be a Romanian lone wolf, was clearly a cover-up for the CYBER BEARS. Lorenzo Franceschi-Bicchierai, a staff writer at VICE Motherboard who covers hacking and information security, writes, "Considering a long trail of breadcrumbs pointing back to Russia left by the hacker, as well as other circumstantial evidence, it appears more likely that Guccifer 2.0 is nothing but a disinformation or deception campaign by Russian state-sponsored hackers to cover up their own hack—and a hasty and sloppy one at that."[12]

Franceschi-Bicchierai, who actually chatted with Guccifer 2.0, points to the blogger's use of certain characters that are popular in Russia and metadata that indicates the blogger might actually be Russian. He also points out other linguistic evidence—such as his seemingly poor Romanian and broken English that wasn't necessarily consistent with a Romanian speaking English as a second language but might bear some resemblance to Russian-English syntax—as indicators that Guccifer 2.0 might not be who he claimed to be.[13]

Regardless of whether or not Guccifer 2.0 really did infiltrate the DNC systems or release the documents to WikiLeaks, CrowdStrike issued an update to its original post in response, reiterating its findings about the presence of the two Russian groups in DNC networks. "Whether or not this posting is part of a Russian Intelligence disinformation campaign, we are exploring the documents' authenticity and origin," Alperovitch wrote. "Regardless, these claims do nothing to lessen our findings relating to the Russian government's involvement, portions of which we have documented for the public and the greater security community."[14]

Fomenting Civil War among Democrats

On July 22, 2016 a few days before the opening of the DNC, WikiLeaks published 19,252 emails alleged to be from the DNC hack.[15] Operation LUCKY-7 was now fully underway. The emails weren't spectacular, mostly mundane discussions that would happen between personnel, including their preferred candidate. However, as released by WikiLeaks it fueled suspicions of the most hardcore Bernie Sanders supporters that the Democratic presidential nomination was engineered and stolen.

Team Trump saw the opportunity and they too piled on in a series of tweets that tried to drive a wedge between the Clinton and Sanders camps. On July 23, Trump tweeted "The WikiLeaks e-mail release today was so bad to Sanders that it will make it impossible for him to support her, unless he is a fraud!"[16] Assange immediately replied to the Trump tweet and linked to the DNC cache so his followers would find it with a cheery "everyone can see for themselves."

The emails revealed that DNC chairperson Debbie Wasserman-Schultz, whose role should make her neutral until the nomination process was complete, had been strongly favoring Hillary Clinton throughout the primary process. The DNC did not dispute the content of the emails themselves.

There was an email thread started on May 5, 2016, with the title "No shit" in which Brad Marshall, the CFO for the DNC, allegedly suggests to get someone to ask Sanders what his beliefs are in order to portray him as an atheist. It read "My Southern Baptist peeps would draw a big difference between a Jew and an atheist."[17] Follow-up emails suggest that Amy Dacey responded with "Amen."

In some of the emails for example, senders made recommendations to diminish the Sanders campaign. An email from May 21, 2016, allegedly from committee communications official Mark Paustenbach, made a suggestion to criticize the Sanders campaign as a "mess" that didn't have its "act together" when it was discovered that they had accessed voter data belonging to the Clinton campaign.[18] He also stated "It's not a DNC conspiracy, it's because they never had their act together" in one email.[19]

In a particularly pointed email dated May 17, 2016, soon-to-be-former DNC Chairwoman Debbie Wasserman-Schultz called Jeff

Weaver, the Sanders campaign manager, "particularly scummy" and a "damn liar."[20] The Sanders campaign had spent many months calling for the resignation of the DNC chairwoman, and the emails provided their chance.

The Response to the Hacks

The storm of outrage among Sanders's supporters exploded on the starting day of the Democratic Convention. The revelation of damaging emails happened just in time for the first news of the morning. It appeared that their release would cause a massive split and tear Sanders's passionate voters away from not only Clinton but the Democratic Party. To quell the danger Chairwoman Debbie Wassermann-Schultz announced her resignation. Senator Sanders had been preparing to endorse Clinton and his supporters were begging him to walk out of the convention and run as a third party candidate. Such an event would split the ticket and catapult a flailing Trump directly into the White House. In the end, common sense prevailed and Clinton did end up receiving Sanders's endorsement, but he seemed very cold during the convention. Pro-Bernie delegates often interrupted the speeches of prominent Democratic key speakers, chanting his name, including House Democratic Whip, Representative Steny Hoyer, former Secretary of Defense and CIA Director Leon Panetta, Representative Elijah Cummings, Senator Al Franken, comedian Sarah Silverman, and even their own economic heroine Senator Elizabeth Warren.

The outrage was so hot in the convention hall that committee CEO Amy Dacey, Communications Director Luis Miranda, and CFO Brad Marshall and other supporting staffers also left their posts at the DNC in an effort to stem the split.[21] Some Sanders delegates staged a walkout and went directly to the press tent to complain about how the system was rigged—exactly as Donald Trump kept saying. Outside the venue in nearby Roosevelt Park, more than a thousand Sanders supporters took to the scalding streets of Philadelphia to vent their frustration. Many Sanders supporters shouted against Mrs. Clinton with the same taunting chant from the previous week's Republican convention: "Lock her up!" Other protesters gathered outside the downtown Ritz-Carlton, where many major donors to Mrs. Clinton's campaign were staying, and attacked her use of a "super PAC" and her reliance on big fund-raising events.[22] Some claimed that they were actually planning to vote for Trump. Initial reactions were much less focused on the hack itself; rather they were focused on reiterating the Republican nominee's claim that the Democratic primaries and the resulting nomination process were illegitimate.

Julian Assange said that WikiLeaks actually timed the release of the leak to coincide with the start of the convention. "That's when we knew there would be maximum interest by readers, but also, we have a responsibility to," Assange told CNN's Anderson Cooper. "If we published after, you can just imagine how outraged the Democratic voting population would have been. It had to have been before."[23] The Assange-friendly media joined in on the disinformation campaign against Clinton too. News articles abounded such as the *Guardian*'s headline "WikiLeaks Proves Primary Was Rigged: DNC Undermined Democracy."[24]

Around the same time, Assange, with the help of Russia Today, also brought another prominent conspiracy theory to promenence when he suggested a DNC staffer who had been murdered in July might have been an informant killed for leaking information to WikiLeaks. "Whistleblowers often take very significant efforts to bring us material and often at very significant risks," Assange said in an interview on a Dutch television program, discovered by BuzzFeed's Andrew Kaczynski. "There's a twenty-seven-year-old who works for the DNC and who was shot in the back, murdered, just a few weeks ago, for unknown reasons as he was walking down the streets in Washington."[25] When asked if he was suggesting Rich might be a WikiLeaks source, Assange replied that they do not comment on their sources. Then,

WikiLeaks announced on Twitter it was offering a $20,000 reward "for information leading to conviction for the murder of DNC staffer Seth Rich." Jeremy Stahl, a senior editor at *Slate* wrote, "Julian Assange and his WikiLeaks organization appear to be actively encouraging a conspiracy theory that a Democratic National Committee staffer was murdered for nefarious political purposes, perhaps by Hillary Clinton."[26] He noted however, that there was "zero evidence" to support these conspiracy theories, and that the fact-checking website Snopes had debunked many of them.[27]

Despite Assange straying off the deep end of conspiracy theory, the most significant aspect of the WikiLeaks dump was a surprise that the CYBER BEARS had given the stir-crazy Assange and his gullible supporters: The Russians had infected the downloadable package of DNC emails with a wide variety of hacking malware. Tens of thousands of people who would download the emails from their WikiLeaks' Global Intelligence Files would find their computers filled with malware and open their lives to exploitation by the CYBER BEARS. It was quickly noticed and warnings went out across the cyber security community to beware of malware embedded in emails from WikiLeaks.[28]

Fomenting a crisis between the two competing candidates of the Democratic Party was the objective, and it looked like it could succeed, if not for Donald Trump himself. During the convention the family of US Army Captain Humayun Khan, a soldier killed in Iraq by a suicide bomber, came to the stage to give a speech. The Khans were Gold Star parents—parents who have lost their children in war. Humayun's father Khzir Khan gave a stirring patriotic speech attacking Trump's knowledge of sacrifice and of the US Constitution. Captain Khan's mother, Ghazala stood next to her husband, devastated in grief under a 20-foot high photo of her son. She was struck speechless. Trump could not resist the opportunity to insult the family, and in an instant the fury over the DNC leaks essentially ended in a plume of Trump-initiated radioactivity.[29]

Though the protests did slowly calm down or were repressed and the persistent interruption of speakers ceased, tensions remained during the convention throughout the entire week. While the Republican Party spent the election season plagued by internal factions, the hacked emails were enough to make internal disputes within the Democratic Party the focus of political media. During President Obama's address to the convention, a shout-out to Senator Sanders met with the televised image of a prickly-looking Sanders.

Ignoring the implications that Russia might be trying to influence the outcomes of this election by taking attention off of Trump and discrediting Clinton, Sanders supporters expressed outrage that the Democratic Party bigwigs had picked a candidate before primary voters had. The doubts about Clinton, amplified by release of the stolen emails, called into question her own campaign's involvement in the election. Though the tensions waned, and the Democratic Party did not suffer a split, a secondary desired effect was that many Sanders supporters now had a hard time supporting Clinton.

For the CYBER BEAR hackers this effect was well on track for what the operation had intended to produce, though a Democratic Party split would have been optimal.

To paraphrase J.K. Rowling's Harry Potter, the mischief had been managed, but the attack was not yet finished. The CYBER BEARS were going to systematically waltz their way through the remaining arms of the Democratic Party's machine and steal, reveal, discredit, and attack anyone who stood against Donald Trump, and by extension, Russia.

Team Trump Tips Its Hand?

The first two days of the Democratic National Convention in Philadelphia had been chaotic. The forces between Clinton and Sanders were engaged in tit-for-tat taunts and accusations of divisiveness. If the hacks were designed to damage the convention it was performing nominally. The entire pathway of Kompromat from surveillance, planning, and hacking, to establishing a legend in Guccifer 2.0 and gaining international credibility by channeling the release through WikiLeaks was happening within planning parameters and with only minor hitches. Even the international media was buying into the belief that it was absolutely unimportant how the information from the hacks was acquired but that the content was critical. So long as the CYBER BEARS could infuse doubt as to their participation, there was little chance for repercussion. Julian Assange hinted at future releases though the Guccifer 2.0 legend and the ever-compliant WikiLeaks. There also remained perfect opportunites to prepare and introduce Black Propaganda—false documents that could be taken from a clean source and modified ever so slightly to make it malicious. Science and Technology Directorate of the FSB's SVR could easily fabricate such documents if the mission required letters, money, deeds, titles, or any other falsely impugning evidence. Working with the SVR political warfare specialists, the cyber warriors of the FSB could also seamlessly change a word or two in an email without a trace and reintroduce it into a flood of legitimate documents. But then that plan was suddenly spoiled.

Speaking to an American press conference when asked about the subject of hacking, Trump brought up the private Hillary Clinton emails deleted from her server. Trump blurted out, "Russia, if you're listening, I hope you're able to find the 30,000 emails that are missing . . . I think you will probably be rewarded mightily by our press."[30] Almost immediately a media storm shook the campaign and people wondered aloud if Trump was actually in league with the Kremlin. It made some wonder if the comments made by Fox News's Andrew Napolitano in May—stating that Russia was engaged in an inter-Kremlin argument about whether to release Clinton's hacked emails—was tied to Trump's call to release them. Did Team Trump have advance knowledge of what the Kremlin was doing?

In another strange twist, Trump ally Roger Stone would later claim to be in direct communication with the WikiLeaks founder Julian

Assange. "I actually have communicated with Assange," Stone said. "I believe the next tranche of his documents pertain to the Clinton Foundation but there's no telling what the October surprise may be."[31] While Stone has no official role in the Trump campaign, *Roll Call* writes that he "might have inadvertently linked the Donald Trump campaign with the WikiLeaks founder Julian Assange."[32]

The Kremlin certainly could no longer express shock and surprise now that they had been asked publically to do what they had been doing since 2015. All that could be done for LUCKY-7 was to keep up the flow of email releases in the hope that Trump does not damage or discredit the hacks any further.

American presidential elections are high-stakes events. Russia would not be the first foreign power, friendly or hostile, to pursue its preferred outcome. Nor would Mr. Trump be the first politician to leverage foreign actors for electoral benefit. But this is the first time that a presidential candidate had openly asked a foreign power to meddle in the democratic process to his benefit. More than that, Mr. Trump seemed to be suggesting that Russia should violate United States espionage laws on his behalf.[33] To members of the US intelligence community, the indications that nefarious practitioners were playing in the most dangerous of games was now confirmed. The first question that popped into the minds of many practitioners was, "What does Trump know that we do not?" The implication would naturally cause counter-intelligence and cyberwarfare operatives to ask themselves if there is there a link between Trump or his supporters and the Russians in the DNC hacks?

The DCCC and ActBlue Hacks

The next day after Trump begged Russia to hack America, the CYBER BEARS complied. On July 28, the Democratic Congressional Campaign Committee announced it was attacked by the CYBER BEARS. The

DCCC is focused on raising funds for Democratic congressional campaigns and managing the finances of the senatorial campaign donations. This hack used Typosquatting, building a fake website identical to the DCCC's where staff and donors sign-in information was stolen. It used spear-phishing techniques to gain entry and was focused on an effort to gain general information from the DCCC. The CYBER BEARS managed to steal much more personal data about the donors and supporters of the party from the DCCC than the DNC, including information on credit card numbers, personal information, and addresses.[34] Since the effort placed so much emphasis on donors, the mission was most likely intended to create doubts about the security of the Democratic Party's control of financial information and reduce donations.

Reuters announced the attack just before the DNC's grand evening, the Hillary Clinton acceptance speech in Philadelphia. On the eve of Clinton's speech, the DCCC's spokeswoman said in a statement, "The DCCC takes this matter very seriously. With the assistance of leading experts, we have taken and are continuing to take steps to enhance the security of our network in the face of these recent events. We are cooperating with the federal law enforcement with respect to their ongoing investigation."[35]

ActBlue.com is the official site for fundraising that donors thought they were going to when they wound up at ActBlues.com which was a fake watering hole site complete with a malware package ready to steal data.[36] ActBlues.com was being hosted on a machine with a Netherlands IP address. The site had been registered to a Gmail account, fisterboks@gmail.com, which had registered three other sites used as German cover for Russian spear-phishing campaigns. Cyber security companies ThreatConnect and Fidelis concluded that the Gmail was tied to domains associated with the DNC hack related to "misdepatrment.com." That domain was registered to frank_merdeux@europe.com and was used as the C2 server in the DNC attack.[37] The CYBER BEARS had struck again.

The administrators of the official ActBlue.com site stated they were never hacked and that no information on donors in their systems was compromised.[38]

The DCCC did not officially disclose what data had been stolen. However, shortly after the leak was announced the account associated with "Guccifer 2.0" claimed responsibility. On August 12, 2016, they published a trove of internal emails, memos, and other data. In particular, there was a memo from Troy Perry, a DCCC employee who advised others on how to handle activists in the Black Lives Matters campaign. He suggested to "listen to their concerns but do not offer support for concrete policy decisions."

As a result of publishing the DCCC information, Twitter suspended the Guccifer 2.0 account.[39] WordPress too took action . . . in a way. They stepped in and scrubbed the website of posts related to the DCCC hack and sent a reminder to Guccifer 2.0 of its Terms of Service related to publishing private information. The laughter in the LUCKY-7 Information Warfare Management cell (IWMC) must have been raucous when the sternly worded letter about monkey-wrenching an entire American election was read aloud.

Clinton Campaign Hack

Trump's wish for Russia to get more data continued apace. On July 29, 2016, Clinton campaign spokesman Nick Merrill said, "Our campaign computer system has been under review by outside cyber security experts. To date, they have found no evidence that our internal systems have been compromised."[40] This was political lingo to say the campaign had been visited by the CYBER BEARS but they hadn't found the actual hack yet.

In fact the CYBER BEARS did attack the Clinton servers, but their access was limited. The attackers managed to access a server used for the campaign's analytics program that stores voter analysis. There is no other sensitive data on those machines, and the campaign said the internal computer systems had not been compromised. Still, the Russians now knew more about how the Clinton campaign analyzed voter data. Nothing is ever too obscure for cyber theft.

The techniques the CYBER BEARS used to attack were the same as the others. An email was sent to 108 Hillary for America email addresses, containing a short link pointing to a fake Google sign-in. The target enters their Gmail email and password and then—poof!—it belongs to Mother Russia.

SecureWorks determined 213 links were sent. Because SecureWorks could only find just over half of the 108 Gmail accounts, they determined the hackers got the emails from another source.[41] The emails were aimed at specific figures that held rank in the campaign. Out of the 213 links generated by the hackers, 20 had been clicked at least once. Eight people clicked the links at least twice; two of those clicked them four times. In addition, 26 personal accounts for Clinton campaign staffers were targeted in 150 short links specifically created to target this group.

The DNC uses dnc.org as its mail server for staff email. SecureWorks reported that sixteen short links were sent to nine specific accounts at the DNC. At least three senior Clinton staff members clicked on these short links. SecureWorks did not link these emails specifically to the DNC hack but did affirm the same spear-phishing technique was used.[42] In its brief on the HillaryClinton.com hack, SecureWorks refers to "TG-4127" and designated it as APT28 COZY BEAR.

Now that their tears of laughter had dried from the stern warning from Wordpress, the CYBER BEARS paid no heed and started to issue more stolen DNC documents, including "DCCC internal docs on primaries in Florida." However, a telling clue of the releases started to reveal itself. While Guccifer 2.0 released some documents randomly in order to incite Sanders die-hards, others followed a certain parameter, indicating that the Russian IWMC was paying close attention to what the Trump campaign said and then released documents to support Trump's statements. The most telling was the week-long storm the Trump campaign made by claiming that if he didn't win in Pennsylvania, then the election was stolen. Speaking in Altoona on August 12, he said "We're going to watch Pennsylvania. Go down to certain areas and watch and study and make sure other people don't come in and vote five times. If you do that, we're not going to lose. The only way we can lose, in my opinion—I really mean this, Pennsylvania—is if cheating goes on." Little more than a week later, Guccifer 2.0 posted "DCCC Docs Pennsylvania." They would soon be followed up with a leak of DNC material from virtually all of the swing states of Florida, Ohio, New Hampshire, Illinois, and North Carolina just when Trump needed a boost in the polls.

More evidence of synchronicity was found on the same day that Trump visited Mexico and then lit a barn burner of a speech on immigration. That night Guccifer 2.0 released the documents "DCCC docs from [Nancy] Pelosi's PC" with discussions on immigration, Black Lives Matters, and other items.[43]

The *New York Times* had set a new editorial policy stipulating that anything Trump said needed fact checking. Editorial writer Charles Blow wrote an article suggesting that if you support Trump, you support racism.[44] Sure enough, within days the CYBER BEARS hacked the *New York Times* in what appears to be an attempt to gain information to discredit Blow and others. What it did was reveal that anyone who publically goes against Trump is subject to attack.

The Intelligence Professionals Weigh In

As the public has come to learn about more cyberattacks, numerous officials and cyber security experts have weighed in on the possibility of Russian interference on the 2016 election cycle. Numerous intelligence officials and government and cyber security experts alike weighed in on possible Russian involvement. They overwhelmingly agreed that though more evidence is needed, the CYBER BEARS paw prints are all over the hacks.

Reuters reported that the US Department of Justice national security division was investigating the attacks as threats on US national security. The FBI also said it was investigating the case, and it was "aware of media reporting on cyber intrusions involving multiple political entities, and is working to determine the accuracy, nature and scope of these matters."[45]

While speaking at the Aspen Security Forum about the Clinton campaign hacks, CIA director John O. Brennan didn't point any fingers to Russia but said, "obviously, interference in the US election process is a very, very serious matter, and I think certainly this government would treat it with great seriousness."[46]

The US government has not yet officially named any culprits, but the general consensus is that Russia is behind the hacks. "The consensus that Russia hacked the DNC is at this point very strong, albeit not unanimous," said cybersecurity consultant Matt Tait. "The consensus that Russia hacked the DNC in support of Trump is, by contrast, plausible, but something for which the jury at this stage is very much still out."[47]

President Obama also said "anything's possible" to NBC, since Russian hackers "on a regular basis, they try to influence elections in Europe."[48]

Yahoo! News reported August 15 that state polling systems had been hacked by foreign agencies. The FBI sent out an internal "flash" alert from the FBI's Cyber division saying that state polling systems had potentially been hacked by Russian state-sponsored hackers, aimed at disrupting the November elections. Homeland Security Secretary Jeh Johnson held a conference call with state elected officials to offer his department's services. Johnson said there were no "specific or credible cybersecurity threats" to the election, but three days later, the FBI released a memo titled "Targeting Activity Against State Board of Election Systems." It revealed that the bureau is investigating attacks on two state election websites this summer that resulted in the theft of voter registration data.[49]

The memo didn't directly name any particular states, but *Yahoo! News* sources claim Arizona and Illinois were affected. In Illinois, officials were forced to shut down the state's voter registration system for ten days in late July, after hackers downloaded personal data on at least 200,000 state voters, according to Ken Menzel, the general counsel of the Illinois Board of Elections. The Arizona attack wasn't as serious; the virus injected into the voter registration system wasn't successful in stealing data.

"The FBI is requesting that states contact their Board of Elections and determine if any similar activity to their logs, both inbound and outbound, has been detected," the alert said. "Attempts should not be made to touch or ping the IP addresses directly."

"This is a big deal," said Rich Barger, chief intelligence officer for ThreatConnect, a cybersecurity firm, on the FBI alert. "Two state election boards have been popped, and data has been taken. This certainly should be concerning to the common American voter." Barger said one of the IP addresses listed in the FBI alert has surfaced before in Russian criminal underground hacker forums. He also compared the hacking methods to that of cyberattacks on the World Anti-Doping Agency. The FBI told *Yahoo! News* that it intended "to help systems administrators guard against the actions of persistent cyber criminals." Menzel, the Illinois election official, said the FBI was investigating a "possible link" to the other hacks. They drew no conclusions in the run-up to the election about the intent of the hack; some say it could just be common cyber criminals looking to steal data for fraud. However, the IPs of where the hackers registered their domains came from a shady company called IT Itch. It registers sites anonymously and is paid in Bitcoins, the currency of the internet underworld. This same company registered the COZY BEAR and FANCY BEAR spear-phishing websites as well. [50]

Even President Barack Obama weighed in on the possibility that Russia was behind the leak. The Associated Press wrote:

> Asked whether Moscow was trying to influence the presidential election, Obama said, "Anything's possible." Obama, who traditionally avoids commenting on active FBI investigations, broke with that protocol and noted that outside experts have blamed Russia for the leak. He leaned heavily into the notion that President Vladimir Putin may have reason to facilitate the attack. "What the motives were in terms of the leaks, all that—I can't say directly," Obama told NBC News. "What I do know is that Donald Trump has repeatedly expressed admiration for Vladimir Putin."[51]

Overall, the CYBER BEARS working in the guise of Guccifer 2.0 publically gave Trump and Clinton detractors illegally obtained opposition research, without it being connected directly to Trump. As former FBI agent and security specialist Ali Soufan noted on Twitter "The nature of breaches appears to be changing from covert info collection to the overt and weaponized use of that info."[52]

I Know Noth-Think!

On September 1, 2016, in a moment of rare candor and perhaps a bit of mischief, Vladimir Putin spoke about the nature and responsibility of the hacks against the United States: "But I want to tell you again, I don't know anything about it, and on a state level Russia has never done this." Putin then added, with a completely straight face, "Listen, does it even matter who hacked this data? . . . The important thing is the content that was given to the public."

9

CYBERWAR TO DEFEND DEMOCRACY

"Always remember: cyber or kinetic, your adversaries prefer your silence,
apathy and inaction. Be the consequence, not the victim."
—ANTHONY COUCHENOUR, HOPLITE CYBER SECURITY

THE 2016 ELECTION CYCLE IN THE United States will be noteworthy for more than just the bombastic rhetoric, the illogic, the lies, and the almost religious fervor of the electorate. The most important part of this election could easily be lost in the short-term memory of the American people, mainly because of the simplistic way our media makes us forget what is truly important.

Without any question, no matter what side of the aisle one sits on, the simple fact is that the United States was attacked by Russian cyber commandos deployed by Vladimir Putin and organized by his intelligence apparatus, the FSB and GRU. It was a serious act of political warfare.

The 2016 cyberattack was not just another case of simple Kompromat—meddling in the political affairs of a satellite nation or an individual dissenter. It was a direct attempt to hijack and derail the traditional processes and norms that held the United States together for more than 240 years. The attempt was even more brazen due to the apparent belief that Putin assumed that he and his oligarchy could charm, groom, and select a candidate, then with the right amount of cybercrime and enough organized propaganda they could actually choose a president of the United States to do their bidding.

The Cyberian Candidate

In terms of Russia's cyber capability its worthy to note that LUCKY-7 managed to fuse together all aspects of the traditional KGB-style operations and then marry them up with the advanced cyberwarfare capabilities of the more modern FSB. Their human intelligence officer, oligarchs, and the Russian news media apparently groomed powerful but friendly American associates over several years through financial, personal, and political patronage. If they sought to create a cadre of fellow travelers in their hatred of Hillary Clinton and deep admiration of Russia's political hardball, they got it in spades. Until 2016 it was unthinkable that Americans could be assembled in mutual endeavor to manipulate the goodwill of the American people in order to further their own personal financial interest at the behest of a hostile government. But it appears to have not only happened but even managed to completely usurp the stridently anti-Communist Republican Party and replace it with a presidential nominee who openly lavishes praise on Russia's leader, disparages NATO, and promises to dismantle America's superiority in order to allow Russia to take the role of world's superpower. The fact that Russia can smile, deny, and at the same time conduct cyber and propaganda operations and still have Donald Trump beg them for cyber espionage assistance to hurt another American is unbelievable. If it reveals anything it proves the old KGB policy that loyalty to one's country is elastic if the money is right.

On September 8, 2016, Trump gushed with admiration and at the same time insulted America's president.[1] He was quickly seconded by vice presidential nominee Mike Pence, who agreed "I think it's inarguable that Vladimir Putin has been a stronger leader in his country than Barack Obama has been in this country."

By publically choosing a known, dangerous, and proven autocratic adversary who has murdered opponents, killed his own citizens, conducted acts of terrorism, and invaded and seized other nations in violation of global norms, Trump and Pence chose Russia's values over America's. It has been said that this election would spell the rise of fascism and end the two-century-long run of American democratic governance. It may be worse than that. The deliberate subversion of America's interests to those of a hostile adversary has never before been suggested aloud in polite company in the history of this nation.

When asked at the Iraq and Afghanistan Veterans of America Commander-in-Chief Forum about Putin, Trump said "Well, he does have an 82 percent approval rating, according to the different pollsters, who, by the way, some of them are based right here." Trump continued,

> If he says great things about me, I'm going to say great things about him. . . . I've already said, he is really very much of a leader. I mean, you can say, "Oh, isn't that a terrible thing—the man has very strong control over a country." Now, it's a very different system, and I don't happen to like the system. But certainly, in that system, he's been a leader, far more than our president has been a leader.

Spoken at a forum of men and women who fought and served against the Soviet Union in the Cold War, Trump's ability to make them forget their service to the nation and agree with him that Russia is a better nation than America because a dictator showed him some love, revealed that the subversion of the unwitting asset appeared complete.

The more excited partisans often misuse the word "treason" when discussing support for the ideals of another nation. The US Code on Treason reads,

> Whoever, owing allegiance to the United States, levies war against them or adheres to their enemies, giving them aid and comfort within the United States or elsewhere, is guilty of treason and shall suffer death, or shall be imprisoned not less than five years and fined under this title but not less than $10,000; and shall be incapable of holding any office under the United States.[2]

No one is accusing Trump or his associates of treason, sedition, or treachery. That kind of talk should be squelched. Unless true evidence of deliberate collusion between the campaign and the Russia government is found by US counterintelligence officers and brought forth in charges by the US Justice Department, and that is highly unlikely, then no one should ever accuse an American citizen of these dangerous and litigious words. Fighting words. We should defend his right under the First Amendment to continue saying any and all the stupid things he will most assuredly continue to do. That is his right.

Nor are any of the statements or activities of the Trump campaign, no matter how distasteful, the behaviors or actions of clandestine agents of the Russian regime. However, even a cursory glance at the evidence reveals to intelligence professionals that the probability that Vladimir Putin has handled Trump and his associates, who were doing Russia's bidding without even knowing it, is well within the KGB playbook. These Americans may not be real agents of the Russian Federation, but they may have unwittingly exposed themselves to a massive intelligence manipulation machine from which, once involved, they may be completely unable to extract themselves. The rhetoric of the 2016 election reveals that damage has already been done.

Worst of all is that the rise of an American ideologue who firmly admires and wishes to emulate the murder-based power politics of America's strategic nuclear opponent with the intent to dismantle the defensive systems and treaties that kept this nation safe for over seventy years, reveals that the intelligence community's ability to detect real national security threats can be defeated through demagoguery.

America under Attack

Russia's capability is so absolutely organized to benefit the regime that it generates billions through authorized cybercrime so long as the Kremlin gets what it wants. Another former NSA member of the elite Tailored Access Operations program warned, "Do not underestimate the food chain that Putin has assembled." That food chain is topped by the CYBER BEARS; every nation below is intended to be consumed. Alex Cochenour, president of Hoplite Security, agreed with this aspect of Russia's cyber capacity:

> So complete is Russia's control over its vast and profitable cybercrime and cyber propaganda campaigns that virtually no collateral damage ever lands within the Russians' own border. This effect is amusingly referred to as the "Russian Cyber Force Field," everything from making their malware exploit kits geo and language aware to manipulating malicious advertising campaigns, the Russians go to great lengths to keep their hands clean. The attached screenshot from Hoplite's global sensor network show this effect visually, notice the lack of activity inside Russia's borders? The activity inside Russia is virtually always from machines owned by Europeans and Americans traveling with already infected machines. If that graphic is at all useful, you have my permission to use it.

What are the nation's options? A few recommendations have been universally recognized by some of the top cyber security people in the world including:

1. The president should address the nation before the election and use the bully pulpit to make the nation aware that an operation has been run against the United States by a hostile intelligence agency, and that the security of the system is paramount. He should allow the law enforcement and intelligence agencies of the United States to assist any and all state and local organizations to use the maximum resources of the nation to ensure the integrity of the election.

2. The Department of Homeland Security and the US Cyber Command should be directed to create a temporary joint public-private partnership, a Priority Infrastructure Cyber Security Cooperative (PICSC), in order to rapidly disseminate detected threats and solutions that will be available industry wide and without cost in order to stop emergent hacks. We require a central organization where anyone who has been hacked can report the incident for analysis. Many cyber security experts believe that we need an international Hackers Defense Network in order to allow academics, researchers, and intelligence agencies to work together to correctly identify, analyze, and score attacks with a single common standard.

3. The administration should make clear that the United States will respond to this attack at a time and place of its choosing. The target should be chosen by US cyber command. If we do not communicate our intent to punish any further meddling, it will occur again. The argument that Russia will attack our infrastructure with a cyber disruption is no reason to allow them to damage our freedom to choose our government without retribution.

4. National recognition and awareness of the enormity and fully-integrated propaganda that emanates from the Russian state entities Russia Today, Sputnik News, and other state disinformation agencies. These agencies should be called out for generating centralized propaganda and influencing our electorate through carefully-timed "conspiracy theory" releases that work to our detriment.

Where the candidates themselves stand is revealing as well. When discussing responses to Russian cyberwarfare Hillary Clinton spoke about the attack and stated "As president, I will make it clear that the United States will treat cyberattacks just like any other attack. . . . We will be ready with serious political, economic and military responses."[3]

On the other hand, Donald Trump seems to admire Russia's capacity to hurt our nation through cyberespionage. Apart from that, there is little evidence that Trump knows or cares about cyberwarfare. In a fluff interview conducted by General Michael Flynn, Trump was asked about cyberwar. He gave a peculiarly ignorant answer:

> Well that's it, and, you know cyber is becoming so big today. It's becoming something that a number of years ago, a short number of years ago, wasn't even a word. And now the cyber is so big. And, you know, you look at what they're doing with the internet, how they're taking recruiting people through the internet. And part of it is the psychology because so many people think they're winning. And, you know, there's a whole big thing. Even today's psychology, where CNN came out with a big poll, their big poll came out today that Trump is winning. It's good psychology.[4]

However, despite the evidence the hacks benefitted him, Trump went on Larry King's interview program that was aired on Russia Today television. When asked, he noted that the hacks were inappropriate, but pled ignorance and tried to pin the blame onto the Democrats, saying, "Maybe the Democrats are putting that out—who knows . . . I don't know who hacked. You tell me: Who hacked?"[5]

Just because Russia now has money, resources, and military technology does not mean that they will ever see America as equals. I believe Donald Trump when he says that Russia has no respect for the United States or its leadership. Russia, like both Trump and Putin, suffers from an inferiority complex that makes them strive to best everyone and talk big beyond their ability to control the results. To them smack talk and chest puffing is enough to make them believe that they are the biggest ape in the jungle. However, when attacked and challenged America has always rallied to its flag and responded as a nation. It would be vitally important for Putin to disable this greatest American strength before endeavoring on to any further adventures. That unity and national will has been critically damaged by Trump as well, only to Russia's benefit.

The key to unraveling the objectives of LUCKY-7 is to accept that Russia is not an ally but a strategic opponent who views America's standing as an obstacle to its own greatness. Should the chicanery of the 2016 election go without response, America would become target number one for Kompromat at even the lowest level elections. Future hacking and political releases would directly affect US policy and could disable the processes that keep us safe. Politicians from both sides of the aisle could find themselves at risk of political blackmail, or they may entertain troll opinions generated by another nation. Russia believes that they have now perfected the tool by which America could be brought down by revealing to the world how easily we are manipulated through propaganda to the point that our own governmental functions cease to work. China will jump into the game with both feet should LUCKY-7 be successful. Imagine two global cyberwars being waged secretly against America and our political establishment incapable of passing a law or allocating funds to stop it because the legislators have already been influenced by a foreign power.

The Next Attack

The Russian ability to launch an attack with a "weapon of Mass Disruption" has yet to occur, but could come at a time of Russia's choosing. Should the Kremlin game out that the time is right to politically and economically destabilize America and finally topple it from being the shining city on the capitalist hill to collapsing under its own ignorance and faith in a parlor tricking, reality show con man, then a massive hack on election day is well within its capability. The LUCKY-7 Information Warfare Management Cell doesn't need to get into the electronic voting machines. The Russian IWMC and its LUCKY-7 operations team just needs to change one column of electoral tallies in one state just long enough to make the tens of millions of Trump voters finally believe that the election was being stolen by Hillary Clinton. No matter what the evidence, no matter who will ask for calm, they won't believe anything other than treachery because Donald Trump has convinced a third of the American electorate that the entire American electoral system has always been corrupt. The greatest danger now is that any outcome other than the election of Donald Trump will not be accepted, and demands for a new election and rejection of the result will cripple the nation in ways not seen since 1860 secession. It could lead some states to suggest just that should the outcome be not to their liking. At that point the prospect of a second American civil war is not only viable, but likely.

The Russian use of cyber weapons to perform criminal acts and damage our electoral process was intended to remove faith in America itself. Along with Donald Trump's claims that the election will be rigged, they have achieved this goal. Due to their meddling, activities that were considered routine politics in America are now suspect. Politics itself is under fire, due to the combination of hacking and demagoguery.

Though we have yet to see an actual disruption that matters in the lives of the average American citizen, one can be sure that it will come at a time when, once recognized, the only alternative to the attack may be a real war.

APPENDIX

THE FOLLOWING SUPPLEMENT FROM THE OFFICE of the Director of National Intelligence (ODNI) entitled "Assessing Russian Activities and Intentions in Recent US Elections" is an intelligence community assessment, presented in an unclassified format, of just a few of the conclusions related to the Russian hacking that could be released to the public.

Many of the conclusions that were included in the consensus opinion of the principal three intelligence agencies, the NSA, the CIA, and the FBI, are identical to *The Plot to Hack America*. It should be noted that the intelligence community conclusions in this and the CIA report were written at the same time that the author was writing this book and delivered to the president on the exact same date, September 23, 2016, *The Plot to Hack America* was released in an online edition. This is because both the intelligence community and the author worked on the exact same subject, for the exact same time period, using the exact same methodologies and came to the exact same conclusions at the exact same time.

It should also be noted that on October 7, 2016, the first day that the book became available in stores, President Obama, Director of National Intelligence James Clapper, and Director of Homeland

Security Jae Johnson announced publically the conclusion that the Russians had attempted to hack the US electoral process.

This ODNI assessment is a dramatic but partial validation of my writing. I say partial because the majority of the conclusions remain highly classified. Yet, new media reports reveal almost daily that *The Plot to Hack America* remains a startlingly prescient book.

The key judgments of this intelligence community found in this assessment will give the reader even deeper insights into the depths of the Russian intelligence efforts to use propaganda and cyberwarfare to undermine and damage American democracy.

Background to "Assessing Russian Activities and Intentions in Recent US Elections": The Analytic Process and Cyber Incident Attribution

6 January 2017

Background to "Assessing Russian Activities and Intentions in Recent US Elections": The Analytic Process and Cyber Incident Attribution

"Assessing Russian Activities and Intentions in Recent US Elections" is a declassified version of a highly classified assessment that has been provided to the President and to recipients approved by the President.

- The Intelligence Community rarely can publicly reveal the full extent of its knowledge or the precise bases for its assessments, as the release of such information would reveal sensitive sources or methods and imperil the ability to collect critical foreign intelligence in the future.

- Thus, while the conclusions in the report are all reflected in the classified assessment, the declassified report does not and cannot include the full supporting information, including specific intelligence and sources and methods.

The Analytic Process

The mission of the Intelligence Community is to seek to reduce the uncertainty surrounding foreign activities, capabilities, or leaders' intentions. This objective is difficult to achieve when seeking to understand complex issues on which foreign actors go to extraordinary lengths to hide or obfuscate their activities.

- On these issues of great importance to US national security, the goal of intelligence analysis is to provide assessments to decisionmakers that are intellectually rigorous, objective, timely, and useful, and that adhere to tradecraft standards.

- The tradecraft standards for analytic products have been refined over the past ten years. These standards include describing sources (including their reliability and access to the information they provide), clearly expressing uncertainty, distinguishing between underlying information and analysts' judgments and assumptions, exploring alternatives, demonstrating relevance to the customer, using strong and transparent logic, and explaining change or consistency in judgments over time.

- Applying these standards helps ensure that the Intelligence Community provides US policymakers, warfighters, and operators with the best and most accurate insight, warning, and context, as well as potential opportunities to advance US national security.

Intelligence Community analysts integrate information from a wide range of sources, including human sources, technical collection, and open source information, and apply specialized skills and structured analytic tools to draw inferences informed by the data available, relevant past activity, and logic and reasoning to provide insight into what is happening and the prospects for the future.

- A critical part of the analyst's task is to explain uncertainties associated with major judgments based on the quantity and quality of the source material, information gaps, and the complexity of the issue.

- When Intelligence Community analysts use words such as "we assess" or "we judge," they are conveying an analytic assessment or judgment.

- Some analytic judgments are based directly on collected information; others rest on previous judgments, which serve as building blocks in rigorous analysis. In either type of judgment, the tradecraft standards outlined above ensure that analysts have an appropriate basis for the judgment.

- Intelligence Community judgments often include two important elements: judgments of how likely it is that something has happened or will happen (using terms such as "likely" or "unlikely") and confidence levels in those judgments (low, moderate, and high) that refer to the evidentiary basis, logic and reasoning, and precedents that underpin the judgments.

Determining Attribution in Cyber Incidents

The nature of cyberspace makes attribution of cyber operations difficult but not impossible. Every kind of cyber operation—malicious or not—leaves a trail. US Intelligence Community analysts use this information, their constantly growing knowledge base of previous events and known malicious actors, and their knowledge of how these malicious actors work and the tools that they use, to attempt to trace these operations back to their source. In every case, they apply the same tradecraft standards described in the Analytic Process above.

- Analysts consider a series of questions to assess how the information compares with existing knowledge and adjust their confidence in their judgments as appropriate to account for any alternative hypotheses and ambiguities.

- An assessment of attribution usually is not a simple statement of who conducted an operation, but rather a series of judgments that describe whether it was an isolated incident, who was the likely perpetrator, that perpetrator's possible motivations, and whether a foreign government had a role in ordering or leading the operation.

Scope and Sourcing

Information available as of 29 December 2016 was used in the preparation of this product.

Scope

This report includes an analytic assessment drafted and coordinated among The Central Intelligence Agency (CIA), The Federal Bureau of Investigation (FBI), and The National Security Agency (NSA), which draws on intelligence information collected and disseminated by those three agencies. It covers the motivation and scope of Moscow's intentions regarding US elections and Moscow's use of cyber tools and media campaigns to influence US public opinion. The assessment focuses on activities aimed at the 2016 US presidential election and draws on our understanding of previous Russian influence operations. When we use the term "we" it refers to an assessment by all three agencies.

- This report is a declassified version of a highly classified assessment. This document's conclusions are identical to the highly classified assessment, but this document does not include the full supporting information, including specific intelligence on key elements of the influence campaign. Given the redactions, we made minor edits purely for readability and flow.

We did not make an assessment of the impact that Russian activities had on the outcome of the 2016 election. The US Intelligence Community is charged with monitoring and assessing the intentions, capabilities, and actions of foreign actors; it does not analyze US political processes or US public opinion.

- New information continues to emerge, providing increased insight into Russian activities.

Sourcing

Many of the key judgments in this assessment rely on a body of reporting from multiple sources that are consistent with our understanding of Russian behavior. Insights into Russian efforts—including specific cyber operations—and Russian views of key US players derive from multiple corroborating sources.

Some of our judgments about Kremlin preferences and intent are drawn from the behavior of Kremlin-loyal political figures, state media, and pro-Kremlin social media actors, all of whom the Kremlin either directly uses to convey messages or who are answerable to the Kremlin. The Russian leadership invests significant resources in both foreign and domestic propaganda and places a premium on transmitting what it views as consistent, self-reinforcing narratives regarding its desires and redlines, whether on Ukraine, Syria, or relations with the United States.

Assessing Russian Activities and Intentions in Recent US Elections

ICA 2017-01D
6 January 2017

Key Judgments

Russian efforts to influence the 2016 US presidential election represent the most recent expression of Moscow's longstanding desire to undermine the US-led liberal democratic order, but these activities demonstrated a significant escalation in directness, level of activity, and scope of effort compared to previous operations.

We assess Russian President Vladimir Putin ordered an influence campaign in 2016 aimed at the US presidential election. Russia's goals were to undermine public faith in the US democratic process, denigrate Secretary Clinton, and harm her electability and potential presidency. We further assess Putin and the Russian Government developed a clear preference for President-elect Trump. We have high confidence in these judgments.

- **We also assess Putin and the Russian Government aspired to help President-elect Trump's election chances when possible by discrediting Secretary Clinton and publicly contrasting her unfavorably to him.** All three agencies agree with this judgment. CIA and FBI have high confidence in this judgment; NSA has moderate confidence.

- Moscow's approach evolved over the course of the campaign based on Russia's understanding of the electoral prospects of the two main candidates. When it appeared to Moscow that Secretary Clinton was likely to win the election, the Russian influence campaign began to focus more on undermining her future presidency.

- Further information has come to light since Election Day that, when combined with Russian behavior since early November 2016, increases our confidence in our assessments of Russian motivations and goals.

Moscow's influence campaign followed a Russian messaging strategy that blends covert intelligence operations—such as cyber activity—with overt efforts by Russian Government agencies, state-funded media, third-party intermediaries, and paid social media users or "trolls." Russia, like its Soviet predecessor, has a history of conducting covert influence campaigns focused on US presidential elections that have used intelligence officers and agents and press placements to disparage candidates perceived as hostile to the Kremlin.

- Russia's intelligence services conducted cyber operations against targets associated with the 2016 US presidential election, including targets associated with both major US political parties.

- We assess with high confidence that Russian military intelligence (General Staff Main Intelligence Directorate or GRU) used the Guccifer 2.0 persona and DCLeaks.com to release US victim data obtained in cyber operations publicly and in exclusives to media outlets and relayed material to WikiLeaks.

- Russian intelligence obtained and maintained access to elements of multiple US state or local electoral boards. **DHS assesses that the types of systems Russian actors targeted or compromised were not involved in vote tallying.**

- Russia's state-run propaganda machine contributed to the influence campaign by serving as a platform for Kremlin messaging to Russian and international audiences.

We assess Moscow will apply lessons learned from its Putin-ordered campaign aimed at the US presidential election to future influence efforts worldwide, including against US allies and their election processes.

> This report is a declassified version of a highly classified assessment; its conclusions are identical to those in the highly classified assessment but this version does not include the full supporting information on key elements of the influence campaign.

Contents

Scope and Sourcing   i

Key Judgments   ii

Contents   iv

CIA/FBI/NSA Assessment: Russia's Influence Campaign Targeting the 2016 US Presidential Election

Putin Ordered Campaign To Influence US Election   1

Russian Campaign Was Multifaceted   2

Influence Effort Was Boldest Yet in the US   5

Election Operation Signals "New Normal" in Russian Influence Efforts   5

Annexes

A: Russia—Kremlin's TV Seeks To Influence Politics, Fuel Discontent in US   6

B: Estimative Language   13

Russia's Influence Campaign Targeting the 2016 US Presidential Election

Russia's Influence Campaign Targeting the 2016 US Presidential Election

Putin Ordered Campaign To Influence US Election

We assess with high confidence that Russian President Vladimir Putin ordered an influence campaign in 2016 aimed at the US presidential election, the consistent goals of which were to undermine public faith in the US democratic process, denigrate Secretary Clinton, and harm her electability and potential presidency. We further assess Putin and the Russian Government developed a clear preference for President-elect Trump. When it appeared to Moscow that Secretary Clinton was likely to win the election, the Russian influence campaign then focused on undermining her expected presidency.

- We also assess Putin and the Russian Government aspired to help President-elect Trump's election chances when possible by discrediting Secretary Clinton and publicly contrasting her unfavorably to him. All three agencies agree with this judgment. CIA and FBI have high confidence in this judgment; NSA has moderate confidence.

- In trying to influence the US election, we assess the Kremlin sought to advance its longstanding desire to undermine the US-led liberal democratic order, the promotion of which Putin and other senior Russian leaders view as a threat to Russia and Putin's regime.

- Putin publicly pointed to the Panama Papers disclosure and the Olympic doping scandal as US-directed efforts to defame Russia, suggesting he sought to use disclosures to discredit the image of the United States and cast it as hypocritical.

- Putin most likely wanted to discredit Secretary Clinton because he has publicly blamed her since 2011 for inciting mass protests against his regime in late 2011 and early 2012, and because he holds a grudge for comments he almost certainly saw as disparaging him.

We assess Putin, his advisers, and the Russian Government developed a clear preference for President-elect Trump over Secretary Clinton.

- Beginning in June, Putin's public comments about the US presidential race avoided directly praising President-elect Trump, probably because Kremlin officials thought that any praise from Putin personally would backfire in the United States. Nonetheless, Putin publicly indicated a preference for President-elect Trump's stated policy to work with Russia, and pro-Kremlin figures spoke highly about what they saw as his Russia-friendly positions on Syria and Ukraine. Putin publicly contrasted the President-elect's approach to Russia with Secretary Clinton's "aggressive rhetoric."

- Moscow also saw the election of President-elect Trump as a way to achieve an international counterterrorism coalition against the Islamic State in Iraq and the Levant (ISIL).

- Putin has had many positive experiences working with Western political leaders whose business interests made them more disposed to deal with Russia, such as former Italian Prime Minister Silvio Berlusconi and former German Chancellor Gerhard Schroeder.

- Putin, Russian officials, and other pro-Kremlin pundits stopped publicly criticizing the US election process as unfair almost immediately after the election because Moscow probably assessed it would be counterproductive to building positive relations.

We assess the influence campaign aspired to help President-elect Trump's chances of victory when possible by discrediting Secretary Clinton and publicly contrasting her unfavorably to the President-elect. When it appeared to Moscow that Secretary Clinton was likely to win the presidency the Russian influence campaign focused more on undercutting Secretary Clinton's legitimacy and crippling her presidency from its start, including by impugning the fairness of the election.

- Before the election, Russian diplomats had publicly denounced the US electoral process and were prepared to publicly call into question the validity of the results. Pro-Kremlin bloggers had prepared a Twitter campaign, #DemocracyRIP, on election night in anticipation of Secretary Clinton's victory, judging from their social media activity.

Russian Campaign Was Multifaceted

Moscow's use of disclosures during the US election was unprecedented, but its influence campaign otherwise followed a longstanding Russian messaging strategy that blends covert intelligence operations—such as cyber activity—with overt efforts by Russian Government agencies, state-funded media, third-party intermediaries, and paid social media users or "trolls."

- We assess that influence campaigns are approved at the highest levels of the Russian Government—particularly those that would be politically sensitive.

- Moscow's campaign aimed at the US election reflected years of investment in its capabilities, which Moscow has honed in the former Soviet states.

- By their nature, Russian influence campaigns are multifaceted and designed to be deniable because they use a mix of agents of influence, cutouts, front organizations, and false-flag operations. Moscow demonstrated this during the Ukraine crisis in 2014, when Russia deployed forces and advisers to eastern Ukraine and denied it publicly.

The Kremlin's campaign aimed at the US election featured disclosures of data obtained through Russian cyber operations; intrusions into US state and local electoral boards; and overt propaganda. Russian intelligence collection both informed and enabled the influence campaign.

Cyber Espionage Against US Political Organizations. Russia's intelligence services conducted cyber operations against targets associated with the 2016 US presidential election, including targets associated with both major US political parties.

We assess Russian intelligence services collected against the US primary campaigns, think tanks, and lobbying groups they viewed as likely to shape future US policies. In July 2015, Russian intelligence gained access to Democratic National Committee (DNC) networks and maintained that access until at least June 2016.

- The General Staff Main Intelligence Directorate (GRU) probably began cyber operations aimed at the US election by March 2016. We assess that the GRU operations resulted in the compromise of the personal e-mail accounts of Democratic Party officials and political figures. By May, the GRU had exfiltrated large volumes of data from the DNC.

Public Disclosures of Russian-Collected Data. We assess with high confidence that the GRU used the Guccifer 2.0 persona, DCLeaks.com, and WikiLeaks to release US victim data obtained in cyber operations publicly and in exclusives to media outlets.

- Guccifer 2.0, who claimed to be an independent Romanian hacker, made multiple contradictory statements and false claims about his likely Russian identity throughout the election. Press reporting suggests more than one person claiming to be Guccifer 2.0 interacted with journalists.

- Content that we assess was taken from e-mail accounts targeted by the GRU in March 2016 appeared on DCLeaks.com starting in June.

We assess with high confidence that the GRU relayed material it acquired from the DNC and senior Democratic officials to WikiLeaks. Moscow most likely chose WikiLeaks because of its self-proclaimed reputation for authenticity. Disclosures through WikiLeaks did not contain any evident forgeries.

- In early September, Putin said publicly it was important the DNC data was exposed to WikiLeaks, calling the search for the source of the leaks a distraction and denying Russian "state-level" involvement.

- The Kremlin's principal international propaganda outlet RT (formerly Russia Today) has actively collaborated with WikiLeaks. RT's editor-in-chief visited WikiLeaks founder Julian Assange at the Ecuadorian Embassy in London in August 2013, where they discussed renewing his broadcast contract with RT, according to Russian and Western media. Russian media subsequently announced that RT had become "the only Russian media company" to partner with WikiLeaks and had received access to "new leaks of secret information." RT routinely gives Assange sympathetic coverage and provides him a platform to denounce the United States.

These election-related disclosures reflect a pattern of Russian intelligence using hacked information in targeted influence efforts against targets such as Olympic athletes and other foreign governments. Such efforts have included releasing or altering personal data, defacing websites, or releasing e-mails.

- A prominent target since the 2016 Summer Olympics has been the World Anti-Doping Agency (WADA), with leaks that we assess to have originated with the GRU and that have involved data on US athletes.

Russia collected on some Republican-affiliated targets but did not conduct a comparable disclosure campaign.

Russian Cyber Intrusions Into State and Local Electoral Boards. Russian intelligence accessed elements of multiple state or local electoral boards. Since early 2014, Russian intelligence has researched US electoral processes and related technology and equipment.

- DHS assesses that the types of systems we observed Russian actors targeting or compromising are not involved in vote tallying.

Russian Propaganda Efforts. Russia's state-run propaganda machine—comprised of its domestic media apparatus, outlets targeting global audiences such as RT and Sputnik, and a network of quasi-government trolls—contributed to the influence campaign by serving as a platform for Kremlin messaging to Russian and international audiences. State-owned Russian media made increasingly favorable comments about President-elect Trump as the 2016 US general and primary election campaigns progressed while consistently offering negative coverage of Secretary Clinton.

- Starting in March 2016, Russian Government–linked actors began openly supporting President-elect Trump's candidacy in media aimed at English-speaking audiences. RT and Sputnik—another government-funded outlet producing pro-Kremlin radio and online content in a variety of languages for international audiences—consistently cast President-elect Trump as the target of unfair coverage from traditional US media outlets that they claimed were subservient to a corrupt political establishment.

- Russian media hailed President-elect Trump's victory as a vindication of Putin's advocacy of global populist movements—the theme of Putin's annual conference for Western academics in October 2016—and the latest example of Western liberalism's collapse.

- Putin's chief propagandist Dmitriy Kiselev used his flagship weekly newsmagazine program this fall to cast President-elect Trump as an outsider victimized by a corrupt political establishment and faulty democratic election process that aimed to prevent his election because of his desire to work with Moscow.

- Pro-Kremlin proxy Vladimir Zhirinovskiy, leader of the nationalist Liberal Democratic Party of Russia, proclaimed just before the election that if President-elect Trump won, Russia would "drink champagne" in anticipation of being able to advance its positions on Syria and Ukraine.

RT's coverage of Secretary Clinton throughout the US presidential campaign was consistently negative and focused on her leaked e-mails and accused her of corruption, poor physical and mental health, and ties to Islamic extremism. Some Russian officials echoed Russian lines for the influence campaign that Secretary Clinton's election could lead to a war between the United States and Russia.

- In August, Kremlin-linked political analysts suggested avenging negative Western reports on Putin by airing segments devoted to Secretary Clinton's alleged health problems.

- On 6 August, RT published an English-language video called "Julian Assange Special: Do WikiLeaks Have the E-mail That'll Put Clinton in Prison?" and an exclusive interview with Assange entitled "Clinton and ISIS Funded by the Same Money." RT's most popular video on Secretary Clinton, "How 100% of the Clintons' 'Charity' Went to...Themselves," had more than 9 million views on social media platforms. RT's most popular English language video about the President-elect, called "Trump Will Not Be Permitted To Win," featured Assange and had 2.2 million views.

- For more on Russia's past media efforts—including portraying the 2012 US electoral process as undemocratic—please see Annex A: Russia—Kremlin's TV Seeks To Influence Politics, Fuel Discontent in US.

Russia used trolls as well as RT as part of its influence efforts to denigrate Secretary Clinton. This effort amplified stories on scandals about Secretary Clinton and the role of WikiLeaks in the election campaign.

- The likely financier of the so-called Internet Research Agency of professional trolls located in Saint Petersburg is a close Putin ally with ties to Russian intelligence.

- A journalist who is a leading expert on the Internet Research Agency claimed that some social media accounts that appear to be tied to Russia's professional trolls—because they previously were devoted to supporting Russian actions in Ukraine—started to advocate for President-elect Trump as early as December 2015.

Influence Effort Was Boldest Yet in the US

Russia's effort to influence the 2016 US presidential election represented a significant escalation in directness, level of activity, and scope of effort compared to previous operations aimed at US elections. We assess the 2016 influence campaign reflected the Kremlin's recognition of the worldwide effects that mass disclosures of US Government and other private data—such as those conducted by WikiLeaks and others—have achieved in recent years, and their understanding of the value of orchestrating such disclosures to maximize the impact of compromising information.

- During the Cold War, the Soviet Union used intelligence officers, influence agents, forgeries, and press placements to disparage candidates perceived as hostile to the Kremlin, according to a former KGB archivist.

Since the Cold War, Russian intelligence efforts related to US elections have primarily focused on foreign intelligence collection. For decades, Russian and Soviet intelligence services have sought to collect insider information from US political parties that could help Russian leaders understand a new US administration's plans and priorities.

- The Russian Foreign Intelligence Service (SVR) Directorate S (Illegals) officers arrested in the United States in 2010 reported to Moscow about the 2008 election.

- In the 1970s, the KGB recruited a Democratic Party activist who reported information about then-presidential hopeful Jimmy Carter's campaign and foreign policy plans, according to a former KGB archivist.

Election Operation Signals "New Normal" in Russian Influence Efforts

We assess Moscow will apply lessons learned from its campaign aimed at the US presidential election to future influence efforts in the United States and worldwide, including against US allies and their election processes. We assess the Russian intelligence services would have seen their election influence campaign as at least a qualified success because of their perceived ability to impact public discussion.

- Putin's public views of the disclosures suggest the Kremlin and the intelligence services will continue to consider using cyber-enabled disclosure operations because of their belief that these can accomplish Russian goals relatively easily without significant damage to Russian interests.

- Russia has sought to influence elections across Europe.

We assess Russian intelligence services will continue to develop capabilities to provide Putin with options to use against the United States, judging from past practice and current efforts. Immediately after Election Day, we assess Russian intelligence began a spearphishing campaign targeting US Government employees and individuals associated with US think tanks and NGOs in national security, defense, and foreign policy fields. This campaign could provide material for future influence efforts as well as foreign intelligence collection on the incoming administration's goals and plans.

Annex A

Russia -- Kremlin's TV Seeks To Influence Politics, Fuel Discontent in US*

RT America TV, a Kremlin-financed channel operated from within the United States, has substantially expanded its repertoire of programming that highlights criticism of alleged US shortcomings in democracy and civil liberties. The rapid expansion of RT's operations and budget and recent candid statements by RT's leadership point to the channel's importance to the Kremlin as a messaging tool and indicate a Kremlin-directed campaign to undermine faith in the US Government and fuel political protest. The Kremlin has committed significant resources to expanding the channel's reach, particularly its social media footprint. A reliable UK report states that RT recently was the most-watched foreign news channel in the UK. RT America has positioned itself as a domestic US channel and has deliberately sought to obscure any legal ties to the Russian Government.

In the runup to the 2012 US presidential election in November, English-language channel RT America -- created and financed by the Russian Government and part of Russian Government-sponsored RT TV (see textbox 1) -- intensified its usually critical coverage of the United States. The channel portrayed the US electoral process as undemocratic and featured calls by US protesters for the public to rise up and "take this government back."

- RT introduced two new shows -- "Breaking the Set" on 4 September and "Truthseeker" on 2 November -- both overwhelmingly focused on criticism of US and Western governments as well as the promotion of radical discontent.

- From August to November 2012, RT ran numerous reports on alleged US election fraud and voting machine vulnerabilities, contending that US election results cannot be trusted and do not reflect the popular will.

Messaging on RT prior to the US presidential election (RT, 3 November)

- In an effort to highlight the alleged "lack of democracy" in the United States, RT broadcast, hosted, and advertised third-party candidate debates and ran reporting supportive of the political agenda of these candidates. The RT hosts asserted that the US two-party system does not represent the views of at least one-third of the population and is a "sham."

---

* This annex was originally published on 11 December 2012 by the Open Source Center, now the Open Source Enterprise.

- RT aired a documentary about the Occupy Wall Street movement on 1, 2, and 4 November. RT framed the movement as a fight against "the ruling class" and described the current US political system as corrupt and dominated by corporations. RT advertising for the documentary featured Occupy movement calls to "take back" the government. The documentary claimed that the US system cannot be changed democratically, but only through "revolution." After the 6 November US presidential election, RT aired a documentary called "Cultures of Protest," about active and often violent political resistance (RT, 1-10 November).

RT new show "Truthseeker" (RT, 11 November)

RT Conducts Strategic Messaging for Russian Government

RT's criticism of the US election was the latest facet of its broader and longer-standing anti-US messaging likely aimed at undermining viewers' trust in US democratic procedures and undercutting US criticism of Russia's political system. RT Editor in Chief Margarita Simonyan recently declared that the United States itself lacks democracy and that it has "no moral right to teach the rest of the world" (*Kommersant*, 6 November).

- Simonyan has characterized RT's coverage of the Occupy Wall Street movement as "information warfare" that is aimed at promoting popular dissatisfaction with the US Government. RT created a *Facebook* app to connect Occupy Wall Street protesters via social media. In addition, RT featured its own hosts in Occupy rallies ("Minaev Live," 10 April; RT, 2, 12 June).

- RT's reports often characterize the United States as a "surveillance state" and allege widespread infringements of civil liberties, police brutality, and drone use (RT, 24, 28 October, 1-10 November).

Simonyan steps over the White House in the introduction from her short-lived domestic show on REN TV (REN TV, 26 December 2011)

- RT has also focused on criticism of the US economic system, US currency policy, alleged Wall Street greed, and the US national debt. Some of RT's hosts have compared the United States to Imperial Rome and have predicted that government corruption and "corporate greed" will lead to US financial collapse (RT, 31 October, 4 November).

RT broadcasts support for other Russian interests in areas such as foreign and energy policy.

- RT runs anti-fracking programming, highlighting environmental issues and the impacts on public health. This is likely reflective of the Russian Government's concern about the impact of fracking and US natural gas production on the global energy market and the potential challenges to Gazprom's profitability (5 October).

- RT is a leading media voice opposing Western intervention in the Syrian conflict and blaming the West for waging "information wars" against the Syrian Government (RT, 10 October-9 November).

RT anti-fracking reporting (RT, 5 October)

- In an earlier example of RT's messaging in support of the Russian Government, during the Georgia-Russia military conflict the channel accused Georgians of killing civilians and organizing a genocide of the Ossetian people. According to Simonyan, when "the Ministry of Defense was at war with Georgia," RT was "waging an information war against the entire Western world" (*Kommersant*, 11 July).

In recent interviews, RT's leadership has candidly acknowledged its mission to expand its US audience and to expose it to Kremlin messaging. However, the leadership rejected claims that RT interferes in US domestic affairs.

- Simonyan claimed in popular arts magazine *Afisha* on 3 October: "It is important to have a channel that people get used to, and then, when needed, you show them what you need to show. In some sense, not having our own foreign broadcasting is the same as not having a ministry of defense. When there is no war, it looks like we don't need it. However, when there is a war, it is critical."

- According to Simonyan, "the word 'propaganda' has a very negative connotation, but indeed, there is not a single international foreign TV channel that is doing something other than promotion of the values of the country that it is broadcasting from." She added that "when Russia is at war, we are, of course, on Russia's side" (*Afisha*, 3 October; *Kommersant*, 4 July).

- TV-Novosti director Nikolov said on 4 October to the Association of Cable Television that RT builds on worldwide demand for "an alternative view of the entire world." Simonyan asserted on 3 October in *Afisha* that RT's goal is "to make an alternative channel that shares information unavailable elsewhere" in order to "conquer the audience" and expose it to Russian state messaging (*Afisha*, 3 October; *Kommersant*, 4 July).

- On 26 May, Simonyan tweeted with irony: "Ambassador McFaul hints that our channel is interference with US domestic affairs. And we, sinful souls, were thinking that it is freedom of speech."

RT Leadership Closely Tied to, Controlled by Kremlin

RT Editor in Chief Margarita Simonyan has close ties to top Russian Government officials, especially Presidential Administration Deputy Chief of Staff Aleksey Gromov, who reportedly manages political TV coverage in Russia and is one of the founders of RT.

- Simonyan has claimed that Gromov shielded her from other officials and their requests to air certain reports. Russian media consider Simonyan to be Gromov's protege (*Kommersant*, 4 July; Dozhd TV, 11 July).

- Simonyan replaced Gromov on state-owned Channel One's Board of Directors. Government officials, including Gromov and Putin's Press Secretary Peskov were involved in creating RT and appointing Simonyan (*Afisha*, 3 October).

- According to Simonyan, Gromov oversees political coverage on TV, and he has periodic meetings with media managers where he shares classified information and discusses their coverage plans. Some opposition journalists, including Andrey Loshak, claim that he also ordered media attacks on opposition figures (*Kommersant*, 11 July).

Simonyan shows RT facilities to then Prime Minister Putin. Simonyan was on Putin's 2012 presidential election campaign staff in Moscow (Rospress, 22 September 2010, Ria Novosti, 25 October 2012).

The Kremlin staffs RT and closely supervises RT's coverage, recruiting people who can convey Russian strategic messaging because of their ideological beliefs.

- The head of RT's Arabic-language service, Aydar Aganin, was rotated from the diplomatic service to manage RT's Arabic-language expansion, suggesting a close relationship between RT and Russia's foreign policy apparatus. RT's London Bureau is managed by Darya Pushkova, the daughter of Aleksey Pushkov, the current chair of the Duma Russian Foreign Affairs Committee and a former Gorbachev speechwriter (*DXB*, 26 March 2009; *MK.ru*, 13 March 2006).

- According to Simonyan, the Russian Government sets rating and viewership requirements for RT and, "since RT receives budget from the state, it must complete tasks given by the state." According to Nikolov, RT news stories are written and edited "to become news" exclusively in RT's Moscow office (Dozhd TV, 11 July; *AKT*, 4 October).

- In her interview with pro-Kremlin journalist Sergey Minaev, Simonyan complimented RT staff in the United States for passionately defending Russian positions on the air and in social media. Simonyan said: "I wish you could see...how these guys, not just on air, but on their own social networks, *Twitter*, and when giving interviews, how they defend the positions that we stand on!" ("Minaev Live," 10 April).

RT Focuses on Social Media, Building Audience

RT aggressively advertises its social media accounts and has a significant and fast-growing social media footprint. In line with its efforts to present itself as anti-mainstream and to provide viewers alternative news content, RT is making its social media operations a top priority, both to avoid broadcast TV regulations and to expand its overall audience.

- According to RT management, RT's website receives at least 500,000 unique viewers every day. Since its inception in 2005, RT videos received more than 800 million views on *YouTube* (1 million views per day), which is the highest among news outlets (see graphics for comparison with other news channels) (*AKT*, 4 October).

- According to Simonyan, the TV audience worldwide is losing trust in traditional TV broadcasts and stations, while the popularity of "alternative channels" like RT or Al Jazeera grows. RT markets itself as an "alternative channel" that is available via the Internet everywhere in the world, and it encourages interaction and social networking (*Kommersant*, 29 September).

- According to Simonyan, RT uses social media to expand the reach of its political reporting and uses well-trained people to monitor public opinion in social media commentaries (*Kommersant*, 29 September).

- According to Nikolov, RT requires its hosts to have social media accounts, in part because social media allows the distribution of content that would not be allowed on television (*Newreporter.org*, 11 October).

- Simonyan claimed in her 3 October interview to independent TV channel Dozhd that Occupy Wall Street coverage gave RT a significant audience boost.

The Kremlin spends $190 million a year on the distribution and dissemination of RT programming, focusing on hotels and satellite, terrestrial, and cable broadcasting. The Kremlin is rapidly expanding RT's availability around the world and giving it a reach comparable to channels such as Al Jazeera English. According to Simonyan, the United Kingdom and the United States are RT's most successful markets. RT does not, however, publish audience information.

- According to market research company Nielsen, RT had the most rapid growth (40 percent) among all international news channels in the United States over the past year (2012). Its audience in New York tripled and in Washington DC grew by 60% (*Kommersant*, 4 July).

- RT claims that it is surpassing Al Jazeera in viewership in New York and Washington DC (*BARB*, 20 November; RT, 21 November).

- RT states on its website that it can reach more than 550 million people worldwide and 85 million people in the United States; however, it does not publicize its actual US audience numbers (RT, 10 December).

TV News Broadcasters: Comparative Social Media Footprint

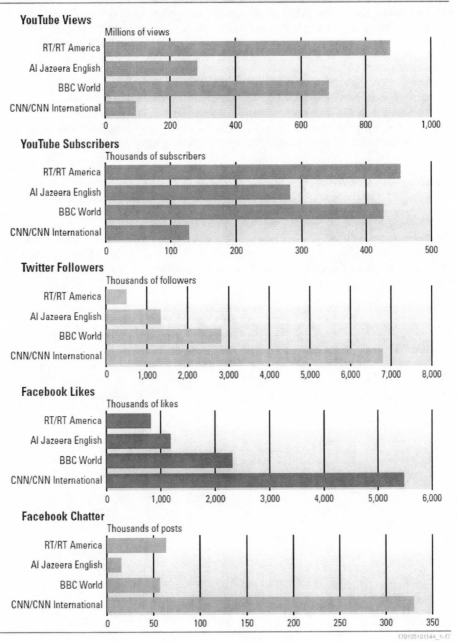

YouTube Views
Millions of views

RT/RT America
Al Jazeera English
BBC World
CNN/CNN International

0 — 200 — 400 — 600 — 800 — 1,000

YouTube Subscribers
Thousands of subscribers

RT/RT America
Al Jazeera English
BBC World
CNN/CNN International

0 — 100 — 200 — 300 — 400 — 500

Twitter Followers
Thousands of followers

RT/RT America
Al Jazeera English
BBC World
CNN/CNN International

0 — 1,000 — 2,000 — 3,000 — 4,000 — 5,000 — 6,000 — 7,000 — 8,000

Facebook Likes
Thousands of likes

RT/RT America
Al Jazeera English
BBC World
CNN/CNN International

0 — 1,000 — 2,000 — 3,000 — 4,000 — 5,000 — 6,000

Facebook Chatter
Thousands of posts

RT/RT America
Al Jazeera English
BBC World
CNN/CNN International

0 — 50 — 100 — 150 — 200 — 250 — 300 — 350

170105101144_1-17

Formal Disassociation From Kremlin Facilitates RT US Messaging

RT America formally disassociates itself from the Russian Government by using a Moscow-based autonomous nonprofit organization to finance its US operations. According to RT's leadership, this structure was set up to avoid the Foreign Agents Registration Act and to facilitate licensing abroad. In addition, RT rebranded itself in 2008 to deemphasize its Russian origin.

- According to Simonyan, RT America differs from other Russian state institutions in terms of ownership, but not in terms of financing. To disassociate RT from the Russian Government, the federal news agency RIA Novosti established a subsidiary autonomous nonprofit organization, TV-Novosti, using the formal independence of this company to establish and finance RT worldwide (Dozhd TV, 11 July).

- Nikolov claimed that RT is an "autonomous noncommercial entity," which is "well received by foreign regulators" and "simplifies getting a license." Simonyan said that RT America is not a "foreign agent" according to US law because it uses a US commercial organization for its broadcasts (*AKT*, 4 October; Dozhd TV, 11 July).

- Simonyan observed that RT's original Russia-centric news reporting did not generate sufficient audience, so RT switched to covering international and US domestic affairs and removed the words "Russia Today" from the logo "to stop scaring away the audience" (*Afisha*, 18 October; *Kommersant*, 4 July).

- RT hires or makes contractual agreements with Westerners with views that fit its agenda and airs them on RT. Simonyan said on the pro-Kremlin show "Minaev Live" on 10 April that RT has enough audience and money to be able to choose its hosts, and it chooses the hosts that "think like us," "are interested in working in the anti-mainstream," and defend RT's beliefs on social media. Some hosts and journalists do not present themselves as associated with RT when interviewing people, and many of them have affiliations to other media and activist organizations in the United States ("Minaev Live," 10 April).

Annex B

ESTIMATIVE LANGUAGE

Estimative language consists of two elements: judgments about the likelihood of developments or events occurring and levels of confidence in the sources and analytic reasoning supporting the judgments. Judgments are not intended to imply that we have proof that shows something to be a fact. Assessments are based on collected information, which is often incomplete or fragmentary, as well as logic, argumentation, and precedents.

Judgments of Likelihood. The chart below approximates how judgments of likelihood correlate with percentages. Unless otherwise stated, the Intelligence Community's judgments are not derived via statistical analysis. Phrases such as "we judge" and "we assess"—and terms such as "probable" and "likely"—convey analytical assessments.

Percent

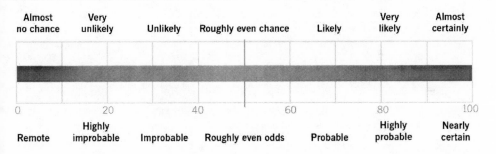

Confidence in the Sources Supporting Judgments. Confidence levels provide assessments of the quality and quantity of the source information that supports judgments. Consequently, we ascribe high, moderate, or low levels of confidence to assessments:

- **High confidence** generally indicates that judgments are based on high-quality information from multiple sources. High confidence in a judgment does not imply that the assessment is a fact or a certainty; such judgments might be wrong.

- **Moderate confidence** generally means that the information is credibly sourced and plausible but not of sufficient quality or corroborated sufficiently to warrant a higher level of confidence.

- **Low confidence** generally means that the information's credibility and/or plausibility is uncertain, that the information is too fragmented or poorly corroborated to make solid analytic inferences, or that reliability of the sources is questionable.

ENDNOTES

Chapter 1

1. Biddle, Sam. "Contrary to DNC Claim, Hacked Data Contains a Ton of Personal Donor Information." *Gawker*. Gawker Media, 17 June 2016. Web. 29 Aug. 2016. gawker.com/contrary-to-dnc-claim-hacked-data-contains-a-ton-of-pe-1782132678

2. Nakashima, Ellen. "Russian Government Hackers Penetrated DNC, Stole Opposition Research on Trump." *Washington Post*. Washington Post Company, 14 June 2016. Web. 29 Aug. 2016. www.washingtonpost.com/world/national-security/russian-government-hackers-penetrated-dnc-stole-opposition-research-on-trump/2016/06/14/cf006cb4-316e-11e6-8ff7-7b6c1998b7a0_story.html

3. Parker, Ashley, and Steve Eder. "Inside the Six Weeks Donald Trump Was a Nonstop 'Birther'." *New York Times*. New York Times Company, 02 July 2016. Web. 29 Aug. 2016. www.nytimes.com/2016/07/03/us/politics/donald-trump-birther-obama.html

4. C-SPAN. "C-SPAN: President Obama at the 2011 White House Correspondents' Dinner." YouTube. C-SPAN, 30 Apr. 2011. Web. 29 Aug. 2016. www.youtube.com/watch?v=n9mzJhvC-8E

5. Roberts, Roxanne. "I Sat next to Donald Trump at the Infamous 2011 White House Correspondents' Dinner." *Washington Post*. Washington Post Company, 28 Apr. 28. Web. 29 Aug. 2016. www.washington post.com/lifestyle/style/i-sat-next-to-donald-trump-at-the-infamous-

2011-white-house-correspondents-dinner/2016/04/27/5cf46b74-0bea-11e6-8ab8-9ad050f76d7d_story.html

6. Ibid.

7. "Night of Comedy." *Fox News*. FOX News Network, 1 May 2011. Web. 29 Aug. 2016. video.foxnews.com/v/4671338/night-of-comedy/?#sp=show-clips

8. Barbaro, Michael. "After Roasting, Trump Reacts In Character." *New York Times*. New York Times Company, 01 May 2011. Web. 29 Aug. 2016. www.nytimes.com/2011/05/02/nyregion/after-roasting-trump-reacts-in-character.html

9. Haberman, Maggie, and Alexander Burns. "Donald Trump's Presidential Run Began in an Effort to Gain Stature." *New York Times*. New York Times Company, 12 Mar. 2016. Web. 29 Aug. 2016. www.nytimes.com/2016/03/13/us/politics/donald-trump-campaign.html

10. Andrews, Wilson, K.K. Lai Rebecca, Alicia Parlapiano, and Karen Yourish. "Who Is Running for President?" *New York Times*. New York Times Company, 26 July 2016. Web. 23 Aug. 2016. www.nytimes.com/interactive/2016/us/elections/2016-presidential-candidates.html

11. Linshi, Jack. "More People Are Running for Presidential Nomination Than Ever." *Time*. Time, 7 July 2015. Web. 29 Aug. 2016. time.com/3948922/jim-gilmore-virginia-2016/

12. Agiesta, Jennifer. "Poll: Bush, Trump Rising for GOP, but Both Trail Clinton." *CNN*. Cable News Network, 1 July 2015. Web. 23 Aug. 2016. www.cnn.com/2015/07/01/politics/donald-trump-poll-hillary-clinton-jeb-bush/

13. "CNN/ORC Poll: Trump Elbows His Way to the Top." *CNN*. Turner Broadcasting System, 26 July 2015. Web. 23 Aug. 2016. www.cnn.com/2015/07/26/politics/cnn-poll-presidential-race/

14. Schreckinger, Ben. "Trump Attacks McCain: 'I like People Who Weren't Captured'" *POLITICO*. POLITICO, 19 July 2015. Web. 23 Aug. 2016. www.politico.com/story/2015/07/trump-attacks-mccain-i-like-people-who-werent-captured-120317

15. Grim, Ryan, and Danny Shea. "A Note About Our Coverage Of Donald Trump's 'Campaign'." *Huffington Post*. Huffington Post, 17 July 2015. Web. 23 Aug. 2016. www.huffingtonpost.com/entry/a-note-about-our-coverage-of-donald-trumps-campaign_us_55a8fc9ce4b0896514d0fd66

16. McDermott, John. "Nate Silver's Election Predictions a Win for Big Data, New York Times." *Advertising Age*. Advertising Age, 07

Nov. 2012. Web. 23 Aug. 2016. adage.com/article/campaign-trail/nate-silver-s-election-predictions-a-win-big-data-york-times/238182/

17. Silver, Nate. "Dear Media, Stop Freaking Out About Donald Trump's Polls." *FiveThirtyEight*. ESPN, 24 Nov. 2015. Web. 23 Aug. 2016. fivethirtyeight.com/features/dear-media-stop-freaking-out-about-donald-trumps-polls/

18. Korotayev, Artyom. "Putin Says He Considers Donald Trump to Be Absolute Leader of US Presidential Race." *TASS*. TASS, 17 Dec. 2015. Web. 23 Aug. 2016. /tass.ru/en/politics/844947

19. CNN/ORC poll results: 2016 election. (2016, May 2). *CNN*. Retrieved August 23, 2016, from http://www.cnn.com/2016/05/02/politics/2016-election-poll-results-cnn-orc/

20. Prokop, A. (2016, May 04). "John Kasich Is Dropping Out of the Republican Race—Leaving Trump as the Last Man Standing." *Vox*. Retrieved August 25, 2016, from http://www.vox.com/2016/5/4/11465204/kasich-drops-out-trump-wins

21. Andrews, Wilson, K.K. Lai Rebecca, Alicia Parlapiano, and Karen Yourish. "Who Is Running for President?" *New York Times*. New York Times Company, 26 July 2016. Web. 23 Aug. 2016. www.nytimes.com/interactive/2016/us/elections/2016-presidential-candidates.html

22. "Debate Schedule for the 2016 Presidential Primaries." *Washington Post*. Washington Post Company, 18 Apr. 2016. Web. 23 Aug. 2016. www.washingtonpost.com/graphics/politics/2016-election/debates/schedule/

23. "Fox News's Prime-Time Presidential Debate." *Fox News*. FOX News Network, 7 Aug. 2015. Web. 25 Aug. 2016. video.foxnews.com/v/4406746003001/watch-a-replay-of-fox-news-prime-time-presidential-debate/#sp=show-clips

24. Ibid.

25. Cirilli, Kevin. "Violence at Trump Rallies Shows No Sign of Abating." *Bloomberg*. Bloomberg LP, 20 June 2016. Web. 21 Sept. 2016. www.bloomberg.com/politics/articles/2016-06-20/violence-at-trump-rallies-shows-no-sign-of-abating

26. Golshan, Tara. "The Mess Surrounding Donald Trump's Campaign Manager, Explained." *Vox*. Vox Media, 14 Apr. 2016. Web. 26 Aug. 2016. www.vox.com/2016/3/29/11325328/michelle-fields-donald-trump-corey-lewandowski-assault-explained

27. Parker, Ashley. "Donald Trump Frowns on Idea of 'Toning It Down,'

Despite Aide's Comments." *New York Times*. New York Times Company, 23 Apr. 2016. Web. 25 Aug. 2016. www.nytimes.com/politics/first-draft/2016/04/23/donald-trump-frowns-on-idea-of-toning-it-down-despite-aides-comments/

28. Ibid.

29. Lee, Jasmine C. and Kevin Quealy. "The 258 People, Places and Things Donald Trump Has Insulted on Twitter: A Complete List." *New York Times*. New York Times Company, 22 Aug. 2016. Web. 23 Aug. 2016. www.nytimes.com/interactive/2016/01/28/upshot/donald-trump-twitter-insults.html

30. "CNN/ORC Poll Results: 2016 Election." *CNN*. Turner Broadcasting System, 2 May 2016. Web. 23 Aug. 2016. www.cnn.com/2016/05/02/politics/2016-election-poll-results-cnn-orc/

31. Ibid.

32. Beauchamp, Zack. "9 Questions about Benghazi You Were Too Embarrassed to Ask." *Vox*. Vox Media, 18 July 2016. Web. 25 Aug. 2016. www.vox.com/2015/10/12/9489389/benghazi-explained

33. Herszenhorn, David. "House Benghazi Report Finds No New Evidence of Wrongdoing by Hillary Clinton." *New York Times*. New York Times Company, 28 June 2016. Web. 24 Aug. 2016. www.nytimes.com/2016/06/29/us/politics/hillary-clinton-benghazi.html

34. Ibid.

35. Gass, Nick. "Trump Sharpens Benghazi Attacks on Clinton." *POLITICO*. POLITICO, 28 June 2016. Web. 24 Aug. 2016. www.politico.com/story/2016/06/donald-trump-benghazi-clinton-224911

36. Tau, Byron. "Hillary Clinton Takes Decisive Lead Over Bernie Sanders in Delegate Count, Popular Vote." *Wall Street Journal*. News Corporation, 08 June 2016. Web. 25 Aug. 2016. www.wsj.com/articles/hillary-clinton-takes-decisive-lead-over-bernie-sanders-in-delegate-count-popular-vote-1465389182

37. Sanders, Bernie. "Forever Forward." *Medium*. Medium, 12 July 2016. Web. 23 Aug. 2016. medium.com/@BernieSanders/forever-forward-ee015b23547a#.ly5te2fne

38. Rutz, David. "Sanders Campaign Manager: It Would Be Difficult for Clinton to Keep Running If Under Indictment."*Washington Free Beacon*.

Washington Free Beacon, 1 June 2016. Web. 23 Aug. 2016. freebeacon. com/politics/sanders-manager-difficult-clinton-running-indicted/

39. Landler, Mark, and Eric Lichtblau. "FBI Director James Comey Recommends No Charges for Hillary Clinton on Email." *New York Times.* New York Times Company, 05 July 2016. Web. 24 Aug. 2016. www.nytimes. com/2016/07/06/us/politics/hillary-clinton-fbi-email-comey.html

Chapter 2

1. Biddle, Sam, and Gabrielle Bluestone. "This Looks Like the DNC's Hacked Trump Oppo File." *Gawker.* Gawker Media, 15 June 2016. Web. 21 Sept. 2016. gawker.com/this-looks-like-the-dncs-hacked-trump-oppo-file-1782040426

2. Dredge, Stuart. "Yahoo to Notify Its Users about 'State-Sponsored' Hacking Attacks." *Guardian.* Guardian News and Media, 24 Dec. 2015. Web. 24 Aug. 2016. www.theguardian.com/technology/2015/dec/24/ yahoo-users-state-sponsored-hacking-attacks

3. Lord, Bob. "Notifying Our Users of Attacks by Suspected State-Sponsored Actors." *Yahoo Security.* Tumblr, 21 Dec. 2015. Web. 24 Aug. 2016. yahoo-security.tumblr.com/post/135674131435/notifying-our-users-of-attacks-by-suspected

4. Ibid.

5. The Kelly File. "Clinton Staffer's Emails Still Missing - The Perfect Storm - Judge Napolitano - The Kelly File." *YouTube.* Fox News, 09 May 2016. Web. 25 Aug. 2016. www.youtube.com/watch?v=oounggTI-jk

6. Faal, Sorcha. "Kremlin War Erupts Over Release Of Top Secret Hillary Clinton Emails." *What Does It Mean.* Sisters of Sorcha Faal, 6 May 2016. Web. 21 Sept. 2016. www.whatdoesitmean.com/index2036.htm

7. Riechmann, Deb. "Correction: Campaign 2016-Foreign Hacking Story." *The Big Story.* Associated Press, 23 May 2016. Web. 21 Sept. 2016. bigstory.ap.org/article/936b3fe969a540559ecc7503a547e2ad/us-intelligence-foreign-hackers-spying-campaigns

8. Nakashima, Ellen. "National Intelligence Director: Hackers Have Targeted 2016 Presidential Campaigns." *Washington Post.* Washington

Post Company, 18 May 2016. Web. 25 Aug. 2016. www.washingtonpost.
com/world/national-security/national-intelligence-director-hackers-
have-tried-to-spy-on-2016-presidential-campaigns/2016/05/18/2b1745c0-
1d0d-11e6-b6e0-c53b7ef63b45_story.html

9. Glendinning, Lee. "Obama, McCain Computers 'Hacked' during Election Campaign." *Guardian*. Guardian News and Media, 07 Nov. 2008. Web. 24 Aug. 2016. www.theguardian.com/global/2008/nov/07/obama-white-house-usa

10. Issakof, Michael. "Chinese Hacked Obama, McCain Campaigns, Took Internal Documents, Officials Say." *NBC Investigations*. NBC News, 6 June 2013. Web. 25 Aug. 2016. investigations.nbcnews.com/_news/2013/06/06/18807056-chinese-hacked-obama-mccain-campaigns-took-internal-documents-officials-say

11. Ibid.

Chapter 3

1. Hackard, Mark. "Inside the KGB's Intelligence School." *Espionage History Archive*. WordPress, 02 Apr. 2015. Web. 24 Aug. 2016. espionagehistoryarchive.com/2015/03/24/the-kgbs-intelligence-school/

2. "Biography." *Vladimir Putin – Personal Website*. Kremlin, 4 Mar. 2012. Web. 22 Sept. 2016. en.putin.kremlin.ru/bio

3. Hoffman, David. "Putin's Career Rooted in Russia's KGB." *Washington Post* 30 Jan. 2000, Foreign Service sec.: A1+. *Washington Post*. Washington Post Company, 30 Jan. 2000. Web. 22 Sept. 2016. www.washingtonpost.com/wp-srv/inatl/longterm/russiagov/putin.htm

4. Rezunkov, Viktor and Tatyana Voltskaya. "15 Years Later, Questions Remain About Death Of The Man Who Made Putin." *Radio Free Europe Radio Liberty*. RFE/RL, 24 Feb. 2015. Web. 25 Aug. 2016. www.rferl.org/content/questions-remain-about-death-of-man-who-made-putin/26867539.html

5. Satter, David. "The Unsolved Mystery Behind the Act of Terror That Brought Putin to Power." *National Review Online*. National Review, Inc., 17 Aug. 2016. Web. 22 Sept. 2016. www.nationalreview.com/article/439060/vladimir-putin-1999-russian-apartment-house-bombings-was-putin-responsible

6. Richelson, Jeffrey. "Cheka and RU." *Sword and Shield: The Soviet Intelligence and Security Apparatus.* 1st ed. Cambridge, MA: Ballinger Pub., 1986. pp. 2-8. Print.

7. Ibid.

8. Soldatov, Andreï and Irina Borogan. *The New Nobility: The Restoration of Russia's Security State and the Enduring Legacy of the KGB.* 1st ed. New York, NY: Public Affairs, 2010. Print.

9. Richelson, Jeffrey. "Structure and Function." *Sword and Shield: The Soviet Intelligence and Security Apparatus.* 1st ed. Cambridge, MA: Ballinger Pub., 1986. p. 21. Print.

10. Owen, Sir Robert. "The Litvinenko Inquiry." (n.d.): n. pag. *The Litvinenko Inquiry.* British Parliament, 21 Jan. 2016. Web. 26 Aug. 2016. www. litvinenkoinquiry.org/files/lit210116.pdf

11. Soldatov, Andreï and Irina Brogan. "The Mutation of the Russian Secret Services." *Agentura.ru.* Agentura.ru, n.d. Web. 25 Aug. 2016. www. agentura.ru/english/dosie/mutation/

12. United States of America v. Anna Chapman, and Mikhail Semenko. U.S. District Court, Southern District of New York. 27 June 2010. *US Department of Justice.* US Department of Justice, 28 June 2010. Web. 26 Aug. 2016. www.justice.gov/sites/default/files/opa/legacy/2010/06/28/062810complaint1.pdf

13. Clark, Andrew. "Anna Chapman's Call to Father Led to FBI Spy Arrests." *Guardian.* Guardian News and Media, 11 July 2010. Web. 26 Aug. 2016. www.theguardian.com/world/2010/jul/12/anna-chapman-call-father-fbi-spy-arrests

14. United States of America v. Anna Chapman, and Mikhail Semenko. U.S. District Court, Southern District of New York. 27 June 2010. *US Department of Justice.* US Department of Justice, 28 June 2010. Web. 26 Aug. 2016. www.justice.gov/sites/default/files/opa/legacy/2010/06/28/062810complaint1.pdf

15. "Ten Alleged Secret Agents Arrested in the United States." *US Department of Justice.* US Department of Justice, Office of Public Affairs, 28 June 2010. Web. 22 Sept. 2016. www.justice.gov/opa/pr/ten-alleged-secret-agents-arrested-united-states

16. Adams, Stephen. "Anna Chapman: Profile of a 'Russian Spy'" *Telegraph.* Telegraph Media Group, 2 July 2010. Web. 27 Aug. 2016. www.telegraph.

co.uk/news/worldnews/europe/russia/7867512/Anna-Chapman-profile-of-a-Russian-spy.html

17. Forrest, Brett. "The Big Russian Life of Anna Chapman, Ex-Spy."
     POLITICO PRO. POLITICO, 4 Jan. 2012. Web. 27 Aug. 2016. www.
     politico.com/states/new-york/albany/story/2012/01/the-big-russian-
     life-of-anna-chapman-ex-spy-067223

18. Katz, Emily Tess. "Anna Chapman, Alleged Russian Spy, Was Dating
     60-Year-Old Divorced Dad Michael Bittan." *Huffington Post.* AOL, 1 July
     2010. Web. 27 Aug. 2016. www.huffingtonpost.com/2010/07/01/anna-
     chapman-alleged-russ_n_632543.html

19. Higgins, Andrew, and Mary Sheridan Beth. "US and Russia Complete
     Spy Swap." *Washington Post.* Washington Post Company, 10 July 2010.
     Web. 27 Aug. 2016. www.washingtonpost.com/wp-dyn/content/article/
     2010/07/09/AR2010070901956.html

20. "Federal Security Service (FSB) Federal'naya Sluzhba Bezopasnosti."
     GlobalSecurity.org. GlobalSecurity.org, n.d. Web. 27 Aug. 2016. global
     security.org/intell/world/russia/fsb.htm

21. Hoffman, David. "Putin's Career Rooted in Russia's KGB." *Washington
     Post* 30 Jan. 2000, Foreign Service sec.: A1+. *Washington Post.*
     Washington Post Company, 30 Jan. 2000. Web. 22 Sept. 2016. www.
     washingtonpost.com/wp-srv/inatl/longterm/russiagov/putin.htm

22. Docherty, Neil. "Putin's Way." *Frontline.* PBS. Arlington, VA, 13 Jan.
     2015. Television.

Chapter 4

1.   Goldstein, Steve. "Trump May Build Hotels In USSR." *Philly.
     com.* Philadelphia Media Network, PBC, 07 July 1987. Web.
     27 Aug. 2016. articles.philly.com/1987-07-07/news/26200012_1_trump-
     tower-second-largest-soviet-city-soviet-officials

2.   "The Donald Trump of Russia." *Closing Bell.* CNBC. Englewood
     Cliffs, NJ, 18 May 2015. *CNBC.* Web. 27 Aug. 2016. video.cnbc.com/
     gallery/?video=3000380510

3.   Stone, Peter, David Smith, Ben Jacobs, Alec Luhn, and Rupert Neate.
     "Donald Trump and Russia: A Web That Grows More Tangled All the

Time." *Guardian*. Guardian News and Media, 30 July 2016. Web. 27 Aug. 2016. www.theguardian.com/us-news/2016/jul/30/donald-trump-paul-manafort-ukraine-russia-putin-ties

4. Wagner, Daniel, and Aram Roston. "The Donald and the Dictator." *BuzzFeed*. BuzzFeed Inc., 7 June 2016. Web. 12 Aug. 2016. https://www.buzzfeed.com/danielwagner/how-trump-tried-to-get-qaddafis-cash?utm_term=.uodEg04Qd4#.lw9AqKxm6x.

5. Trump, Donald. "Do you think Putin will be going to The Miss Universe Pageant in November in Moscow - if so, will he become my new best friend?." 18 Jul. 2013, 8:17 PM. Tweet.

6. Trump, Donald. "I just got back from Russia-learned lots & lots. Moscow is a very interesting and amazing place! U.S. MUST BE VERY SMART AND VERY STRATEGIC." 10 Nov. 2013, 6:44 PM. Tweet.

7. Richter, Greg. "Trump Trashes Other Candidates, Praises Putin on 'O'Reilly'" *Newsmax*. Newsmax Media, 16 June 2015. Web. 27 Aug. 2016. http://www.newsmax.com/Politics/Donald-Trump-Bill-OReilly-respects-Putin/2015/06/16/id/650840/#ixzz4Io7IAyVD.

8. Crowley, Michael. "When Donald Trump Brought Miss Universe to Moscow." *POLITICO*. POLITICO, 15 May 2016. Web. 28 Aug. 2016. www.politico.com/story/2016/05/donald-trump-russia-moscow-miss-universe-223173

9. "Yuri Bezmenov - KGB Defector on "Useful Idiots" and the True Face of Communism." *YouTube*. Saturnus Lateinos, 17 Dec. 2014. Web. 28 Aug. 2016. www.youtube.com/watch?v=K4kHiUAjTvQ

10. Schreyer, Natalie. "Donald Trump Got Duped by a Gorbachev Impersonator." *Mother Jones*. Foundation for National Progress, 5 July 2016. Web. 28 Aug. 2016.www.motherjones.com/politics/2016/06/donald-trump-mikhail-gorbachev-impersonator

11. Burkett, Randy. "An Alternative Framework for Agent Recruitment: From MICE to RASCLS." *Studies in Intelligence* 57.1 (2013): n. pag. *Central Intelligence Agency*. Central Intelligence Agency, Mar. 2013. Web. 28 Aug. 2016. www.cia.gov/library/center-for-the-study-of-intelligence/csi-publications/csi-studies/studies/vol.-57-no.-1-a/vol.-57-no.-1-a-pdfs/Burkett-MICE%20to%20RASCALS.pdf

12. Fontova, Humberto. "What's Behind the Trump-Putin "Bromance?" *Townhall*. Salem Communications Corporation, 22 Jan. 2016. Web. 28

Aug. 2016. townhall.com/columnists/humbertofontova/2016/01/22/whats-behind-the-trumpputin-bromance-n2108551

13. Nguyen, Tina. "Putin Endorses Trump, Says Disgraced FIFA Chief Should Win the Nobel Prize." *Vanity Fair*. Conde Nast, 17 Dec. 2015. Web. 29 Aug. 2016 www.vanityfair.com/news/2015/12/putin-trump-endorsement

14. Korotayev, Artyom. "Putin Says He Considers Donald Trump to Be Absolute Leader of US Presidential Race." *TASS*. TASS, 17 Dec. 2015. Web. 23 Aug. 2016. /tass.ru/en/politics/844947

15. Foer, Franklin. "Putin's Puppet." *Slate*. Slate Group, 21 July 2016. Web. 12 Aug. 2016. www.slate.com/articles/news_and_politics/cover_story/2016/07/vladimir_putin_has_a_plan_for_destroying_the_west_and_it_looks_a_lot_like.html

16. Helderman, Rosalind S. and Tom Hamburger. "Former Mafia-Linked Figure Describes Association with Trump." *Washington Post*. Washington Post Company, 17 May 2016. Web. 12 Aug. 2016. www.washingtonpost.com/politics/former-mafia-linked-figure-describes-association-with-trump/2016/05/17/cec6c2c6-16d3-11e6-aa55-670cabef46e0_story.html

17. Ibid.

18. Mcintire, Mike. "Donald Trump Settled a Real Estate Lawsuit, and a Criminal Case Was Closed." *New York Times*. New York Times Company, 05 Apr. 2016. Web. 12 Aug. 2016. www.nytimes.com/2016/04/06/us/politics/donald-trump-soho-settlement.html?_r=1

19. Helderman, Rosalind S. and Tom Hamburger. "Former Mafia-Linked Figure Describes Association with Trump." *Washington Post*. Washington Post Company, 17 May 2016. Web. 12 Aug. 2016. www.washingtonpost.com/politics/former-mafia-linked-figure-describes-association-with-trump/2016/05/17/cec6c2c6-16d3-11e6-aa55-670cabef46e0_story.html

20. Bagli, Charles V. "Brass Knuckles Over to Broadway; MTA and Landlord Are Fighting It Out over Rent and Renovations." *New York Times*. New York Times Company, 08 Aug. 2000. Web. 12 Aug. 2016. www.nytimes.com/2000/08/09/nyregion/brass-knuckles-over-2-broadway-mta-landlord-are-fighting-it-over-rent.html

21. Schreckinger, Ben. "Trump's Mob-Linked Ex-Associate Gives $5,400 to Campaign." *POLITICO.* POLITICO, 26 Aug. 2016. Web. 31 Aug. 2016. www.politico.com/story/2016/08/donald-trump-russia-felix-sater-227434

22. Stempel, Jonathan and Deepa Seetharaman. "Donald Trump Sued for Fraud over Trump SoHo Condo." *Reuters.* Thomson Reuters, 03 Aug. 2010. Web. 31 Aug. 2016. www.reuters.com/article/us-trumpsoho-lawsuit-idUSTRE67232X20100803

23. McIntire, Mike. "Donald Trump Settled a Real Estate Lawsuit, and a Criminal Case Was Closed." *New York Times.* New York Times Company, 05 Apr. 2016. Web. 12 Aug. 2016. www.nytimes.com/2016/04/06/us/politics/donald-trump-soho-settlement.html?_r=1

24. Karmin, Craig. "Trump SoHo Hotel Lender Plans to Put Property Up for Sale." *Wall Street Journal.* News Corporation, 16 Sept. 2014. Web. 31 Aug. 2016. www.wsj.com/articles/trump-soho-hotel-lender-plans-to-put-property-up-for-sale-1410885344

25. Stone, Peter. "Trump's New Right-Hand Man Has History of Controversial Clients and Deals." *Guardian.* Guardian News and Media, 27 Apr. 2016. Web. 12 Aug. 2016. www.theguardian.com/us-news/2016/apr/27/paul-manafort-donald-trump-campaign-past-clients

26. Ibid.

27. Mufson, Steven, and Tom Hamburger. "Inside Trump Adviser Manafort's World of Politics and Global Financial Dealmaking." *Washington Post.* Washington Post Company, 26 Apr. 2016. Web. 12 Aug. 2016. www.washingtonpost.com/politics/in-business-as-in-politics-trump-adviser-no-stranger-to-controversial-figures/2016/04/26/970db232-08c7-11e6-b283-e79d81c63c1b_story.html

28. Stone, Peter. "Trump's New Right-Hand Man Has History of Controversial Clients and Deals." *Guardian.* Guardian News and Media, 27 Apr. 2016. Web. 12 Aug. 2016. www.theguardian.com/us-news/2016/apr/27/paul-manafort-donald-trump-campaign-past-clients>.

29. Smith, Ben, and Meredith Kennedy. "Trump Adviser's Ties Raise Security Questions." *BuzzFeed.* BuzzFeed Inc., 6 May 2016. Web. 22 Sept. 2016. www.buzzfeed.com/bensmith/manafort-russia?utm_term=.psV0doRgKR#.prQ8J0EWbE

30. Stone, Peter. "Trump's New Right-Hand Man Has History of

Controversial Clients and Deals." *Guardian*. Guardian News and Media, 27 Apr. 2016. Web. 11 Aug. 2016. www.theguardian.com/us-news/2016/apr/27/paul-manafort-donald-trump-campaign-past-clients>.

31. Harding, Luke. "WikiLeaks Cables Link Russian Mafia Boss to EU Gas Supplies." *Guardian*. Guardian News and Media, 01 Dec. 2010. Web. 12 Aug. 2016. www.theguardian.com/world/2010/dec/01/wikileaks-cables-russian-mafia-gas

32. "US Embassy Cables: Gas Supplies Linked to Russian Mafia." *Guardian*. Guardian News and Media, 01 Dec. 2010. Web. 12 Sept. 2016. www.theguardian.com/world/us-embassy-cables-documents/182121

33. Stone, Peter. "Trump's New Right-Hand Man Has History of Controversial Clients and Deals." *Guardian*. Guardian News and Media, 27 Apr. 2016. Web. 11 Aug. 2016. www.theguardian.com/us-news/2016/apr/27/paul-manafort-donald-trump-campaign-past-clients>.

34. Ibid.

35. Kramer, Andrew E., Mike Mcintire, and Barry Meier. "Secret Ledger in Ukraine Lists Cash for Donald Trump's Campaign Chief." *New York Times*. New York Times Company, 14 Aug. 2016. Web. 17 Aug. 2016. www.nytimes.com/2016/08/15/us/politics/paul-manafort-ukraine-donald-trump.html?_r=0

36. Ibid.

37. Garver, Rob. "Is this Why Trump Is Changing Gears? Report Says Manafort Organized Anti-NATO Protests." *Fiscal Times*. Fiscal Times Media Group, LLC, 17 Aug. 2016. Web. 17 Aug. 2016. www.thefiscaltimes.com/2016/08/17/Trump-s-Campaign-Chair-Organized-Anti-NATO-Protests-Ukraine-Report

38. Mider, Zachary. "Trump Russia Adviser Carter Page Interview." *Bloomberg*. Bloomberg LP, 30 Mar. 2016. Web. 12 Aug. 2016. www.bloomberg.com/politics/articles/2016-03-30/trump-russia-adviser-carter-page-interview

39. Page, Carter. "New Slaves, Global Edition: Russia, Iran and the Segregation of the World Economy | Global Policy Journal - Practitioner, Academic, Global Governance, International Law, Economics, Security, Institutions, Comment & Opinion, Media, Events, Journal." *Global Policy*. Wiley Blackwell, 10 Feb. 2015. Web. 13 Aug. 2016. www.globalpolicyjournal.com/blog/10/02/2015/new-slaves-global-edition-russia-iran-and-segregation-world-economy

40. Wilkie, Christina, and S.V. Date. "Trump Foreign Policy Adviser Travels to Russia Prior to Changes in GOP Platform."*Huffington Post.* AOL, 3 Aug. 2016. Web. 12 Aug. 2016.www.huffingtonpost.com/entry/ carter-page-trump-russia_us_57a0f329e4b0693164c2fb41

41. "Richard Burt." *McLarty Associates.* N.p., n.d. Web. 17 Aug. 2016. maglobal.com/about-us/our-team/richard-burt/

42. Carden, James. "Trump Attempted a Foreign Policy Makeover Today. Did It Work?" *Nation.* Nation Company, L.P., 27 Apr. 2016. Web. 17 Aug. 2016. www.thenation.com/article/trump-attempted-a-foreign-policy-makeover-today-did-it-work/

43. "Dimitri K. Simes." *Center for the National Interest.* N.p., n.d. Web. 17 Aug. 2016. cftni.org/expert/dimitri-k-simes-2/

44. Kirchick, James. "Donald Trump's Russia Connections." *POLITICO.* POLITICO, 29 Apr. 2016. Web. 17 Aug. 2016. www.politico.eu/article/ donald-trumps-russia-connections-foreign-policy-presidential-campaign/

45. Ibid.

46. Priest, Dana. "Trump Adviser Michael T. Flynn on His Dinner with Putin and Why Russia Today Is Just like CNN." *Washington Post.* Washington Post Company, 15 Aug. 2016. Web. 29 Aug. 2016. /www.washington-post.com/news/checkpoint/wp/2016/08/15/trump-adviser-michael-t-flynn-on-his-dinner-with-putin-and-why-russia-today-is-just-like-cnn/

47. Diamond, Jeremy, and Greg Botelho. "Putin Praises 'Bright and Talented' Donald Trump." *CNN.* Turner Broadcasting System, 17 Dec. 2015. Web. 30 Aug. 2016. www.cnn.com/2015/12/17/politics/russia-putin-trump/

48. Dickey, Jeffrey V., Thomas Everett B., Zane Galvach M., Matthew Mesko J., and Anton Soltis V. "Russian Political Warfare: Origin, Evolution, and Application." *Calhoun.* Dudley Knox Library, June 2015. Web. 30 Aug. 2016. calhoun.nps.edu/bitstream/handle/10945/45838/15Jun_Dickey_ Everett_Galvach_Mesko_Soltis.pdf?sequence=1&isAllowed=y

49. Taub, Amanda. "DNC Hack Raises a Frightening Question: What's Next?" *New York Times.* New York Times Company, 29 July 2016. Web. 30 Aug. 2016. www.nytimes.com/2016/07/30/world/europe/dnc-hack-russia.html

50. Ibid.

51. Ibid.

52. Remnick, David. "Trump and Putin: A Love Story." *New Yorker*. Conde Nast, 03 Aug. 2016. Web. 30 Sept. 2016. www.newyorker.com/news/news-desk/trump-and-putin-a-love-story

53. Remnick, David. "Danse Macabre." *New Yorker*. Conde Nast, 18 Mar. 2013. Web. 30 Sept. 2016. www.newyorker.com/magazine/2013/03/18/danse-macabre

54. Foer, Franklin. "Vladimir Putin Has a Plan for Destroying the West— and It Looks a Lot Like Donald Trump." *Slate Magazine*. Slate Group, 21 July 2016. Web. 30 Aug. 2016. www.slate.com/articles/news_and_politics/cover_story/2016/07/vladimir_putin_has_a_plan_for_destroying_the_west_and_it_looks_a_lot_like.html

55. Applebaum, Anne. ""I Didn't Think It Could Be Done in the United States"." Interview by Jacob Weisberg. *Slate*. Slate Group, 28 July 2016. Web. 30 Aug. 2016.

56. Ibid.

57. Gregory, Paul Roderick. "What If Vladimir Putin Has Hillary Clinton's Emails?" Forbes. Forbes, Inc., 12 Feb. 2016. Web. 30 Aug. 2016. www.forbes.com/sites/paulroderickgregory/2016/02/12/vladimir-putin-hillary-clinton-emails/#4ec4e9e57fe6

58. Ibid.

59. Ibid.

60. Morell, Michael J. "I Ran the CIA. Now I'm Endorsing Hillary Clinton." *New York Times*. New York Times Company, 04 Aug. 2016. Web. 26 Aug. 2016. www.nytimes.com/2016/08/05/opinion/campaign-stops/i-ran-the-cia-now-im-endorsing-hillary-clinton.html

Chapter 5

1. Meeks, Karen Robes. "Hillary Clinton Compares Vladimir Putin's Actions in Ukraine to Adolf Hitler's in Nazi Germany." Long Beach Press Telegram. Digital First Media, 05 Mar. 2014. Web. 30 Aug. 2016. www.presstelegram.com/general-news/20140304/hillary-clinton-compares-vladimir-putins-actions-in-ukraine-to-adolf-hitlers-in-nazi-germany

2. Diamond, Jeremy, and Greg Botelho. "Putin Praises 'Bright and Talented' Donald Trump." CNN. Turner Broadcasting System, 17 Dec. 2015. Web. 30 Aug. 2016. www.cnn.com/2015/12/17/politics/russia-putin-trump/

3. Kreutz, Liz. "Hillary Clinton Psychoanalyzes Vladimir Putin." ABC News. Disney-ABC Television Group, 08 Apr. 2014. Web. 30 Aug. 2016. abcnews.go.com/blogs/politics/2014/04/hillary-clinton-psychoanalyzes-vladimir-putin/

4. Aron, Leon. "The Putin Doctrine." *Foreign Affairs*. Council on Foreign Relations, 11 Mar. 2013. Web. 26 Aug. 2016. www.foreignaffairs.com/articles/russian-federation/2013-03-08/putin-doctrine

5. "Russia Security Paper Designates Nato as Threat." *BBC News*. British Broadcasting Corporation, 31 Dec. 2015. Web. 28 Aug. 2016. www.bbc.com/news/world-europe-35208636

6. Rose, Charlie. "Charlie Rose on How Vladimir Putin Sees the World." *Charlie Rose*. PBS. Arlington, VA, 19 June 2015. *PBS Newshour*. Web. 22 Sept. 2016. www.pbs.org/newshour/bb/charlie-rose-vladimir-putin-sees-world/

7. Lazar, Alex, and Alexey Eremenko. "Here's Why Russians Like Donald Trump (Sort of)." *NBC News*. NBCUniversal News Group24, 24 Aug. 2016. Web. 30 Aug. 2016. www.nbcnews.com/news/world/why-russians-donald-trump-sort-n634626

8. Rose, Charlie. "Charlie Rose on How Vladimir Putin Sees the World." *Charlie Rose*. PBS. Arlington, VA, 19 June 2015. *PBS Newshour*. Web. 22 Sept. 2016. www.pbs.org/newshour/bb/charlie-rose-vladimir-putin-sees-world/

9. "Relations with Russia." *NATO*. NATO, 18 May 2016. Web. 27 Aug. 2016.

10. www.nato.int/cps/en/natolive/topics_50090.htm

11. "Ukraine Crisis: Obama Orders Ban on Crimea Trade." *BBC News*. British Broadcasting Corporation, 20 Dec. 2014. Web. 27 Aug. 2016. www.bbc.com/news/world-europe-30558502

12. "Ukraine Crisis: Russia and Sanctions." *BBC News*. British Broadcasting Corporation, 19 Dec. 2014. Web. 27 Aug. 2016. www.bbc.com/news/world-europe-26672800

13. Trump, Donald. "Transcript: Donald Trump on NATO, Turkey's Coup Attempt and the World." Interview by David E. Sanger and Maggie Haberman. *New York Times*. New York Times Company, 21 July 2016. Web. 27 Aug. 2016.

14. Ibid.

15. Meeks, Karen Robes. "Hillary Clinton Compares Vladimir Putin's Actions in Ukraine to Adolf Hitler's in Nazi Germany." Long Beach Press Telegram. Digital First Media, 05 Mar. 2014. Web. 30 Aug. 2016. www.presstelegram.com/general-news/20140304/hillary-clinton-compares-

vladimir-putins-actions-in-ukraine-to-adolf-hitlers-in-nazi-germany

16.   Diamond, Jeremy. "Timeline: Donald Trump's Praise for Vladimir Putin." *CNN*. Turner Broadcasting System, 21 July 2016. Web. 29 Aug. 2016. www. cnn.com/2016/07/28/politics/donald-trump-vladimir-putin-quotes/

17.   Kalb, Marvin L. *Imperial Gamble: Putin, Ukraine, and the New Cold War*. 1st ed. Washington, D.C.: Brookings Institution Press, 2015. Print.

18.   Lazar, Alex, and Alexey Eremenko. "Here's Why Russians Like Donald Trump (Sort of)." *NBC News*. NBCUniversal News Group, 24 Aug. 2016. Web. 30 Aug. 2016. www.nbcnews.com/news/world/why-russians-donald-trump-sort-n634626

19.   Schreckinger, Ben. "Clinton Urges More Financial, Military Aid to Ukraine." *POLITICO*. POLITICO, 21 Jan. 2015. Web. 28 Aug. 2016.www.politico. com/story/2015/01/hillary-clinton-ukraine-aid-military-financial-114462

20.   Bradner, Eric and David Wright. "Trump Says Putin Is 'Not Going to Go into Ukraine,' Despite Crimea." *CNN*. Turner Broadcasting System, 1 Aug. 2016. Web. 28 Aug. 2016. www.cnn.com/2016/07/31/politics/donald-trump-russia-ukraine-crimea-putin/

Chapter 6

1.   Zetter, Kim. "Russian 'Sandworm' Hack Has Been Spying on Foreign Governments for Years." *Wired*. Conde Nast, 14 Oct. 2014. Web. 28 Aug. 2016. www.wired.com/2014/10/russian-sandworm-hack-isight

2.   Bejtlich, Richard. "Putting the A, P, and T in the APT." 2011 Business Security Conference. Honolulu Design Center, Honolulu. 7 Sept. 2011. *Hawaiian Telcom*. Web. 12 Aug. 2016. www.hawaiiantel.com/Portals/1/Bejtlich.pdf

3.   Alperovitch, Dmitri. "Bears in the Midst: Intrusion into the Democratic National Committee." Web log post. *CrowdStrike*. N.p., 15 June 2016. Web. 28 Aug. 2016. www.crowdstrike.com/blog/bears-midst-intrusion-democratic-national-committee/

4.   Reuvers, Paul and Marc Simons. "IBM Selectric Bug." *Crypto Museum*. N.p., Aug.-Sept. 2010. Web. 29 Aug. 2016. cryptomuseum.com/covert/bugs/selectric/

5.   Kaplan, Fred M. "'Could Something Like This Really Happen?'" *Dark Territory: The Secret History of Cyber War*. 1st ed. New York, NY: Simon & Schuster, 2016. p. 16. Print.

6.   Kaplan, Fred M. "Solar Sunrise, Moonlight Gaze." *Dark Territory: The Secret History of Cyber War*. 1st ed. New York, NY: Simon & Schuster, 2016. pp. 78-88. Print.

7.   Cutler, Terry. "The Anatomy of an Advanced Persistent Threat | SecurityWeek.Com." *Security Week*. Wired Business Media, 06 Dec. 2010. Web. 27 Aug. 2016. www.securityweek.com/anatomy-advanced-persistent-threat

8.   "Microsoft Security Intelligence Report: Strontium." Web log post. *TechNet*. Microsoft, 16 Nov. 2015. Web. 28 Aug. 2016. blogs.technet.microsoft.com/mmpc/2015/11/16/microsoft-security-intelligence-report-strontium/

9.   Hacquebord, Feike. "Pawn Storm's Domestic Spying Campaign Revealed; Ukraine and US Top Global Targets." Web log post. *Trend Labs Security Intelligence Blog*. Trend Micro, 18 Aug. 2015. Web. 30 Aug. 2016. blog.trendmicro.com/trendlabs-security-intelligence/pawn-storms-domestic-spying-campaign-revealed-ukraine-and-us-top-global-targets/

10. Kharouni, Loucif, Feike Hacquebord, Numaan Huq, Jim Gogolinski, Fernando Mercês, Alfred Remorin, and Douglas Otis. *Operation Pawn Storm: Using Decoys to Evade Detection*. *Trend Micro*. Trend Micro Inc., 22 Oct. 2014. Web. 9 Aug. 2016. www.trendmicro.com/cloud-content/us/pdfs/security-intelligence/white-papers/wp-operation-pawn-storm.pdf

11. Ibid.

12. Ibid.

13. Ibid.

14. Ibid.

15. Hacquebord, Feike. "Pawn Storm's Domestic Spying Campaign Revealed; Ukraine and US Top Global Targets." Web log post. *Trend Labs Security Intelligence Blog*. Trend Micro, 18 Aug. 2015. Web. 30 Aug. 2016. blog.trendmicro.com/trendlabs-security-intelligence/pawn-storms-domestic-spying-campaign-revealed-ukraine-and-us-top-global-targets/

16. F-Secure Labs. *THE DUKES: 7 Years of Russian Cyberespionage*. Rep. F-Secure, 5 Sept. 2015. Web. 30 Aug. 2016. www.f-secure.com/documents/996508/1030745/dukes_whitepaper.pdf

17. Ibid.

18. Silva, Cristina. "Meet Turla, the Russian Hacking Group Using Commercial Satellites to Spy on US, Europe." *International Business Times*. IBT Media, 09 Sept. 2015. Web. 30 Aug. 2016.www.ibtimes.com/ meet-turla-russian-hacking-group-using-commercial-satellites-spy-us-europe-2089116

19. "Breaking the Code on Russian Malware." Web log post. *Recorded Future Blog*. Recorded Future, 20 Nov. 2016. Web. 28 Aug. 2016.www.recorded-future.com/russian-malware-analysis/

20. Ibid.

21. Nakashima, Ellen. "Cyber-Intruder Sparks Response, Debate." *Washington Post*. Washington Post Company, 8 Dec. 2011. Web. 28 Aug. 2016. www.washingtonpost.com/national/national-security/cyber-intruder-sparks-response-debate/2011/12/06/gIQAxLuFgO_story.html

22. *The Waterbug Attack Group*. Security Response. Symantec, 14 Jan. 2016. Web. 28 Aug. 2016. www.symantec.com/content/en/us/enterprise/ media/security_response/whitepapers/waterbug-attack-group.pdf

23. *2015 Global Threat Report*. Rep. CrowdStrike, 14 Jan. 2016. Web. 31 Aug. 2016.   go.crowdstrike.com/rs/281-OBQ-266/images/15GlobalThreat Report.pdf

24. "Denial-of-Service: The Estonian Cyberwar and Its Implications for US National Security." *International Affairs Review*. Elliott School of International Affairs, n.d. Web. 30 Aug. 2016. www.iar-gwu.org/node/65

25. Traynor, Ian. "Russia Accused of Unleashing Cyberwar to Disable Estonia." *Guardian*. Guardian News and Media, 16 May 2007. Web. 29 Aug. 2016. www.theguardian.com/world/2007/may/17/topstories3. russia

26. "Estonia Fines Man for 'Cyber War.'" *BBC News*. British Broadcasting Corporation, 25 Jan. 2008. Web. 29 Aug. 2016. news.bbc.co.uk/2/hi/ technology/7208511.stm

27. *"Georgia: Avoiding War in South Ossetia"*. Rep. International Crisis Group, 26 Nov. 2014. Web. 29 Aug. 2016. unpan1.un.org/intradoc/groups /public/documents/UNTC/UNPAN019224.pdf

28. "If Kosovo Goes Free." *Economist*. Economist Group, 29 Nov. 2007. Web. 29 Aug. 2016. www.economist.com/node/10225052.

29. Hollis, David, "Cyberwar Case Study: Georgia 2008." *Small Wars*

Journal. Small Wars Foundation, 6 Jan. 2011. Web 29 Aug. 2016. http://smallwarsjournal.com/blog/journal/docs-temp/639-hollis.pdf.

30. Schachtman, Noah. "Top Georgian Official: Moscow Cyber Attacked Us – We Just Can't Prove It." *Wired.* Conde Nast, 6 Jan. 2011. Web. 29 Aug. 2016. www.wired.com/2009/03/georgia-blames

31. F-Secure Labs. *BLACKENERGY & QUEDAGH: The Convergence of Crimeware and APT Attacks.* Rep. F-Secure, n.d. Web. 29 Aug. 2016. www.f-secure. com/documents/996508/1030745/blackenergy_whitepaper.pdf

32. US-CCU. *Overview by the US-CCU of the Cyber Campaign Against Georgia in August of 2008.* Campaign Overview. The U.S. Cyber Consequences Unit, Aug. 2009. Web. 29 Aug. 2016. www.registan.net/wp-content/uploads/2009/08/US-CCU-Georgia-Cyber-Campaign-Overview.pdf

33. *APT28: A Window Into Russia's Cyber Espionage Operations?* Rep. FireEye, 5 Feb. 2016. Web. 29 Aug. 2016. www.fireeye.com/content/dam/fireeye-www/global/en/current-threats/pdfs/rpt-apt28.pdf

34. United States of America. Library of Congress. Global Legal Monitor. *Lithuania: Ban on Nazi and Soviet Symbols.* By Peter Roudik. Law Library of Congress, 2 July 2008. Web. 29 Aug. 2016. www.loc.gov/law/foreign-news/article/lithuania-ban-on-nazi-and-soviet-symbols/

35. Rhodin, Sara. "Hackers Tag Lithuanian Web Sites with Soviet Symbols." *New York Times.* New York Times Company, 30 June 2008. Web. 29 Aug. 2016. www.nytimes.com/2008/07/01/world/europe/01baltic.html ?_r=1

36. Danchev, Dancho. "300 Lithuanian Sites Hacked by Russian Hackers | ZDNet." *ZDNet.* CBS Interactive, 2 July 2008. Web. 29 Aug. 2016. www. zdnet.com/article/300-lithuanian-sites-hacked-by-russian-hackers/

37. Krebs, Brian. "Lithuania Weathers Cyber Attack, Braces for Round 2." *Washington Post.* Washington Post Company, 3 July 2008. Web. 29 Aug. 2016. voices.washingtonpost.com/securityfix/2008/07/lithuania_weathers_cyber_attac_1.html

38. Counter Threat Unit Research Team. "Kyrgyzstan Under DDoS Attack From Russia." Web log post. *Secure Works Blog.* Secure Works Corp, 27 Jan. 2009. Web. 29 Aug. 2016. www.secureworks.com/blog/research-20957

39. Blomfield, Adrian. "US Troops Ordered Out of Kyrgyzstan after Russia Deal." *Telegraph.* Telegraph Media Group, 4 Feb. 2009. Web. 29 Aug.

2016. www.telegraph.co.uk/news/worldnews/asia/kyrgyzstan/4513296/US-troops-ordered-out-of-Kyrgyzstan-after-Russia-deal.html

40. Constantin, Lucian. "Macro-Based Malware Is Making a Comeback, Researchers Warn." *Computerworld*. IDG News Service, 07 Jan. 2015. Web. 29 Aug. 2016. www.computerworld.com/article/2866055/macro-based-malware-is-making-a-comeback-researchers-warn.html

41. Muncaster, Phil. "Sandworm Team Went After Firms Running SCADA." *Infosecurity Magazine*. Infosecurity Group, 20 Oct. 2014. Web. 29 Aug. 2016. www.infosecurity-magazine.com/news/sandworm-team-went-after-firms/

42. Zetter, Kim. "Inside the Cunning, Unprecedented Hack of Ukraine's Power Grid." *Wired*. Conde Nast, 3 Mar. 2016. Web. 29 Aug. 2016. www.wired.com/2016/03/inside-cunning-unprecedented-hack-ukraines-power-grid/

43. Stone, Jeff. "Russian Hacking Group Sandworm Targeted US Before Knocking Out Power In Ukraine." *International Business Times*. IBT Media, 11 Jan. 2016. Web. 25 Aug. 2016. www.ibtimes.com/russian-hacking-group-sandworm-targeted-us-knocking-out-power-ukraine-2257194

44. Finkle, Jim. "US Firm Blames Russian 'Sandworm' Hackers for Ukraine Outage." *Reuters*. Thomson Reuters, 07 Jan. 2016. Web. 29 Aug. 2016. www.reuters.com/article/us-ukraine-cybersecurity-sandworm-id USKBN0UM00N20160108

45. Prabhu, Vijay. "Warsaw Stock Exchange Hacked by ISIS Cyber Criminals?" *TechWorm*. TechWorm, 24 Oct. 2014. Web. 29 Aug. 2016. www.techworm.net/2014/10/warsaw-stock-exchange-hacked-isis-cyber-criminals.html

46. Riley, Michael. "Cyberspace Becomes Second Front in Russia's Clash With NATO." *Bloomberg*. Bloomberg L.P., 14 Oct. 2015. Web. 31 Aug. 2016. www.bloomberg.com/news/articles/2015-10-14/cyberspace-becomes-second-front-in-russia-s-clash-with-nato

47. Prabhu, Vijay. "Warsaw Stock Exchange Hacked by ISIS Cyber Criminals?" *TechWorm*. TechWorm, 24 Oct. 2014. Web. 29 Aug. 2016. www.techworm.net/2014/10/warsaw-stock-exchange-hacked-isis-cyber-criminals.html

48. Melvin, Don and Greg Botelho. "French TV Network TV5Monde Hit by Massive Cyberattack." *CNN*. Turner Broadcasting System,

9 Apr. 2015. Web. 8 Sept. 2016.www.cnn.com/2015/04/09/europe/french-tv-network-attack-recovery/

49. "Who Are the Cybercaliphate Hackers Who Claimed Responsibility for TV5Monde Cyberattack?" *France 24 English*. YouTube, 09 Apr. 2015. Web. 8 Aug. 2016. www.youtube.com/watch?v=gM-6r8L8SZQ

50. "Russian Hackers Suspected in Cyberattack on German Parliament | News | DW.COM | 19.06.2015." *DW*. ARD, 16 June 2015. Web. 29 Aug. 2016. www.dw.com/en/russian-hackers-suspected-in-cyberattack-on-german-parliament/a-18528045

51. Paganini, Pierluigi. "Alleged Russian Hackers behind the EFF Spear Phishing Scam." *Security Affairs*. N.p., 30 Aug. 2015. Web. 30 Aug. 2016. securityaffairs.co/wordpress/39686/cyber-crime/eff-spear-phishing-apt28.html

52. Bishara, Motez. "Russian Doping: 'Unprecedented Attack on Olympic Games'" *CNN*. Turner Broadcasting System, 21 July 2016. Web. 23 Sept. 2016. edition.cnn.com/2016/07/18/sport/russia-doping-sochi-2014-olympic-games-rio-2016/

53. Threatconnect Research Team. "Russian Cyber Operations on Steroids." Web log post. *ThreatConnect Blog*. ThreatConnect, Inc., 19 Aug. 2016. Web. 31 Aug. 2016. www.threatconnect.com/blog/fancy-bear-anti-doping-agency-phishing/

54. Engel, Richard and Aggelos Petropoulos. "Russian Doping Whistleblowers Fear for Their Lives after Cyber Attack."*NBC News*. NBCUniversal News Group, 28 Aug. 2016. Web. 31 Aug. 2016. www.nbcnews.com/storyline/2016-rio-summer-olympics/russian-doping-whistleblowers-fear-their-lives-after-cyber-attack-n638746

55. "Russian Doping: Who Is Whistleblower Grigory Rodchenkov?" *BBC News*. British Broadcasting Corporation, 19 July 2016. Web. 23 Aug. 2016. www.bbc.com/news/world-europe-36833962?_ga=1.190104555.19 62198461.1471990212

56. Hacquebord, Feike. "Pawn Storm's Domestic Spying Campaign Revealed; Ukraine and US Top Global Targets." Web log post. *TrendLabs Security Intelligence Blog*. Trend Micro, 18 Aug. 2015. Web. 30 Aug. 2016. blog.trendmicro.com/trendlabs-security-intelligence/pawn-storms-domestic-spying-campaign-revealed-ukraine-and-us-top-global-targets/

57. Yadron, Danny. "Three Months Later, State Department Hasn't Rooted Out Hackers." *Wall Street Journal*. News Corporation, 19 Feb. 2015. Web. 31 Aug. 2016. www.wsj.com/articles/three-months-later-state-department-hasnt-rooted-out-hackers-1424391453

58. Hackett, Robert. "Report: US Officials Say Russians Hacked White House Computer System." *Fortune*. Time Inc., 06 Apr. 2015. Web. 30 Aug. 2016. fortune.com/2015/04/07/russians-hacked-white-house/

59. Fryer-Biggs, Zachary. "Operation Watersnake: Hacking the US by Ship." *Jane's*. IHS, 8 Aug. 2016. Web. 28 Aug. 2016.janes.ihs.com/Janes/Display/1780967

60. *Global Threat Intel Report 2014*. Rep. CrowdStrike, 17 Jan. 2014. Web. 31 Aug. 2016. *go.crowdstrike.com/rs/281-OBQ-266/images/ReportGlobal ThreatIntelligence.pdf*

61. *2015 Global Threat Report*. Rep. CrowdStrike, 14 Jan. 2016. Web. 31 Aug. 2016. go.crowdstrike.com/rs/281-OBQ-266/images/15GlobalThreat Report.pdf

62. Chen, Adrian. "The Agency." *New York Times*. New York Times Company, 06 June 2015. Web. 29 Aug. 2016. www.nytimes.com/2015/06/07/magazine/the-agency.html

63. Ibid.

64. "The Power of Propaganda." *Psychology Of*. Haverford College, 2015. Web. 29 Aug. 2016. sites.google.com/a/haverford.edu/the-psychology-of/workshops/the-power-of-propaganda

65. Chen, Adrian. "The Agency." *New York Times*. New York Times Company, 06 June 2015. Web. 29 Aug. 2016. www.nytimes.com/2015/06/07/magazine/the-agency.html

66. Ibid.

67. Ibid.

68. Ibid.

69. "Why Are Russian Trolls Spreading Online Hoaxes in the US?" *Newshour*. Ed. Jeffrey Brown. PBS, 8 June 2015. Web. 29 Aug. 2016. www.pbs.org/newshour/bb/russian-trolls-spreading-online-hoaxes-u-s/

70. Seddon, Max. "Documents Show How Russia's Troll Army Hit America." *BuzzFeed*. BuzzFeed, Inc., 2 June 2014. Web. 29 Aug. 2016. www.buzzfeed.com/maxseddon/documents-show-how-russias-troll-army-hit-america

71. Ibid.

72. Ibid.

73. Chen, Adrian. "The Real Paranoia-Inducing Purpose of Russian Hacks." *New Yorker*. Conde Nast, 27 July 2016. Web. 29 Aug. 2016. www.newyorker.com/news/news-desk/the-real-paranoia-inducing-purpose-of-russian-hacks

Chapter 7

1. Assange, Julian. "We Are Drowning in Material." Interview by Michael Sontheimer. *Der Spiegel*. Spiegel-Verlag, 20 July 2015. Web. 25 Aug. 2016.

2. WikiLeaks. "What Is Wikileaks?" *WikiLeaks*. N.p., 3 Nov. 2015. Web. 25 Aug. 2016. wikileaks.org/about*WikiLeaks:About*. WikiLeaks, 5 Dec. 2008. Web. 24 Aug. 2016. www.wikileaks.com/wiki/Wikileaks:About

3. Khatchadourian, Raffi. "No Secrets." *New Yorker*. Conde Nast, 31 May 2010. Web. 24 Aug. 2016. www.newyorker.com/magazine/2010/06/07/no-secrets

4. Ibid.

5. Ibid.

6. Ibid.

7. WikiLeaks. "Collateral Murder." *WikiLeaks*. N.p., 5 Apr. 2010. Web. 24 Aug. 2016. collateralmurder.wikileaks.org/

8. Cohen, Noam, and Brian Stelter. "Iraq Video Brings Notice to a Web Site." *New York Times*. New York Times Company, 06 Apr. 2010. Web. 25 Aug. 2016. www.nytimes.com/2010/04/07/world/07wikileaks.html?_r=0

9. Courson, Paul, and Matt Smith. "WikiLeaks Source Manning Gets 35 Years, Will Seek Pardon." *CNN*. Turner Broadcasting System, 22 Aug. 2013. Web. 22 Sept. 2016. www.cnn.com/2013/08/21/us/bradley-manning-sentencing/

10. Ibid.

11. "The Defense Department's Response." *New York Times*. New York Times Company, 22 Oct. 2010. Web. 25 Aug. 2016. www.nytimes.com/2010/10/23/world/middleeast/23response.html?_r=1

12. Shane, Scott, and Andrew Lehren W. "Leaked Cables Offer Raw Look at U.S. Diplomacy." *New York Times*. New York Times Company, 28 Nov.

2010. Web. 25 Aug. 2016. www.nytimes.com/2010/11/29/world/29cables.
html

13. Erlanger, Steven. "Europeans Criticize Fierce U.S. Response to Leaks."
New York Times. New York Times Company, 09 Dec. 2010. Web. 22 Aug.
2016. www.nytimes.com/2010/12/10/world/europe/10wikileaks-react.
html

14. Ibid.

15. Friedman, Megan. "Julian Assange: Readers' Choice for TIME's
Person of the Year 2010 | TIME.com." *Time.* Time Inc., 13
Dec. 2010. Web. 22 Aug. 2016. newsfeed.time.com/2010/12/13/
julian-assange-readers-choice-for-times-person-of-the-year-2010/

16. Keller, Bill. "Dealing with Assange and the WikiLeaks Secrets." *New York
Times.* New York Times Company, 26 Jan. 2011. Web. 25 Aug. 2016. www.
nytimes.com/2011/01/30/magazine/30Wikileaks-t.html?

17. Khatchadourian, Raffi. "No Secrets." *New Yorker.* Conde Nast, 31 May
2010. Web. 24 Aug. 2016. www.newyorker.com/magazine/2010/06/07/
no-secrets

18. Ibid.

19. Assange, Julian. "Assange: Why I Founded WikiLeaks." *Newsweek.*
Newsweek LLC, 10 Mar. 2016. Web. 25 Aug. 2016. www.newsweek.com/
julian-assange-why-i-founded-wikileaks-294283

20. Christopher, Hitchens. "Why I Founded WikiLeaks." *Slate.* Slate Group,
6 Dec. 2010. Web. 26 Aug. 2016. www.slate.com/articles/news_and_
politics/fighting_words/2010/12/turn_yourself_in_julian_assange.
html

21. Vick, Karl. "WikiLeaks Is Getting Scarier Than the NSA." *Time.*
Time Inc., 12 Aug. 2016. Web. 25 Aug. 2016. time.com/4450282/
wikileaks-julian-assange-dnc-hack-criticism/

22. Bittner, Jochen. "How Julian Assange Is Destroying WikiLeaks." *New York
Times.* New York Times Company, 07 Feb. 2016. Web. 25 Aug. 2016. www.
nytimes.com/2016/02/08/opinion/how-julian-assange-is-destroying-
wikileaks.html

23. "Julian Assange Sex Assault Allegations: Timeline." *BBC News.* British
Broadcasting Corporation, 5 Feb. 2016. Web. 26 Aug. 2016. www.bbc.
com/news/world-europe-11949341

24. Chopping, Dominic. "Julian Assange to Be Questioned at Ecuador's Embassy in London." *Wall Street Journal*. News Corporation, 11 Aug. 2016. Web. 25 Aug. 2016. www.wsj.com/articles/julian-assange-to-be-questioned-at-ecuadors-embassy-in-london-1470914241

25. Wallace, Arturo. "Julian Assange: Why Ecuador Is Offering Asylum." *BBC News*. British Broadcasting Corporation, 16 Aug. 2012. Web. 22 Aug. 2016. www.bbc.com/news/world-europe-19289649

26. Ibid.

27. "Is Russia Secretly Influencing Wikileaks? I Don't Think It Started as a Russian Operation, but I'm Starting to Wonder Why Assange and Crew Only Focus on NATO Countries • /r/conspiracy." *R/conspiracy*. Reddit, Oct. 2015. Web. 22 Sept. 2016. www.reddit.com/r/conspiracy/comments/3pobtq/is_russia_secretly_influencing_wikileaks_i_dont/

28. Ioffe, Julia. "What Is Russia Today?" *Columbia Journalism Review*. Columbia University Graduate School of Journalism, Sept.-Oct. 2010. Web. 23 Aug. 2016. www.cjr.org/feature/what_is_russia_today.php

29. Ibid.

30. Harding, Luke. "The World Tomorrow: Julian Assange Proves a Useful Idiot." *Guardian*. Guardian News and Media, 17 Apr. 2012. Web. 25 Aug. 2016. www.theguardian.com/media/2012/apr/17/world-tomorrow-julian-assange-wikileaks

31. Ibid.

32. Assange, Julian. "Assange: I'll Be Called a Traitor, Interviewing Radicals." Interview by RT. *RT International*. TV Novosti, 16 Apr. 2012. Web. 25 Sept. 2016.

33. Ibid.

34. Wilentz, Sean. "Would You Feel Differently About Snowden, Greenwald, and Assange If You Knew What They Really Thought?" *New Republic*. N.p., 19 Jan. 2014. Web. 24 Aug. 2016. newrepublic.com/article/116253/edward-snowden-glenn-greenwald-julian-assange-what-they-believe

35. Bittner, Jochen. "How Julian Assange Is Destroying WikiLeaks." *New York Times*. New York Times Company, 07 Feb. 2016. Web. 25 Aug. 2016. www.nytimes.com/2016/02/08/opinion/how-julian-assange-is-destroying-wikileaks.html

36. Gayle, Damien. "Julian Assange 'Told Edward Snowden Not to Seek

Asylum in Latin America.'" *Guardian*. Guardian News and Media, 29 Aug. 2015. Web. 24 Aug. 2016. www.theguardian.com/media/2015/aug/29/julian-assange-told-edward-snowdon-not-seek-asylum-in-latin-america

37. WikiLeaks. "A Vote Today for Hillary Clinton Is a Vote for Endless, Stupid War." *WikiLeaks*. N.p., 9 Feb. 2016. Web. 24 Aug. 2016. wikileaks.org/hillary-war/

38. Savage, Charlie. "Assange, Avowed Foe of Clinton, Timed Email Release for Democratic Convention." *New York Times*. New York Times Company, 26 July 2016. Web. 26 Aug. 2016. www.nytimes.com/2016/07/27/us/politics/assange-timed-wikileaks-release-of-democratic-emails-to-harm-hillary-clinton.html

39. Assange, Julian. "Assange: WikiLeaks to Release 'Significant' Clinton Material." Interview by Megyn Kelly. *Fox News*. News Corporation, 24 Aug. 2016. Web. 25 Aug. 2016.

40. Ibid.

41. Mook, Robby. "Clinton Camp: DNC Hack a Russian Plot to Help Trump." Interview by Jake Tapper. *CNN*. Turner Broadcasting System, 24 July 2016. Web. 24 Aug. 2016.

42. Assange, Julian. "Julian Assange: We Have More Material on Clinton." Interview by Anderson Cooper. *CNN*. Turner Broadcasting System, 29 July 2016. Web. 25 Aug. 2016.

43. Assange, Julian. "Julian Assange: 'A Lot More Material' Coming on US Elections." Interview by Matthew Chance.*CNN*. Turner Broadcasting System, 26 July 2016. Web. 25 Aug. 2016.

44. Ibid.

45. Ibid.

46. Assange, Julian. "Assange on Peston on Sunday: 'More Clinton Leaks to Come.'" Interview by Robert Peston. *ITV*. ITV Network Limited, 12 June 2016. Web. 25 Aug. 2016.

Chapter 8

1. Perez, Evan. "Sources: US Officials Warned DNC of Hack Months before the Party Acted." *CNN*. Turner Broadcasting System, 7 July 2016. Web. 25

Aug. 2016. www.cnn.com/2016/07/25/politics/democratic-convention-dnc-emails-russia/

2. Nakashima, Ellen. "National Intelligence Director: Hackers Have Targeted 2016 Presidential Campaigns."*Washington Post*. Washington Post Company, 18 May 2016. Web. 01 Sept. 2016. www.washingtonpost. com/world/national-security/national-intelligence-director-hackers-have-tried-to-spy-on-2016-presidential-campaigns/2016/05/18/2b1745c0-1d0d-11e6-b6e0-c53b7ef63b45_story.html?tid=a_inl

3. Gallagher, Sean. "DNC Staffers: FBI Didn't Tell Us for Months about Possible Russian Hack." *Ars Technica*. Conde Nast, 03 Aug. 2016. Web. 01 Sept. 2016. arstechnica.com/security/2016/08/dnc-staffers-fbi-didnt-tell-us-for-months-about-possible-russian-hack/

4. Nakashima, Ellen. "Russian Government Hackers Penetrated DNC, Stole Opposition Research on Trump." *Washington Post*. The Washington Post Company, 14 June 2016. Web. 29 Aug. 2016. www.washingtonpost.com/world/national-security/russian-government-hackers-penetrated-dnc-stole-opposition-research-on-trump/2016/06/14/cf006cb4-316e-11e6-8ff7-7b6c1998b7a0_story.html

5. Alperovitch, Dmitri. "Bears in the Midst: Intrusion into the Democratic National Committee." Web log post.*CrowdStrike*. N.p., 15 June 2016. Web. 28 Aug. 2016. www.crowdstrike.com/blog/bears-midst-intrusion-democratic-national-committee/

6. Ibid.

7. Rid, Thomas (@RidT). ".@pwnallthethings Remarkably the same C2 IP actually is hardcoded in the DNC and BUNDESTAG APT28 samples.." 8 Jul. 2016,1:03 AM. Tweet.

8. Alperovitch, Dmitri. "Bears in the Midst: Intrusion into the Democratic National Committee." Web log post. *CrowdStrike*. N.p., 15 June 2016. Web. 28 Aug. 2016. www.crowdstrike.com/blog/bears-midst-intrusion-democratic-national-committee/

9. Ibid.

10. Nakashima, Ellen. "National Intelligence Director: Hackers Have Targeted 2016 Presidential Campaigns." *Washington Post*. Washington Post Company, 18 May 2016. Web. 25 Aug. 2016. www.washington post.com/world/national-security/national-intelligence-director-

hackers-have-tried-to-spy-on-2016-presidential-cam-paigns/2016/05/18/2b1745c0-1d0d-11e6-b6e0-c53b7ef63b45_story.html

11. Ibid.

12. Franceschi-Bicchierai, Lorenzo. "'Guccifer 2.0' Is Likely a Russian Government Attempt To Cover Up Their Own Hack." *Motherboard*. Vice Media, 23 June 2016. Web. 25 Sept. 2016. motherboard.vice.com/read/guccifer-20-is-likely-a-russian-government-attempt-to-cover-up-their-own-hack

13. Ibid.

14. Alperovitch, Dmitri. "Bears in the Midst: Intrusion into the Democratic National Committee." Web log post. *CrowdStrike*. N.p., 15 June 2016. Web. 28 Aug. 2016. www.crowdstrike.com/blog/bears-midst-intrusion-democratic-national-committee/

15. Coldewey, Devin. "WikiLeaks Publishes 19,252 DNC-Related Emails Packed with Personal Information." *TechCrunch*. AOL, 22 July 2016. Web. 01 Sept. 2016. techcrunch.com/2016/07/22/wikileaks-publishes-19252-dnc-related-emails-packed-with-personal-information/

16. Trump, Donald. "The Wikileaks e-mail release today was so bad to Sanders that it will make it impossible for him to support her, unless he is a fraud!" 23 Jul. 2016, 2:20 PM. Tweet.

17. WikiLeaks. "No Shit." *WikiLeaks*. N.p., 5 May 2016. Web. 1 Sept. 2016. wikileaks.org/dnc-emails/emailid/11508

18. Shear, Michael D. and Matthew Rosenberg. "Released Emails Suggest the D.N.C. Derided the Sanders Campaign." *New York Times*. New York Times Company, 22 July 2016. Web. 31 Aug. 2016. www.nytimes.com/2016/07/23/us/politics/dnc-emails-sanders-clinton.html?_r=0

19. WikiLeaks. "Bernie Narrative." *WikiLeaks*. N.p., n.d. Web. 1 Sept. 2016. wikileaks.org/dnc-emails/emailid/11056

20. WikiLeaks. "Re: Sanders If I'm Elected, DNC Would Be Out." *WikiLeaks*. N.p., n.d. Web. 1 Sept. 2016. wikileaks.org/dnc-emails/emailid/9999

21. Rappeport, Alan. "3 Top DNC Officials Leave as Upheaval After Email Breach Continues." *New York Times*. New York Times Company, 02 Aug. 2016. Web. 31 Sept. 2016. www.nytimes.com/2016/08/03/us/politics/dnc-email-hack-hillary-clinton-bernie-sanders.html?_r=0

22. Healy, Patrick, and Jonathan Martin. "Democrats Struggle for Unity on First Day of Convention." *New York Times*. New York Times Company, 25

July 2016. Web. 31 Aug. 2016. www.nytimes.com/2016/07/26/us/politics/
dnc-speakers-protests-sanders.html?_r=0

23. Assange, Julian. "Julian Assange: We Have More Material on Clinton."
Interview by Anderson Cooper. *CNN*. Turner Broadcasting System, 29
July 2016. Web. 25 Aug. 2016.

24. Sainato, Michael. "Wikileaks Proves Primary Was Rigged: DNC
Undermined Democracy." *Observer*. Observer Media, 22 July 2016. Web. 26
Aug. 2016. observer.com/2016/07/wikileaks-proves-primary-was-rigged-
dnc-undermined-democracy/

25. Kaczynski, Andrew. "Julian Assange Floats Theory That Murdered DNC
Employee Was Informant In Dutch Interview." *BuzzFeed*. BuzzFeed, Inc.,
9 Aug. 2016. Web. 26 Aug. 2016. www.buzzfeed.com/andrewkaczynski/
julian-assange-floats-theory-murdered-dnc-employee-was-infor?utm_
term=.cgkB3qzOW#.nkbwrvB08

26. Stahl, Jeremy. "WikiLeaks Is Fanning a Conspiracy Theory That Hillary
Murdered a DNC Staffer." *Slate Magazine*. Slate Group, 09 Aug. 2016. Web.
26 Aug. 2016. www.slate.com/blogs/the_slatest/2016/08/09/wikileaks_
is_fanning_a_conspiracy_theory_that_hillary_murdered_a_dnc_
staffer.html

27. Ibid.

28. Das, Samburaj. "Malware Alert: Files on WikiLeaks Can Infect Your
Computer | Hacked." *Hacked*. N.p., 26 Aug. 2015. Web. 26 Aug. 2016.
hacked.com/malware-alert-files-wikileaks-can-infect-computer/

29. Burns, Alexander, Maggie Haberman, and Ashley Parker. "Donald
Trump's Confrontation With Muslim Soldier's Parents Emerges as
Unexpected Flash Point." *New York Times*. New York Times Company, 31
July 2016. Web. 1 Sept. 2016. www.nytimes.com/2016/08/01/us/politics/
khizr-khan-ghazala-donald-trump-muslim-soldier.html

30. Parker, Ashley, and David Sanger E. "Donald Trump Calls on Russia
to Find Hillary Clinton's Missing Emails." *New York Times*. New York
Times Company, 27 July 2016. Web. 27 Aug. 2016. http://www.nytimes.
com/2016/07/28/us/politics/donald-trump-russia-clinton-emails.html?

31. Smith, Jeremy Silk. "Roger Stone Claims To Be in Contact with
WikiLeaks Founder." *Roll Call*. Economist Group, 09 Aug. 2016. Web.
26 Sept. 2016. www.rollcall.com/news/politics/roger-stone-claims-to-
be-in-contact-with-wikileaks-founder.

32. Ibid.

33. Fisher, Max. "Donald Trump's Appeal to Russia Shocks Foreign Policy Experts." *New York Times*. New York Times Company, 28 July 2016. Web. 26 Aug. 2016. www.nytimes.com/2016/07/29/world/europe/russia-trump-clinton-email-hacking.html

34. King, Bob, and Tim Starks. "Hackers Suspected in New Attack on Democrats." *POLITICO*. POLITICO, 28 July 2016. Web. 1 Sept. 2016. www.politico.com/story/2016/07/dccc-hack-fbi-226398

35. Meyer, Josh, Alex Moe, and Tracy Connor. "New Democratic Party Hack 'Similar' to Earlier Breach." *NBC News*. NBCUniversal News Group, 29 July 2016. Web. 1 Sept. 2016. www.nbcnews.com/news/us-news/hack-democratic-congressional-campaign-committee-tied-earlier-breach-n619786

36. "FANCY BEAR Has an (IT) Itch That They Can't Scratch." *'Threat Geek'* Fidelis Cyber Security, 1 Aug. 2016. Web. 28 Aug. 2016. www.threatgeek.com/2016/08/fancy-bear-has-an-it-itch-that-they-cant-scratch.html

37. Ibid.

38. Frenkel, Sheera. "Hackers behind Leaked DNC Emails Are Still Trying to Hack Democratic Party Members."*BuzzFeed*. BuzzFeed, Inc., 2 Aug. 2016. Web. 31 Aug. 2016. www.buzzfeed.com/sheerafrenkel/the-dncs-hackers-are-targeting-democratic-party-members-in-a?utm_term=.yyJlKwpbP#.oeL9YyXN8

39. David, Javier E. "Twitter Suspends Guccifer 2's Account in Wake of DCCC Hack." *CNBC*. NBCUniversal News Group, 13 Aug. 2016. Web. 1 Sept. 2016. www.cnbc.com/2016/08/13/twitter-suspends-guccifer-2-after-dccc-hack.html

40. Hosenball, Mark. "Exclusive: Clinton Campaign Also Hacked in Attacks on Democrats." *Reuters*. Thomson Reuters, 30 July 2016. Web. 1 Sept. 2016.www.reuters.com/article/us-usa-cyber-democrats-investigation-exc-idUSKCN1092HK

41. CTU Research Team. "Threatgroup 4127 Targets Hillary Clinton Presidential Campaign." *Secure Works Research*. Tech. Secure Works, 16 June 2016. Web. 11 Aug. 2016. www.secureworks.com/research/threat-group-4127-targets-hillary-clinton-presidential-campaign

42. Ibid.

43. Guccifer. "DCCC Docs from Pelosi's PC." *GUCCIFER 2.0*. WordPress,

31 Aug. 2016. Web. 1 Sept. 2016. guccifer2.wordpress.com/2016/08/31/pelosi/

44. Hosenball, Mark, Joseph Menn, and John Walcott. "Exclusive: Clinton Campaign Also Hacked in Attacks on Democrats." *Reuters*. Thomson Reuters, 30 July 2016. Web. 1 Sept. 2016. www.reuters.com/article/us-usa-cyber-democrats-investigation-exc-idUSKCN1092HK

45. Lichtblau, Eric. "Computer Systems Used by Clinton Campaign Are Said to Be Hacked, Apparently by Russians." *New York Times*. New York Times Company, 29 July 2016. Web. 1 Sept. 2016.www.nytimes.com/2016/07/30/us/politics/clinton-campaign-hacked-russians.html?_r=0

46. Carroll, Lauren. "What We Know about Russia's Role in the DNC Email Leak." *PolitiFact*. Tampa Bay Times, 31 July 2016. Web. 1 Sept. 2016. www.politifact.com/truth-o-meter/article/2016/jul/31/what-we-know-about-russias-role-dnc-email-leak/

47. NBCNews. "President Obama on Russian DNC Hack Involvement: 'Anything's Possible' - NBC News." *NBC News*. NBCUniversal News Group, 26 July 2016. Web. 1 Sept. 2016. www.nbcnews.com/nightly-news/video/president-obama-on-russian-dnc-hack-involvement-anything-s-possible-732675139636

48. Isikoff, Michael. "FBI Says Foreign Hackers Penetrated State Election Systems." *Yahoo News*. Yahoo Inc., 29 Aug. 2016. Web. 1 Sept. 2016. www.yahoo.com/news/fbi-says-foreign-hackers-penetrated-000000175.html

49. Ibid.

50. Salter, Raphael, and Josh Lederman. "'Anything's Possible'—Obama Points to Russia on DNC Hack." *The Big Story*. Associated Press, 26 July 2016. Web. 25 Aug. 2016. bigstory.ap.org/article/a4be29bc14954dbabe2d968ba4a1bf68/cybersecurity-experts-see-merit-claims-russian-hacking

51. *The Evolving Nature of Cyber-Espionage*. Issue brief. The Soufan Group, 3 Aug. 2016. Web. 31 Aug. 2016. soufangroup.com/tsg-intelbrief-the-evolving-nature-of-cyber-espionage/

Chapter 9

1. Martin, Jonathan, and Amy Chozick. "Donald Trump's Campaign Stands by Embrace of Putin." *New York Times*. New York Times Company,

08 Sept. 2016. Web. 31 Aug. 2016. www.nytimes.com/2016/09/09/us/politics/hillary-clinton-donald-trump-putin.html?_r=0

2.   18, LII § 115-2381 (Cornell University Law School 1948). Web.

3.   Williams, Katie Bo. "Clinton: Treat Cyberattacks 'Like Any Other Attack.'" *Hill*. Capitol Hill Publishing Corp., 31 Aug. 2016. Web. 1 Sept. 2016. thehill.com/policy/cybersecurity/293970-clinton-treat-cyberattacks-like-any-other-attack

4.   "WATCH: Donald Trump's Terrifying Response When Asked about Cybersecurity." *New Statesman*. Progressive Digital Media, 8 Sept. 2016. Web. 10 Sept. 2016. www.newstatesman.com/politics/media/2016/09/watch-donald-trump-s-terrifying-response-when-asked-about-cybersecurity

5.   Trump, Donald. "On Russian TV, Trump Says It's 'Unlikely' Putin Trying to Sway Election." Interview by Larry King. *CNN*. Turner Broadcasting System, 9 Sept. 2016. Web. 10 Sept. 2016.

ALSO BY
MALCOLM NANCE

DEFEATING
ISIS

WHO THEY ARE, HOW THEY FIGHT, WHAT THEY BELIEVE

MALCOLM NANCE

INTERNATIONAL EXPERT, COUNTERTERRORISM INTELLIGENCE

FOREWORD BY **RICHARD ENGEL**
CHIEF FOREIGN CORRESPONDENT FOR NBC NEWS

DEFEATING ISIS
Who They Are, How They Fight, What They Believe

Malcolm Nance, Richard Engel

A *New York Times* bestseller!

This reference shows the history and tactics of the global terror group ISIS—and how to use that knowledge to defeat it.

ISIS—the Islamic State of Iraq and Syria—has become the single most dangerous terrorist threat to global security since al-Qaeda. In *Defeating ISIS*, internationally renowned intelligence veteran and counterterrorism expert Malcolm Nance gives an insider's view on the origins of this organization, its violent propaganda, and how it spreads its ideology throughout the Middle East and to disaffected youth in the Western world.

Defeating ISIS gives a step-by-step analysis of the street-level tactics the group has employed in assaults against fortified targets, in urban combat, and during terrorist operations such as those in Paris. Nance describes ISIS's true danger as a heretical death cult that seeks to wrest control of Islam through young ideologues and redefine Islam as a fight to the death against all comers. Defeating ISIS is the first highly detailed and fully illustrated look into the organization by one of the world's foremost authorities in counterterrorism.

$27.99 | Hardcover | ISBN: 978-1-5107-1184-6

FINAL REPORT OF THE TASK FORCE ON

COMBATING TERRORIST AND FOREIGN FIGHTER TRAVEL

HOMELAND SECURITY
COMMITTEE

FINAL REPORT OF THE TASK FORCE ON COMBATING TERRORIST AND FOREIGN FIGHTER TRAVEL

Homeland Security Committee, Malcolm Nance

The report addresses the urgent and growing threat of terrorist travel by Americans to Syria and Iraq. Despite the government's efforts to control this travel, hundreds of Americans have attempted to reach conflict zones to join jihadists. Using numerous briefings, interviews, site visits, and document analysis, the Task Force makes thirty-two key findings dealing with government strategy, identification of terrorists, and disruption of foreign fighter travel, including:

Key Finding 1: The United States lacks a comprehensive strategy for combating terrorist and foreign fighter travel.

Key Finding 14: State and local law enforcement personnel continue to express concern that they are not provided with the appropriate security clearances to assist with counterterrorism challenges.

Key Finding 29: Gaping security weaknesses overseas—especially in Europe—are putting the US homeland in danger by making it easier for aspiring foreign fighters to migrate to terrorist hotspots and for jihadists to return to the West.

This report is the primary source for explaining the critical need for effective strategy in combating terrorist travel from the United States.

$12.99 | Trade Paperback | ISBN: 978-1-5107-1238-6

ALSO FROM
SKYHORSE PUBLISHING

THE MIND OF A TERRORIST
David Headley,
The Mumbai Massacre,
and His European Revenge

Kaare Sørensen
Translated by Cory Klingsporn

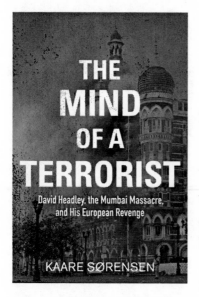

Written with the pacing of a thriller, a veteran journalist's account of the terrorist behind the Mumbai attacks.

David Headley, the American-Pakistani also known as Daood Gilani, lived a double life. One day he would stroll through Central Park in his tailored Armani suit as a true New Yorker, and the next he would browse in the bazaar in Lahore wearing traditional Pakistani clothes.

Born in 1960, the son of an American mother and Pakistani father, Headley grew up between East and West. He was attracted to both worlds, even working as an informant for the US government, until one day he found he had to choose between the place of his birth and a radical form of Islam preaching global jihad. This is the disturbing story of the mastermind behind the 2008 attacks in Mumbai that killed 166 people.

Veteran journalist Kaare Sørensen has reconstructed his movements and planning in a tense feat of reportage. His account, based on extensive reporting, eyewitness interviews, and documentation, offers unprecedented insight into the mind of the terrorist. The author has provided updates and a new preface for the English-language edition.

$24.99 | Hardcover | ISBN: 978-1-62872-514-8

CPSIA information can be obtained
at www.ICGtesting.com
Printed in the USA
LVOW12*1443011017

550761LV00003B/21/P